The Complete Book of
ATHLETICS

The Complete Book of ATHLETICS

Tom McNab

Ward Lock Limited · London

Acknowledgments

The author would like to thank Susan Campbell for contributing Chapter 2 'Women in athletics'.
The author and publishers would like to thank the following for kindly providing photographs for the book.
Colour photographs: Allsport page 123; Allsport/Tony Duffy pages 50, 105 below, 106; Gerry Cranham pages 67, 68, 88, 157, 158, 176; E. D. Lacey page 70; Mark Shearman pages 49, 69, 87, 105 top, 124, 175.
Black and white photographs:
Allsport pages 25, 42, 143, 170; Allsport/Tony Duffy pages 55, 80, 81, 89, 102, 104, 112, 133, 152, 159, 167, 178, 180; Central Press Photos Ltd title page, pages 100, 115; Colorsport pages 37, 45, 52, 54, 58, 86, 92, 94, 96, 98, 136, 137, 138, 140, 179; Mary Evans Picture Library pages 6, 11, 12, 16, 35, 60, 131, 156; E. D. Lacey pages 29, 61, 65, 72, 111, 121, 122, 151; Mansell Collection pages 8, 150; Popperfoto pages 27, 77, 108, 110, 132, 145, 177; Radio Times Hulton Picture Library pages 13, 17, 33, 64, 75, 78, 91; Mark Shearman pages 22, 39, 44, 57, 83, 118, 130, 144, 148, 154, 155, 163 top and below, 166, 168, 172; Mike Street/Essex Sport Picture Services pages 46, 127; United Press International (UK) Ltd pages 43, 82.
We are grateful to the I.A.A.F. for the table on page 116 and the material in Part VI.
Line illustrations by Nils Solberg.

First published in Great Britain in 1980
by Ward Lock Limited, 116 Baker Street,
London W1M 2BB, a Pentos Company.

Designed by Chris Walker
House editor Gill Freeman
Text filmset in 11/13 pt Plantin 110
by Elliott Bros. & Yeoman Ltd., Speke, Merseyside

Printed and bound in USA by
R. R. Donnelley & Sons Company

British Library Cataloguing in Publication Data

McNab, Tom
The complete book of athletics.
1. Track-athletics
1. Title
796.4'2 GV1060.5

ISBN 0-7063-5927-5

Contents

PART I
Introduction

1. Track & field athletics: the long, broken road from Olympia

Track and field athletics is not essentially a sport; rather, it is a collection of separate sports which have, by historical accident, found themselves sharing the same arena. Just as the ancient Olympics and their mass of supporting games contained running, jumping and throwing, so they also contained such events as wrestling, pancratium and chariot-racing. Athletics, itself a complex of sports, therefore existed within a greater complex of sports within the same general competitive area.

No unbroken thread links the Ancient Games with modern athletics. This is because the Greek games are separated by at least a thousand years from even the first rural sports of the medieval period. What is more, the mere span of time is not sufficient to explain this lack of continuity, for the Greek games had a central religious philosophy which has never existed in modern athletics, which have always been essentially secular in nature.

The central religious belief of the Greek Olympics (which date from AD 390 only because this is the first Games of which we have record) is quite unique, and although the creator of the modern Olympic movement, Baron Pierre de Coubertin, attempted to create his own secular version of this belief, it has never translated itself into any coherent humanistic philosophy, if only because de Coubertin's brand of nineteenth century liberalism was rapidly overtaken by the politics of fascism, socialism, communism and a chauvinism common to all nations regardless of political belief.

1936. The Olympic flame is carried from Olympia by relay for the first time.

The Ancient Olympic Games were running based, with field events (discus, long jump and javelin) occurring only in pentathlon, which was itself an event of minor importance, if relative prize-monies are any guide. The three central events were the *stade,* a 192 m (200 yd) sprint, the *diaulos* (an out and back run of double this distance) and the distance run, the *dolichos,* which was probably about 5000 m (5500 yd). The athletic content of the Games was therefore, by modern standards, relatively small.

As will be explained in specific chapters, the rules of the Greek games are obscure, as most of the evidence is in the form of sculpture or pottery, with the aesthetic demands and limitations of these art-forms undoubtedly taking precedence over technical accuracy. There is, however, strong evidence of official control over the technical conduct of the Games.

Amateurism is essentially a nineteenth century concept and the Greeks made no differentiation between paid and unpaid performers. Part of modern Olympic mythology

Here, on the surface of a vase, a Greek artist captures the range and dynamism of Olympic sprinters in the stade *race.*

has been the belief that the Olympics were first participated in by high-born 'amateurs' and were later taken over by 'professionals' from the lower classes, thus falling into inevitable decay. Alas, there is little historical evidence to support this. On the contrary, there is ample evidence that the leisured classes competed throughout most of the history of the Games, albeit with diminished success. Most of the history of the Greek Games (of which the Olympics were only a part), is a professional one, in that prize-money or expensive prizes in kind were given throughout most of their history. The Greek Games offer a direct parallel with the English and Scottish rural sports of the early nineteenth century, where prizes of gloves and stockings were given during their early period, to be replaced with money prizes for the rest of their existence. Similarly, what began as local games soon developed into a 'circuit' with travelling groups of professional athletes, who later formed themselves into unions to negotiate with games organizers. The Greek and the British rural games therefore followed identical paths, with the British games circuits' development accelerated by the rapid growth in the railway system and increased leisure time.

The essential difference between Greek and modern athletics development lay in the intervention, in the last quarter of the nineteenth century, of the Victorian middle classes, who created a separate amateur system which lost all contact with sport's rural roots, and which later became the focal point for the development of an international amateur movement. In contrast, the Greeks, with no amateur/professional semantics to trouble them, simply went about the business of compensating athletes for their skill by offering money prizes, by sponsoring them through the agencies of rich patrons or city subsidies, and by rewarding their success with systems of local pensions. The Greeks thus anticipated modern capitalist and socialist aid to athletes without the heart-searching hypocrisy and semantic gymnastics which have troubled modern sports administrators. The ease with which this was accomplished can be explained by the fact that the Greeks were concerned only with fair competition, and did not saddle themselves with elusive and unworkable amateur definitions. There is no evidence, (though human nature has changed little over the past two thousand years) that the Greek Games were any less fair, in the strictly technical sense, than their modern counterparts. Indeed, it might be argued, with recent developments in the intake of illegal drugs, that it is now impossible to find fair competition at the highest levels.

Another myth that must be nailed to the wall is that the Greeks supported the Bishop of Pennsylvania's contention that taking part was more important than victory. This idea would have been incomprehensible to the Greeks, whose practical expression of their attitude towards losers was to award only first prizes. The concept of valuing a man's competitive effort rather than only his success, though admirable, is therefore a modern one. It should not be classed with the amateur/professional Victoriana which has survived into the last quarter of the twentieth century, but it is a valuable addition to modern sports philosophy, as it places a high value on effort and commitment rather than only on success.

Essentially a rural sports meeting, Robert Dover's Cotswold Games *was the first of several English 'Olympic' Games before de Coubertin's 1896 Athens Olympics.*

The final myth which should be discussed is that the Romans, in their absorption of the Greek Empire, completed the corruption of the Games. To the Romans, the Greek Games and the Greek love of physical culture, had two central flaws. The first was the religious nature of the Games, which related, of course, to a specifically Greek pantheistic view. The second was the unquestioned homosexuality which prevailed in the Greek gymnasia. This last factor was one over which, like many others, Pierre de Coubertin and his followers have passed a discreet veil, but the evidence is inescapable. It is understandable that a religion-based sports culture steeped in homosexuality, and one which made no distinction between amateurs and professionals, was hardly one on which a modern Olympic movement could be based. De Coubertin therefore used the Olympics as a convenient, if one-dimensional, scenario for what was essentially a drama based on nineteenth century humanism, heavily laced with the values of English public schools. This does not mean that the Olympics have not 'done the State some service', but it does call into question the basis of the 'Olympism' which has grown like ectoplasm around the figure of Baron Pierre de Coubertin.

Early British developments

The origins of the modern track and field movement must not, therefore, be looked for in the narrow *stade*-length of Olympia. Rather, we must look to nineteenth century Scotland and England where the first recorded athletics meetings took place in the 1820s. Thom's *Pedestrianism* (1812) does, however, give us an insight into a running-based athletics culture which pre-dates this by at least one hundred years. There are also several sixteenth-century accounts of hammer throwing (most, alas, relating fatalities) and Robert Dover's *Cotswold Games* was undoubtedly early seventeenth century in origin.

Until the early 1820s, it would be reasonable to assume that rural athletics meetings took place, but that there is simply no record of them. There are, however, ample records of running matches between men, usually beyond a mile, on turnpike roads or racecourses, and the most important of these are detailed in *Pedestrianism.* We hear, for instance, that the celebrated Lancashire runner, Joseph Headley, ran 9 min 45 sec at Knavismire in 1777, and that Curley, the Brighton Shepherd, ran 110 m (120 yd) in 12 sec in 1805 at Hampton Court Green. Thom also records that 'A mile was performed in four minutes and ten seconds by John Todd, a Scotchman, in 1803, who ran from Hyde Park corner to the first mile post on the Uxbridge Road'. Despite Todd's nationality, his performance is unlikely, though that of Headley was undoubtedly possible. Also, though it is possible that 'even timers' existed in the early nineteenth century, lack of spiked shoes and the fact that the stop-watch had not yet been invented, makes his performance as unlikely as that of Todd.

The main theme of *Pedestrianism* is the career of the Scot, Captain Barclay Allardice, who might well be called the father of modern athletics, though light years from the beliefs and attitudes of Pierre de Coubertin. Barclay, in matches from a quarter of a mile (56 sec) to his famous 'one thousand miles in a thousand hours' feat on Newmarket Heath in 1809, brought foot-racing from impromptu matches on turnpike roads to a certain level of public respectability. One feature of Thom's book is that he is not in the least concerned with field events and, indeed, does not apparently consider or discuss the existence of track and field athletics.

The first mention of track and field athletics as an entity is in the Scottish Border Games of the early 1820s, and though it is certain that the comprehensive programme which they offered could not have simply been plucked from the ether, the records of these games, with high jumps of 1.70 m (5 ft 5½ in) and triple jumps of close on 14 m (46 ft 2 in), are the first of modern athletics.

Indeed, the conventional view that modern athletics is derived from English public schools and universities is essentially a piece of middle class mythology, and no one has asked how such events as hammer, shot, long jump and hurdles suddenly appeared in mid-nineteenth century university athletic programmes, unless they were simply the

Early English hurdling. Rigid, heavy hurdles fixed in rough grass meant that hurdling was a series of jumps rather than a sprint.

C.D

C. B. Fry, one of the great all-rounders of Victorian sport, takes the world long jump record. Note the marker in the pit, which the rules no longer permit.

inspired invention of undergraduates. No; the public schools of the mid-nineteenth century and the undergraduates of a few years later, simply selected events from the existing rural sports culture. All that rural sportsmen lacked was someone to record and organize their endeavours. In contrast, there was no lack of interest in the feats of Victorian undergraduates.

By the mid-nineteenth century, five separate athletics cultures had come into existence:

1 The rural sports meeting, epitomized by the Scottish Highland Games, and the Scottish Border Games. These were well recorded by the 1850s, possibly because of the increased interest in Scottish culture created by Queen Victoria.

2 Two-man matches in running and jumping between professional athletes. These were a continuation of the matches of the Captain Barclay period, their existence being dependent on betting.

3 Open professional athletics meetings consisting entirely of running events. These reached the peak of public interest in the early 1860s with the great races between the American Indian, 'Deerfoot' (Louis Bennett) and the best English distance runners. Although there was at that time no definition of an 'amateur', these events

were participated in entirely by working-class athletes and were betting based.

4 Open athletics meetings involving the middle classes. Prize values were kept low and there was no encouragement given to the working classes to compete in these meetings. The West London Rowing Club Sports of 1862 is often given as the first open amateur athletics meeting ever held, but there is good evidence of other open amateur meetings held before this date.

5 Competitions within universities and public schools. The first Oxford university sports took place in 1864, and internal college competitions were held before that date.

These streams of competition seem to have operated almost independently of each other, with the possible exception of the embryonic University-open amateur meetings. Nothing prevented university athletes taking part in rural games, but there is little evidence that they did so. The seedy, seamy atmosphere of professional running matches and meetings was hardly, for obvious reasons, the stage on which the amateurs wished to display their talents.

It is not surprising, bearing in mind the relationships between the classes that obtained during the Victorian period, that the middle-class undergraduate, seeking adult recreation, should try to develop associations of his own within which to develop his prowess. Equally, it is not surprising that he should try to keep an increasingly leisured working-class out of these associations. Fortunately, in 1880, when the universities of Oxford and Cambridge brought together the disparate amateur groups which had developed throughout Britain, to form the Amateur Athletic Association, a proposal to exclude 'artisans and labourers' from amateur status, was rejected. The definition, therefore, concerned only payment for athletic performance.

Robert Musgrove, one of the first of the great Lake District pole vaulters.

The story so far is almost entirely British. This can be explained by the fact of rural sports cultures unrestrained by serfdom, with a plethora of public holidays. It can also be explained by an early industrial revolution which created a railway system, which in turn enabled local rural sports, such as the Highland Games, to develop rapidly into a national circuit. The athletes from these rural sports were displaying their talents as early as the 1850s in the main towns of England and Scotland.

Similary, the British were exporting their games and sports by means of emigrants, as early as the first years of the nineteenth century, and Australians were running in professional matches as early as 1809. The first Highland Games were held in Boston in 1842, and there is strong evidence that the Highland Games culture established by immigrant Scots on the East Coast of the United States, was the seminal influence upon the university programmes of the East Coast.

The first international meetings

International athletics, in the form of foot-races between English professionals and American athletes, had taken place as early as 1849, and reached their peak in 1862 with the visit to England of the American Indian, Louis 'Deerfoot' Bennett. It is often forgotten that the first man to break 30 min for 6 miles was Jack ('The Gateshead Clipper') White, in an epic match with Deerfoot, and that this performance, with Deerfoot's 12 mile run of 1 hr 2½ min in 1854, was not approached until the appearance of Nurmi in the 1920s.

Athletics meetings, often prompted by English residents, were taking place in Europe as early as the 1850s, and in 1872 a comprehensive meeting was conducted in Rio de Janeiro at the Rio de Janeiro Cricket Club. There were, however, no governing bodies to regulate and stimulate the development of athletics competition as there was in England, and it was in the post-1896 Athens Olympics period that most continental governing bodies were to spring up.

The first truly full-scale international athletics meeting took place at Travers Island, New York, in the blistering heat of June 1895, between London AC and New York AC. The comprehensive quality of American athletics had not until this time been fully appreciated by English athletes who had, despite the visits of such athletes as the sprinter, Myers, and the high jumper, Byrd Page, tended to doubt the reports of outstanding performances by East Coast American club athletes.

Travers Island was to change that view for ever for the English team was comprehensively trounced.

Compared to this, the 1896 Athens Olympics, hurriedly put together by Baron Pierre de Coubertin and a committee of Greek businessmen and aristocrats, was a modest affair indeed. Held on the cramped, crumbling track of the Averoff stadium, with only a fraction of the world's best athletes in attendance, it had more in common with a Scottish rural meeting than with the quality of a truly international competition such as that which had been held at Travers Island. Nevertheless, the Olympics had taken their first faltering steps. The 1900 Paris Olympics were a disaster, while the 1904 Olympics in St Louis were hardly a representative international meeting. The 1906 Intercalated Games in Athens, possibly the best-organized Olympics to that time, gave de Coubertin breathing space; the 1908 London Olympics finally made de Coubertin's Games a meeting of international class, and the 1912 Stockholm Games set the seal upon the Olympic movement.

1912: the watershed

1912 was, in a way, a watershed. The Olympic movement was now firmly established, and the majority of the world's leading nations now possessed governing bodies. For the first time, a country (Sweden) had successfully employed a professional coach, Hjertberg, to prepare its Olympic team. Within two years, two other nations, Great Britain and Germany, had appointed national coaches (the Canadian, W. R. Knox, and the German Jew, Meyer Prinstein) to prepare their teams for the 1916 Berlin Olympics.

Equally important, in 1913 the International Amateur Athletic Federation was formed, and in the same year it set out those events which were to form the Olympic programme. Thus, such events as the standing jumps and the aggregate throws vanished from sight.

The professional preparation of national teams did not, alas, take place. World War I meant that there were no Berlin Olympics, and by the 1920 Antwerp Games, all thoughts of such preparations had been cast aside, not to be revived until the next Berlin Olympics, in 1936.

The world of athletics was at this point a tiny one, both in national terms and within nations. Neither Russia, still reeling from its revolution, nor China, Africa, the Middle East, nor South America were yet seriously involved in athletics competition. Within major nations, such as the United States and Great Britain, athletics opportunities related directly to social class, with the exception of Germany and Scandinavia. Thus, in the 1924 Olympics, close on 20 per cent of the British team came from the universities of Oxford and Cambridge.

Another central omission was the lack of development in women's athletics. Women were not to appear in the athletics events of the Olympic movement until 1928, when a modest programme was introduced.

The world of athletics until 1930 was therefore a narrowly-based male world, with a large number of countries still socially and economically incapable of taking part in athletics beyond local level.

From a technological point of view, athletics had advanced little since the nineteenth century. Tracks, approach-runs and throwing-circles were still made of cinder and the basic structure of these tracks had changed little since the death of the master track-maker, the Englishman, Charles Perry. Discus, javelin and hammer had not improved substantially in design since 1908, whilst landing-pits for the vertical jumps were still ground-level affairs of no great resilience.

Technical developments

The technical development of the sport still operated on a purely empirical basis, and the western roll, the straddle, the hitch-kick and the running-rotation discus turn, were all products of trial and error. The richest source of development was the colleges of the West Coast of the United States. There, a system of athletics scholarships, linked with an intense competitive structure, produced magnificent performances yearly in the power events, though it was less successful in the middle and long distances. The American club system, the source of its strength in the late nineteenth century, had shrivelled to nothing by the 1920s, and the United States now relied almost entirely on college athletes for its Olympic team. The United States was always to be oriented to college rather than Olympic athletics, but this was of no consequence when the products of its college system could demolish the world every four years at the Olympic Games. For the present, the American college system, however lacking in coaching specialization, was the only effective athletics system in the world.

In 1936, the Olympics gave a hint of things to come when the German team, the first to formally prepare for the Olympics since Sweden in 1912, performed outstandingly well, winning shot, javelin and hammer. As in 1912, war was to intervene and carry the German type of team preparation to its logical conclusion.

The Berlin Olympics 1500 m. The New Zealander, Jack Lovelock (467), the eventual winner, trails the American, Glen Cunningham (746), who finished second.

The entry of the Russians

The 1948 Olympics were an innocent Games, one in which the majority of competitors were, even by pre-war standards, only half-trained, recreational athletes. It was to be the last of the innocent Games; in 1952 the USSR sent a well-trained team which performed successfully in the men's events and dominated the women's programme. What the Russians showed the world in the 1952–60 period was merely the logical extension of what the Nazis had begun in 1936. The Nazis had simply not had the time to go into detailed technical analysis of each event, or to analyse training methods in detail. The Russians did, and in the 1952–60 period more was discovered about athletics techniques and training methods than had been unearthed in the previous two thousand years.

A classic example was the high jump, an event which the United States had dominated since the time of M. F. Sweeney in the late 1890s. In 1952 the Russians arrived in Helsinki with three eastern cut-off jumpers, using inferior versions of the technique which Sweeney had used in 1895. The Russians came back from Helsinki to the drawing-board and analysed the technical structure of the event in detail. They decided that the approach-run and take-off were central to the event, with bar-clearance technique of secondary importance. They therefore aimed at a stereotyped, automatic approach-run and take-off, and within four years the world record was in their grasp.

The entry of the Russians in 1954. Stepanov, later to straddle to a world record, uses the outmoded eastern cut-off technique to win in a London versus Moscow match.

This type of analysis was applied to every event and produced outstanding results in high jump, triple jump and hammer, in particular.

The British had initiated a professionally-staffed coaching scheme in 1947, and in the early 1950s, led the world in general technical knowledge and in its practical expression in club and school coaching. The British scheme leant heavily on physical education for a voluntary coaching system and laid great stress on technical analysis. Its national coaches, whose own coaching experience was general in nature, were virtually untrained for their role and received almost no in-service training. They did not control the scheme and were often not even on central advisory committees. They therefore lived in a limbo between education and sport, and spent much of their time in unproductive work of a general nature. Other Western nations, such as France and Germany, also developed coaching programmes, the central difference in Germany being that the clubs were not purely dependent on voluntary labour, but had a limited number of paid coaching staff. There was in such countries (as there was in Communist societies) the necessary coaching infrastructure within which knowledge could be both applied and developed.

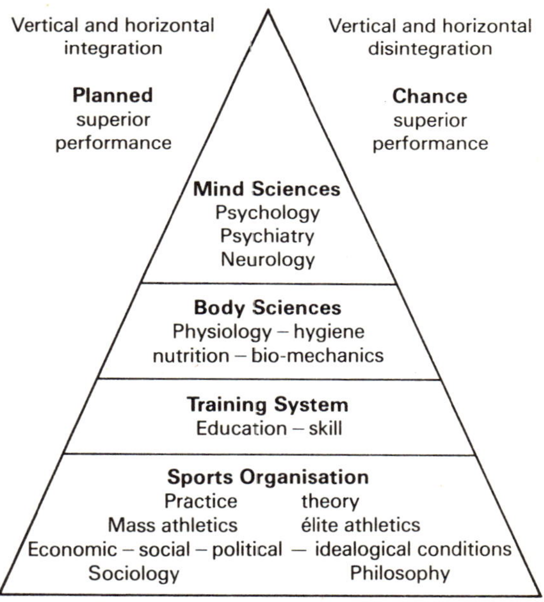

National sports development model.

The United States made no formal response to the challenge of Communist USSR and its satellites in the 1952–60 period, because the means for such a response were simply not there. The Amateur Athletic Union of the United States, essentially a conservative, Eastern-based organization, was three thousand miles from the centre of the action in the colleges of the Western seaboard and had never played any role in the development of college athletes. In any case, United States athletes were still taking the lion's share of medals from the Olympics even if, as in 1960, a Russian named Brumel should break their hold on the Olympic crown, and they lost both men's sprints.

The 1960 Games were the first to be televised on a world basis, and it was the increasing demand for televised sport which was to transform athletics in the Western world. Television attracted attention, and attention attracted sponsors. The money from sponsors went into other competitions, into development programmes, into coaching systems and ultimately back into improved performance.

Increased state involvement

At another level, there was increased state involvement, particularly in totalitarian societies, where sport was seen as a logical extension of political activity. Thus research establishments, sports schools, professional coaching and facilities were all advanced through the state. Western involvement at government level was more tentative, the argument being that sport was the concern and responsibility of governing bodies, rather than of central government. There was some aid to coaching schemes, but specialist facilities were usually left to local authorities, sometimes with modest government aid, and research was left to isolated departments of physical education. Few effective coaching resource centres, or specialized facilities, were built, the notable exception here being West Germany. In the main, Western governments have put their resources into low-level recreational schemes, whilst paying lip-service to the need to develop excellence.

Increased state aid in the East and an increase in sponsorship money and sports scholarships in the West, have increasingly made the term 'amateur' irrelevant and meaningless. If the word 'amateur' has any meaning at all, it relates to someone for whom sport is a recreation, rather than a way of life. There is, therefore, no way in which the world's best athletes can any longer be called amateurs, for they receive directly, or in kind, more help than is required to pursue their sport. This takes the form of government support in the East and sponsorship and undercover performance payments in the West. This is the natural result of increased state, public, and commercial interest in the sport, but it has created a generation of dishonest athletes. There is nothing immoral about taking money to compete in amateur sport, but the operations take place in an atmosphere of corruption, distrust and hypocrisy that can only be damaging to the moral fibre of both athlete and administrator. There is also something essentially rotten about systems in which officials ignore, condone or even involve themselves in the breaking of their own rules.

The rise of East Germany

The period 1960–68 saw a diminishing of the authority of the USSR although this was less noticeable in women's athletics. To some extent, this was because her satellites had learnt their lessons only too well and were now picking up medals at Mother Russia's expense. From 1968 on, the dominant force was to be East Germany, where the methods used by the USSR were to be refined and sharply focussed upon a small, well-disciplined population.

East Germany's improvements since the 1968 Olympics have been quite staggering. In 1968 they won a total of four Olympic track and field medals, whilst in 1976 they won twenty-six. In eight short years they had come to a position where they outpointed even the United States in the total points gained by their men's and women's teams. This has, of course, meant a massive financial commitment (2 per cent of national income) to sport, and the cost per medal is undoubtedly higher than in any country in the world, even if these technical resources are also at the disposal of their recreational system.

Technological changes

The technological changes since 1960 have been massive. In 1964, the first flexible fibre-glass poles were used in the Olympics, with the first primitive foam landing-areas. By 1968 in Mexico City we had sophisticated foam landing-areas and the first Olympics to be held on a synthetic track. Javelin and hammer, and to a lesser degree, discus, have all been brought to a high degree of sophistication. Similarly, methods of measurement (triangulation in the long throws, optical measurement in the horizontal jumps) and the complete accuracy of electrical timing, have taken the subjective element from the judging of events.

All of the above have improved performance, safety and fairness, but there are other factors which have cut at the heart of athletics competition in the 1964–76 period. Whatever differences of environment (Kenyans living at high altitude), or culture (Communist state support), existed until 1964, the athlete depended on his own inherited or trained qualities for success. There was certainly no hint that his performance might have been materially affected by pharmaceutical means. Alas, it is now no longer possible to accept any world-class performance outside the long endurance events, as having occurred without the influence of drugs. The best known of these drugs are the anabolic steroids, whose main effect is to improve work-rate and, therefore, the effects of the training stimulus. The table on page 141 shows the increase in the average weights of shot, discus and hammer throwers from the 1960 to the 1976 Olympics.

It would be wrong to concentrate on the 'heavy' events merely because the athletes in these events have shown the most obvious changes in physique, for steroids have a strong effect on every event in the speed-power area. The IAAF has stepped up its programme of drug detection, and several athletes have now been suspended, albeit only for periods of a year, though the sentence has now been raised to eighteen months. Such derisory sentences possibly give some hint of the importance which the Federation attaches to this matter. An amateur who wins £5 in a professional Highland Games, or who over-claims the same amount in expenses at an amateur meeting, is banned for life from competing in international athletics, while the drug offender can be back in competition within eighteen months.

A central problem is that many governing bodies are, in fact, the agents of drug-intake programmes within their own associations. The 'police' are therefore the criminals. It is inconceivable, for instance, that athletes such as the shot putter Slupianek (East Germany) took steroids as a matter of personal choice, just as it is inconceivable that any American athlete would take drugs under the control and supervision of the AAU. This is not to say that Western athletes do not take proscribed drugs; rather, it is to say that their decision is a personal one.

Drug detection occurs only at major competitions, a time when offending athletes have been off steroids a sufficiently long time for the drug to have cleared their systems.

Since steroids are essentially training drugs, it is virtually pointless to test them merely in competitive situations. There is, in fact, no law against athletes taking steroids in training and the testing and banning of an athlete in a training situation would probably have no validity in law. Alas, methods of avoiding drug detection (and in particular the use of diuretics to 'wash out' steroids) have now reached such an advanced level, it is unlikely that many athletes will be detected in future so steroid intake is unlikely to decrease.

The development of athletics performance relies heavily, first, on the exposure of the world's population to the basic elements of the sport under suitable conditions, and it cannot be said that this process is yet complete. Secondly, there is a need for facilities, coaching and competitive structures to develop and, as yet, these resources are unevenly spread. Communist Cuba has shown that a Caribbean nation can, with organization, take on the best in the world. On the other hand, Australia, once capable of the highest levels of performance (particularly in women's athletics), has completely failed to keep up with world developments.

Women's athletics

Women's athletics records probably have much more 'stretch' in them than their male counterparts, if only because, for social reasons, just a small fraction of the world's female population have as yet been exposed to athletics. It is likely that women's physical capacities are much closer to those of men than has been realized. The table above shows the percentage position of women's world records relative to men's world records, and the position relative to men's world records of the past. Greta Waitz's marathon time would have won gold in all Olympics until 1952, and this is an event which is not yet in the Olympic programme.

	Percentage of men's world record	Year of attainment by male athletes
100 m	91.8%	1912
200 m	90.6%	1910
400 m	90%	1881
800 m	89%	1888
1500 m	89.5%	1912
3000 m	91%	1922
Marathon	87.1%	1952
High jump	86%	1914
Long jump	79%	1883
4 x 100 m relay	90%	1924
4 x 400 m relay	87%	1911

Percentage position of women's world records relative to men's world records, and their position relative to men's world records of the past.

Competition

Although the major impact upon athletics performances has undoubtedly derived from the increased knowledge of techniques and training theory created by the investment of the Eastern bloc nations, the substantial increase in international competition since World War II must be considered a factor of almost equal importance. Before World War II, there were the Olympics, the first European Games (1938), and the Empire Games (1934), a handful of dual international meetings, and a thin film of major individual meetings, mostly on the American indoor circuit. Since then, international competition, sustained by sponsorship and increased government investment, and facilitated by the rapid development of air travel, has grown a hundred-fold. Although the United States versus Europe meetings proved to be unsuccessful, the more competitive European Cup (1965), and the World Cup (1978), have been welcome additions to the international calendar. There are now no fallow years and high-calibre athletes are often forced to rest from intense competition in pre-Olympic years, in order to prepare for Olympic events. The success of this type of policy has been shown in the performances of the Finn, Lasse Viren.

Amateurism

Any discussion of modern track and field athletics without mention of amateurism is like Hamlet without the ghost. Let me first make my position clear. There is nothing preventing a group of men deciding to limit entry to their group by one means or another. That limitation may be religion, age, or one of amateur status. Just so long as the members of the group agree upon the basis for membership, abide by the rules, and exclude those who break them, then all is well. It is also, however, essential that the group remain aware of external factors which may necessitate changes in their conditions of membership.

There is little doubt, given the social and sporting conditions which existed in late nineteenth-century England, that there was a need for some separation from the sport of pedestrianism (professional running) which existed at that time, parallel with the athletics of the middle classes. Whether or not the line should have been drawn at the earning of money, as distinct from competitions at which betting was permitted, is another matter.

The central corruption of pedestrianism was caused, not by money prizes, (which were often quite modest in size), but rather because of betting, which often made it more profitable to lose than to win. Not surprisingly, this corruption did not extend to the Highland Games and English rural sports of the period, where little betting took place. These rural sports constituted the bulk of the British professional programme, offered only modest cash prizes, and in no way made it possible for athletes to make a profession of athletics. Indeed, there has never been a period in the history of athletics since Greek times when anyone was able to make a living out of the sport. The 'professional' has therefore always been a figment of the imagination.

The original Victorian amateur definition, though a liberal one, (in that artisans and mechanics were not, as in other sports, excluded) still drew the line at the acceptance of money and did nothing to prevent amateur athletes from earning money from betting, and therefore nothing to limit the real cause of corruption.

Early in the 1890s, only a decade after the creation of the Amateur Athletic Association in 1880, a small 'circus' of English shamateurs developed, travelling from meeting to meeting in the April–October period to compete in a rapidly-developing network of popular rural meetings. In 1895, a group of these athletes was suspended, but the practice continued unabated into the late 1950s, when the rural programme went into decline. A similar 'circus' developed within the indoor programme on the American East Coast during this period, and was described graphically in a series of articles by the brilliant American sprinter, Barney Wefers, at the turn of the century.

As is still customary, Wefers described 'shamateur' practices in which he claimed to have played no part and was roundly denounced by the bully boy of the AAU, James J. Sullivan, and pressed to provide the type of concrete evidence which Sullivan well knew was not available. Wefers was eventually suspended, and the dust settled on the matter.

Fifty years and a handful of shamateur scapegoats later, there occurred the 'Glenlivet affair', in which it was claimed that illegal payments were made to amateur athletes at the 1978 Edinburgh Highland

Marita Koch (East Germany), a powerful example of East German women's sprinting in the 1970s.

Games, sponsored by Glenlivet Whisky. Since the payments were undoubtedly made in cash, since there were at least three quite separate and contradictory sets of accounts, and since leading amateur officials conducted or condoned the payments, and since it is unlikely that any revelations could be confined to the Glenlivet meeting alone, it is unlikely that anything will be done.

What has happened is simply an extension of the 'shamateurism' which prevailed at the rural sports of the 1850–1960 period. Television has attracted meet-sponsors, and since there is a limited number of 'stars', the sponsors have made available funds for the payment of leading athletes. It has, therefore, been a simple matter of supply and demand.

This has been the Western way, a natural and logical expression of Western capitalism. No such traditions existed in Eastern Europe, where state socialism has simply provided material incentives to successful athletes, in the form of housing, job opportunities and other perquisites. The Victorian definition of amateurism, created in a world in which a totalitarian state was inconceivable, is, of course, irrelevant in such a society. And that is what the amateur definition is; not wrong, but simply irrelevant.

It really makes no difference whether or not an athlete achieves material gain from his performances. What *does* make a difference is the moral climate within which such payments are made. Putting it simply, the present position stinks. It corrupts both athlete and official, and poisons relationships between them, and little of real worth or dignity can be done in such a climate of hypocrisy and deceit.

If we return to the analogy of my first paragraph, it is essential that any group not merely make rules but also effectively police them. If they fail to do so, then the rules in the end cease to exist. Even worse, if, as in amateur athletics, some of the members actively conspire to have other members break the rules, then there is, in effect, a state of anarchy.

This is the point which has now been reached in amateur athletics, a sport in which the gap between precept and practice has become massive and untenable. Much has been said about 'open' athletics and it is certain that the first step is to allow athletes to profit from their endeavours in an indirect manner, by means of advertising, broadcasting and writing. From there it is a short step to allowing athletes to accept appearance money, thus legitimizing existing practice. However, at every step it is important that the overall needs of the sport are safeguarded, in that some fraction of the athlete's earnings should come back to the sport. Similarly, there should be a minimum basic requirement of the 'star' athlete that he supports his key national fixtures. What I am therefore suggesting is an 'open' form of athletics involving certain formal responsibilities to the sport by the athlete. The development of this relationship will not be an easy one, but it may at least be conducted in an atmosphere of honesty, which is not at present possible.

2. Women in athletics

by Susan Campbell

Yesterday's athlete

The Ancient Olympic Games were all-male affairs. However, it would appear that the women took part in their own special festivals called Heraean. They were named after one of Zeus' consorts Hera, who became known as the patron saint of women runners. The main types of competition in which women took part were running and chariot driving. The athletes wore high-waisted, short tunics reaching half-way down to the knee with the right shoulder and breast left bare (was this the original sex test?). They ran bare footed with their hair loose and the victors received a wreath of olive leaves and a share of a sacrificed heifer.

After the fall of the Roman Empire until the beginning of the nineteenth century women were discouraged from taking part in any physical activity. During the Dark Ages asceticism branded anything pleasurable as 'sinful' and later the feudal concept of chivalry permitted nothing of a physical nature to be done by women of the higher social classes.

Later, the Victorian era did little to encourage women to participate in sport. By avoiding exercise and cultivating a pale face and an incapacity to do work, women portrayed the desired image of 'gentility' and helplessness. Despite this, it was from races held at fairs and local festivals at this time that women's athletics took its roots. As physical activity became a compulsory part of the education programme, so schools began organizing races for girls as well as boys. The first modern athletics meetings for women seem to have been held in 1904 in Germany, although it was another ten years before they acquired a recognized national organization. France and Austria also formed national associations in 1917 and this eventually led to the founding of the Fédération Sporting Féminine Internationale in 1921 by Madame A. Milliat (France). Under Madame's direction the first International meeting for women was held in Monte Carlo in 1921 and subsequently every four years until 1934. In England many advocates were emerging to promote women's sport which consequently led to the formation of the Women's Amateur Athletics Association of Great Britain in 1922 and the first Championship meeting a year later.

Women in the modern Olympic Games

There were many people who felt that women should be excluded from the Games. Most notable was the founder of the Modern Olympics, Pierre de Coubertin, who was quoted as saying 'women have but one task, that of the role of crowning the winner with garlands as was their role in Ancient Greece.' Coubertin believed that it was shocking to see women lightly clad, engaging in strenuous activity.

Nevertheless, women were admitted for the first time in Amsterdam in 1928. The initial programme contained only five events: 100 m, 800 m, 4 × 100 m relay, high jump and discus. Unfortunately, the competitors taking part in the 800 m were relatively untrained and most of them collapsed from exhaustion at the end of the race. This served to reinforce the anti-feminists' beliefs that women were incapable of taking part in competitive sport and it was not until 1960 that women were 'allowed' to compete over this distance again. Track and field events continued to be unpopular with many influential people. In 1930 the President of the International Olympic Committee, Count Baillet-Latour of Belgium commented, 'Women should only be permitted to participate in the aesthetical events – gymnastics, swimming, skating and tennis'. Despite these protests, two more events, hurdles and javelin, were included in the programme for the Games in Los Angeles (1932). The debate continued and it was only by two votes to nine that the International Olympic Committee kept women's events in the 1936 Berlin Games. Immediately after the Olympics, Avery Brundage was heard to say, 'I am fed up to the ears with women as track and field competitors . . . their charms sink to something less than zero . . . girls are ineffective and unpleasing on the track'.

During World War II women proved that they had both the strength and endurance to do the most arduous jobs while their husbands fought on the battlefields of the world. This was reflected in the increased number of events and competitors at the London Olympics in 1948. Perhaps one of the most significant developments occurred four years later when athletes from the Soviet Union entered the Olympics for the first time. Their initial impact at the Helsinki Games has been followed by an enviable record of success by Communist athletes at all subsequent Games.

Deprived of Olympic competition in the years of World War II, Fanny Blankers-Koen (Holland) takes four gold medals at the 1948 London Olympics.

Despite the rapid improvement of women's performances it was still not everyone's wish to see females competing at international level. 'There is no place for women today in the hard grind of competition like the Commonwealth Games, the European Games and the Olympic Games. Women running, jumping or throwing was all right when it was the province of schoolgirls . . . Who wants straight-legged, narrow-hipped, big-shouldered, powerful women, aggressive and ferocious in physique and attitude', (Percy Cerutty, Australian Athletics Coach).

This cynical view of the woman athlete has proved to be completely misguided. Women have not only managed to retain their physical attraction, but have shown that they are equally capable of total commitment and dedication to training and competition. It would be impossible and unfair to attempt to highlight any particular individuals, but it should be stressed that they have *all* made an immense contribution to the overall advancement of women's sport.

The position of women in society has continued to change as equal opportunities have gradually become a reality. The subsequent changes in the ever-expanding women's Olympic programme have included the re-introduction of the 800 m at Rome in 1960, and the inclusion of the 1500 m at Munich in 1972. By studying the results of the Games in the table below, it can be observed that there has been a gradual improvement in most events. However, although some performances are no longer showing significant advances, there are two noticeable exceptions. The first is in the throwing events where size, power and technique play such a crucial part. It would appear that more sophisticated training methods and greater scientific knowledge have helped performance levels to continue rising. Rapid improvements are also still taking place in the relatively 'new' middle distance events. Many of the myths about the possible dangers to women from competing over long distances have been dispelled and rigorous training has resulted in very fast times.

Winning performances at the Olympic Games

	Stockholm 1912	Antwerp 1920	Paris 1924	Amsterdam 1928	Los Angeles 1932	Berlin 1936	London 1948	Helsinki 1952	Melbourne 1956	Rome 1960	Tokyo 1964	Mexico 1968	Munch 1972	Montreal 1976
100 m				12.2	11.9	11.5	11.9	11.5	11.5	11.0	11.4	11.0	11.07	11.08
200m							24.4	23.7	23.4	24.0	23.0	22.5	22.40	22.37
400m											52.0	52.0	51.08	49.29
800m				2m 16.8						2m 4.3	2m 1.1	2m .09	1m 58.5	1m 54.94
1500m													4m 1.4	4m 05.48
4 x 100m relay				48.4	47.0	46.9	47.5	45.9	44.5	44.5	43.6	42.8	42.81	42.55
4 x 400m relay													3m 23	3m 19.23
80/100m hurdles					11.7	11.7	11.2	10.9	10.7	10.8	10.5	10.3	12.59*	12.77
High jump				1.57	1.65	1.60	1.68	1.66	1.76	1.85	1.90	1.82	192	1.93
Long jump							5.60	6.24	6.35	6.36	6.76	6.82	6.80	6.72
Shot							13.75	15.60	16.47	17.10	18.0	19.61	21.03	21.16
Discus				39.35	40.54	47.56	41.77	51.23	53.65	55.10	57.03	58.22	66.46	69.0
Javelin					43.60	45.12	45.43	50.47	53.67	55.80	60.37	60.35	63.72	65.94
Pentathlon (points)											5,246	5,098	4,801	4,745

The great Yolande Balas (Rumania), the last athlete to hold a world high jump record using the eastern cut-off technique.

Today's athlete

Nowadays, the barriers restricting female participation in sport have been largely removed and there has been an ever-growing acceptance of women in athletics. However, women are affected by factors other than the external restraints placed on them by administrators.

Female image

Most people need the approval of others and it is important that women athletes do not feel that their femininity is threatened because of their participation in sport. Different athletics events demand very different physiques and it is far easier for some athletes to conform to the stereotyped female image than it is for others. The original concept of the ideal woman was based on the ancient goddesses who displayed both grace and beauty, but were rarely portrayed as powerful or muscular.

The image created by top performers has always been recognized as an important tool for encouraging new recruits. The 'golden girl' tag has often been used to describe star athletes. The women who have been given this label have been great athletes and most attractive people. Their popularity and the publicity they have been given certainly increased participation as many youngsters attempted to emulate their heroines. Unfortunately, some events have never achieved these glamorous heights in Europe or America and have, therefore, become the poor relations in terms of publicity. Bearing this in mind, it is interesting to compare the women of Eastern Europe with those of the West. Every society has its own idea of what a female should do and what is appropriate behaviour for a woman. This has affected the occupations and life style of the women and consequently their athletic ambitions and performances. In the West, women are rarely found in manual jobs, particularly those requiring strength, whereas in Eastern Europe women are expected to work alongside men in every sphere of life.

At least part of the reason for the West's international failure in certain events is due to the fact that it takes an exceptional woman to train and develop a physique which is not readily admired by the society in which she lives.

Females and drugs

Today, competition is extremely intense and winning has become all important. This has particularly affected top performers, who have been subjected to great psychological and physical pressures. In an attempt to extract the maximum performance from their bodies some athletes have resorted to the use of drugs. This is, of course, a controversial matter, and one which cannot be ignored.

There are many drugs used and abused by athletes and it is beyond the scope of this chapter to discuss them in detail. There are, however, two major areas which have a particular relevance for women in athletics. Perhaps the most publicized drugs are anabolic steroids, which have been closely associated with power events. Basically, they reduce nitrogen loss and increase protein synthesis, thus enlarging the muscular contraction force. Their main effect in terms of performance is greater strength as a result of increased muscle bulk. The advantages for women, particularly those competing in power events, is abundantly obvious. No one really knows what long-term damage these drugs may cause, but their side effects have definitely had serious repercussions for women's athletics. The image created by the 'masculinization' of some females has almost certainly deterred many youngsters from taking up the events in which those athletes compete.

The menstrual cycle is an obstacle that women alone have to overcome. In recent years the pill has been used to regulate and control the cycle. This has obvious advantages for women athletes, as their competition time may be safeguarded against any possible problems. The pill itself can produce side effects, but it would appear that by taking the pill some athletes may be at an advantage psychologically as well as physiologically.

The use of drugs raises many moral questions because it is clear that while winning is the primary goal, some athletes and coaches will resort to any means to achieve their objective.

The female and her body

A study of the structure and function of the human body reveals that men and women are far more alike than they are different. The 'human engine' is well adapted to the performance of muscular work regardless of sex and there is no biological basis for the view that vigorous physical activity is more appropriate for men than women. Like men, women are capable of performing work demanding strength, speed or endurance. In the great majority of athletics events, men will always achieve higher levels of performance, but this is a separate issue.

Judgements about the unsuitability of certain athletic events for females are founded in dogma or myth, rather than in an objective assessment of physiological capacities. It is becoming clear, as social barriers are removed, that women can compete successfully at events previously assumed to be too strenuous. Participation in long distance running, for instance, has increased dramatically over the last decade, demonstrating that the female musculo-skeletal system can, with suitable preparation, sustain submaximal aerobic activity over hours. In fact, it is hypothesized that the female may be particularly well adapted to endurance activity using energy released aerobically from ample fuel stores of fat in preference to the limited carbohydrate reserve. Confirmation of this increased reliance on fat metabolism in the female and clarification of the mechanisms involved are still needed, but the fact that so many women now complete the marathon distance is evidence that they have this capacity to sustain physical work over long periods.

There are no structural or physiological reasons why women should not take part in the triple jump, the hammer or the pole vault, events which are at present excluded from the women's programme. Because these events are denied the approval of the governing bodies of athletics there is little evidence of female participation. However, none of these events demands any strength or agility not already demonstrated by women gymnasts and divers. Nor do they subject the body to greater stresses than in those sports. Perhaps, as with distance running, wider acceptance of the suitability of these events for women will only be achieved when female athletes show that they can cope successfully. Continued restriction of women's athletics programmes cannot be justified on any biological ground.

Concern is often expressed that athletic training interferes with the normal menstrual cycle, and amenorrhoea (absence of periods) is seen in some distance runners covering a very high mileage. Groups of female athletes generally exhibit a similar incidence of menstrual problems to other,

Helena Fibingerova (USSR) typifies East European shot-putting strength.

non-athletic groups. The effects of cyclic hormonal changes on performance show considerable inter-individual variation; whilst women have achieved record breaking and medal winning performances at all stages of the menstrual cycle, many do report performance variations. The evidence is presently so ambivalent that one can only conclude that each individual athlete needs to make a personal assessment of the variability, if any, of her performance in relation to the cycle. Exposure to a very intense training stress can, as can other forms of stress, induce menstrual problems but, on the other hand, exercise is often recommended by doctors for women who have painful periods. For many female athletes training and competition may go on with little or no regard to the menstrual cycle while others may need to take account of performance variations; remembering that these could be psychological rather than physiological in origin.

Involvement in athletics does not bring greater risk of injury to women than men. Recent surveys of sports injuries conclude that in general female athletes sustain the same numbers as their male counterparts. The female body is not a delicate thing incompatible with sporting activity and, in fact, it benefits from activity rather than suffering from it. Possible injuries to the female breast have always been of concern, but where such injuries do occur they are minor, taking the form of contusions. Nor is there any evidence that injury predisposes to malignancy. Injuries to genital organs are, in fact, less likely in women than men because of the protection offered by the bony pelvis. The female athlete is certainly at no greater risk than the male and the many benefits accruing from participation outweigh the possible disadvantages.

In summary, there are no physiological barriers to women who have a commitment to improving their standard of performance in the whole range of athletic events. However, if women are to fulfill their potential in the sport there must be changes in attitudes to their performance. Constant, often disparaging, comparisons of performance standards between the sexes are not valid. Women certainly want the same standards of behaviour to apply; for example, aggression and competitiveness should be seen as human traits rather than a male preserve. In most areas of athletic performance the best man will always achieve higher absolute standards than the best woman. Most of this advantage accrues from differences in body composition as the male has a larger proportion of muscle tissue. This gives him greater strength and a better power to weight ratio, and also makes available larger shares of the high energy phosphates which are used to release the energy for events requiring a brief, explosive effort. In events which tax the oxygen transport system heavily, such as the 1500 m, the proportionately larger heart and higher haemoglobin content of the male advantages him. So, despite the fact that considerable overlap is evident with some women achieving higher standards than some men, in most areas of athletic performance it is unfair to judge female performance against standards set by males.

Tomorrow's athlete

As old prejudices are slowly eroded, no doubt more events will be added to the women's programme. However, social attitudes are slow to change, as demonstrated by the International Olympic Committee's rejection of a proposal to include the 3000 m in the 1980 Moscow Games, on the grounds that the race was a 'little too strenuous' for women. Unless there is any new medical evidence to the contrary, it would seem that there is no logical reason why women should not compete in similar events to men. One example of the kind of change which is taking place is the growing number of women marathon runners. Since the first world record time was officially recorded in 1967 there has been phenomenal progress and it would seem that, contrary to popular belief, women are particularly suited to endurance events.

Any discussion about the future always leads to the question of men and women competing together. It seems that women's records are improving more rapidly than men's and this has led to conjecture about the closing gap between male and female performances. Although there is no doubt that recent records have reached new heights it cannot be denied that there are basic physical differences between the sexes which will inevitably affect results. Instead of striving to compete with their male counterparts, it is more important for female athletes to be concerned with the qualities and strengths of their own sex. In the future, women's performances will undoubtedly continue to improve before eventually reaching a plateau. However, athletics should be about individual combat; woman versus woman; man versus man; rather than an obsessive pursuit of times and distances.

It is hoped that the opportunities for women of every country will continue to improve and that new nations will begin to take an active part in international athletics. There has already been a remarkable imprint made by men from the African continent and perhaps it will not be too long before women's athletics feels a similar impact? There are also other countries where, due to religious or cultural reasons, women are far less liberated than in the developed nations, but perhaps in the future these restrictions will be removed.

The future undoubtedly holds many exciting prospects, but there must also be several areas of concern. Firstly, there is the fear that women will be subjected to an even greater use of artificial aids and stimulants, thus reducing the contest to a scientific battle in the 'laboratory': the athletic arena. Secondly, women need to guard against simply attempting to mimic men. 'It is important to see that the fight against sexism in sports, or in society generally, is not won by fitting a few females into the slots of the same repressive system' (Paul Hoch). Finally, it is vital for the future of women's athletics that more females are involved in coaching and administration. The fear here is that not enough women will have the time or the inclination to devote themselves to these positions.

Women's athletics has come out of the starting blocks very strongly and has overcome many of the hurdles put in its way, but it still has a long way to go before the race is won.

3. The world of the professional

The only period in the history of athletics when it can be truly said that professional competition existed was in pre-Christian times. Here I use the word professional in the narrow sense of a person whose income is primarily gained from his athletics ability. As we shall see in a subsequent description of Victorian athletics, no such possibility existed when the amateur rules were framed and (in Western society at least) no such possibility has ever existed.

The professional class of athlete of the pre-Christian period developed on the economic basis of the city-state rather than on that of prize money alone, for then, as now, there was insufficient prize money to sustain more than a handful of athletes. The Mediterranean circuit of major and minor Games, though dense, involved much travel over the May–October period and it must have been difficult for an athlete to remain in good condition over a long programme of Games. A 'circus' of performers, (similar in nature to that which developed in the nineteenth-century Scottish Games) developed. Like the Scots, they formed themselves into craft unions to protect their interests, but unlike the Scots these unions became extremely powerful. It is impossible to put a figure on the number of professional athletes who existed at the peak of the Greek Games' popularity, but it should be remembered that in the narrower sense of 'professional' (the acceptance of money prizes) the whole Greek circuit (excluding Crown Games such as those at Olympia and Delphi) was professional in nature. Most of the competing athletes were, for most of the history of the Greek Games, 'professional' within the modern definition of the term.

It is important to understand that the Greeks had no definition of a professional athlete, for it was of no concern to them whether an athlete won money or not. Neither was it a concern of the English of the pre-1850 period, a period during which the nobility were prominent in backing themselves and their nominees for large wagers. Here the only distinction was one of class; 'gentlemen' had the prefix 'Mr' whilst other classes did not.

The period of wagering backed by the English upper classes probably ended before the coronation of Victoria in 1838, but by that time the backing of professional athletes had passed into the hands of bookmakers and the landlords of public houses. This 'professional' class of athletes which had developed was essentially a part-time group

In 1862, Louis Bennett ('Deerfoot') came from the United States of America to set professional distance records which last to this day, and even had a dance, 'The Deerfoot Galop', dedicated to him.

DEERFOOT GALOP.
THE ESCAPE OF DEERFOOT THE INDIAN RUNNER FROM THE CHIPPEWAYS
ARRANGED BY
W. LEWIS.

of performers, many of them of only modest athletic ability, who were simply involved in a sporting facet of a gambling culture. This was reflected in the number of events which were on a handicap basis.

This was undoubtedly a seedy and dishonest world, one which interlocked with prize fighting, cock fighting, horse racing, and a variety of other gambling, tavern-based activities of the period. Separate from this were local rural cultures, such as the running-based culture of Kent, or the field events cultures of Cumbria, southern Scotland, and the Scottish Highlands. These rural cultures undoubtedly had roots going deep into the eighteenth century, but only that of Kent has been accurately recorded in that century. The first Scottish Border Games are recorded as the St Ronan's Games of 1827 and the first Highland Games were only a few years later, but it is quite certain that these rural cultures based on field events pre-date this by many years.

It must be said that none of these cultures were at that time able to support even a handful of full-time professional athletes. The world of tavern-based running matches had as its competitive population the proletarians of the rapidly developing industrial cities, and offered the most hope for such a development, but it was not until the 1850s, which saw the development of full-scale 'Pedestrian Carnivals' (of which Sheffield and Powderhall were to become the leaders) that such meetings were ever able to offer the hope of full-time employment to professional athletes. The rural cultures (which were, with their comprehensive programmes of running, jumping, throwing and hurdling, to provide the true genesis of modern

PEDESTRIANISM.

MATCHES TO COME.

SEPTEMBER.

7.—Barker and Jones—to run 10 miles, £10 a side, at Brompton, Jones to have half a minute start.
7.—Heywood and Marshall—100 yards, £20 a side, Higginshaw Grounds Oldham.
7.—Howcroft and Lund—to run a mile, £10 a side, St Thomas's Ground, Stanningley, Leeds.
7.—Jarrot and Kirkman—440 yards, £15 a side, Copenhagen Grounds, Manchester.
7.—Culpun and Day—120 yards, £10 a side, St Thomas's Ground, Stanningly, Leeds.
9.—Andrews and Bull—to run four miles, £5 a side, Bull to have one minute start, Holloway.
9.—Deerfoot (the Indian) and Mills—to run six miles, £25 a side and the champion's belt, Hackney Wick.
9.—Dockeray and Peel—to run a mile, £5 a side, Victoria Grounds, Leeds.
9.—One Mile Handicap, for a time piece and money prizes, Copenhagen Grounds, Holloway.
9.—Martin and Sherwood—100 yards, Sherwood staking £15 to £10, within five miles of Worcester.
9.—Boater and Williams—100 yards, £5 a side, Aston Cross.
9, 10.—All England Handicap Race, quarter of a mile, for £15, St Helena Gardens, Balsall Heath.
11.—Green and Maddox—100 yards, £25 a side, Stockton-on-Tees, Maddox to have a yard start.
14.—Five Miles Handicap—£25 in money prizes, Victoria Grounds, Newcastle.
14.—Hunt and Turner—115 yards, £10 a side, Ash Inn, Stockport.
14.—Bently and Shaw—440 yards, £10 a side, Snipe Inn, Audenshaw.
14.—Jarrott and Kirkman—440 yards, £25 a side, Higginshaw Grounds, Oldham.
14.—Cox and Hancock—140 yards, £25 a side, Salford.
14, 21.—Handicap race of 120 yards, £5 and other money prizes, Victoria Grounds, Leeds.
16.—C. Perry—to run 440 yards in 57sec, £10 a side, Brompton.
16.—Lambert and Simcox—120 yards, £10 a side, Aston Cross.
16.—Deerfoot (the Indian) and White—to run four miles, £25 a side, Deerfoot to have 50 yards start, Salford.
16.—Faultless and Robinson—to walk seven miles, £10 a side, Hackney Wick.
16.—Baxter and Bridge—150 yards, £10 a side, Wandsworth.
16.—Several races and various sports, at Hackney Wick, for the benefit of the Spitalfield Weavers.
16.—Coleman and Holden—to walk three miles, £5 a side, within ten miles of Walsall.
16.—Browning and Clarke—to run a mile, £5 a side, St Helena Gardens, Balsall Heath.
16.—Tinsley and Whitty—120 yards, £10 a side, Waterfall Gardens, Endon.
16.—Dorrington and Hatley—to walk four miles, £5 a side, King's Arms, Norwood.
16, 17.—All England Handicap Race, 120 yards, £13 in money prizes, St Helena Gardens, Balsall Heath, Birmingham.
21.—Jones and Mills—to run 10 miles, £15 a side, at Brompton, Jones to have two minutes start.
21.—One Mile Handicap, for £10 in money prizes, George and Dragon, Honley, Yorkshire.
21.—Minns and Stewart—120 yards, £25 a side, Victoria Grounds, Newcastle-on-Tyne.
21, 23.—All England Handicap Race, 130 yards, for £25 and other money prizes, Salford.
23.—Firth and Stewart—to run a mile, £20 a side, George and Dragon, Honley, Yorkshire.
23.—Clynes and Hudson—120 yards, £5 a side, Aston Cross.
23.—120 yards Handicap, for several money prizes, White Hart, Red Hill, Arnold.
23.—Salt and Sumner—100 yards, £10 a side, High Park, Fenton.
23.—Jones and Roberts—to run a mile, £10 a side, Aston Cross.
23.—Albison and Lang—to run half a mile, £50 a side, Lang to have 10 yards start, Copenhagen Grounds, Manchester.
23.—The Ten Mile Champion Cup and £20, also a Sweepstakes of £10 each man, Hackney Wick.
23, 24.—All England Handicap Race, 300 yards, £15 in money prizes, St Helena Gardens, Balsall Heath, Birmingham.
23, 24.—All England Handicap Race, 245 yards, £35 in money prizes, Hyde Park, Sheffield.
23, 24.—Handicap race, 315 yards, £35 in money prizes, Hyde Park, Sheffield.
28.—Barlow and Entwistle—to run a mile, £10 a side, Ash Inn, Stockport.
28.—Crompton and Jepson—440 yards, £10 a side, Copenhagen Grounds, Manchester.
28, Oct 5.—All England Handicap, 400 yards, £11 10s in money prizes, Warren House, Lindley Moor.
30, and Oct 1.—Handicap race of 260 yards, £23 in money prizes, Queen's Hotel, Sheffield.
30.—Croby and Johns—100 yards, £5 a side, Brompton, Johns to have one yard start.
30.—Ireland and Walshaw—to walk two miles and a half, £10 a side, Higginshaw Grounds, Oldham.
30.—Myatt and Roberts—to run a mile, £5 a side, St Helena Gardens, Balsall Heath, Myatt to have six yards start.

A typical programme of pedestrian running matches of the 1860s.

athletics) had low prize values, took place in the May–September period, and did not possess, until the middle of the century, the necessary railway system to enable athletes to go much beyond their local games.

Just as the development of cheap plane travel was to revolutionize international sport in the 1950s, so a century earlier, the creation of a comprehensive capillary system of cheap railway travel was to develop the sport of Victorian Britain. A 'circus' of top level field events athletes travelled the Scottish and Border Games; large crowds gathered at pedestrian carnivals in London, Sheffield, Manchester and Edinburgh, and at the same centres to see man-versus-man matches.

There were three peaks in the development of professional foot-racing. The first was in 1809, when public attention was excited by the feats of Captain Barclay Allardice, culminating in his 'one thousand miles in a thousand hours' in 1809 at Newmarket. The second was in 1862, when Louis 'Deerfoot' Bennett came from the United States to challenge the greatest British distance runners. The third and final phase was in the 1885–95 period when such amateurs as W. G. George, A. R. Downer, F. E. Bacon and E. C. Bredin gave a temporary fillip to a fading sport.

The last period was one of intense public interest and the George versus Cummings contests resulted in George's 4 min 12¾ sec mile. It must be said, however, that even the George versus Cummings series was viewed with some cynicism by the sporting public, and the disastrous Hutchens versus Gent sprint match (which resulted in the destruction of part of London's Lillie Bridge ground) sealed the fate of professional athletics in southern England. The sport therefore retreated further and further north, to Sheffield and Edinburgh.

The George versus Cummings match-races of 1885 marked the high point of Victorian professional running.

The central problem of professional foot-racing was not the money prizes, but the existence of betting. If a strong governing body, similar to the Jockey Club, had arisen to control the sport in the late nineteenth century, then it is quite possible that the AAA (formed 1880) could have governed *all* aspects of the sport and not merely the amateur one. Other national governing bodies would have followed suit and the IAAF would have become the IAF. The hypocrisy and the barren semantics which have surrounded the 'amateur' definition would have had less fertile ground in which to breed and the true relationship between committed sportsmen and recreational sportsmen might have become clearer.

This did not, of course, happen, as the dividing line was drawn by the AAA in 1880 at the mere acceptance of money, thus separating British amateur athletics from its innocent rural roots. What in fact the creators of the AAA really wanted was a governing body which was an extension of university athletics. They sensibly saw that social exclusivity was impossible, but drew a line at the 'professional', the athlete who had accepted money. By 1894, when de Coubertin put to the Paris Congress his proposal to re-establish the Olympics, the 1880 definition was already being given a moral status, a quality of holy writ.

The alternative path for professional athletics was the formation of a world governing body, but this never happened, and the sport therefore pursued a lonely, diminishing existence in Great Britain, Australia, New Zealand, South Africa and the East Coast of the United States until World War I.

There was, however, one faltering flicker in 1908, in the aftermath of the Dorando Marathon at the London Olympics. The interest created in marathon running by Dorando's race brought into being a flurry of professional marathons all over the world, but by 1910 this boom, which was not controlled by a central governing body, was over, and another opportunity was lost.

The carnage of World War I destroyed many of the rural sports of Scotland and northern England and they were slow in reviving, but Powderhall, which had become the world centre of professional handicap foot-racing, maintained its high ethical level and its New Year Handicap yearly attracted some of the best professional runners in the world. Match racing was dead by 1933, and since professional foot-racing was based on handicap events rather than scratch racing, the sport had now dwindled to summer handicaps and rural sports with the Powderhall Handicap in the middle of the winter.

In 1947, the Scottish Games Association was formed under the leadership of T. A. Young, and it soon came to be accepted as the governing body of a loose confederation of local Games in Scotland and northern England. Similar associations were formed at state level in Australia and loose links with the SGA were formed.

The world of amateur athletics changed little in the period from 1900 to 1936 in terms of the relationship between amateurs and professionals. The Berlin Olympics were, however, to see in the German team the first national team whose members were given work concessions to enable them to prepare for the Games. The post-war period was to see the extension of the principle of state intervention, with the entry of the USSR to the 1950 European Championships and the 1952 Olympics. World War II had changed the map of Europe and nowhere were these changes to be more evident than in the world of sport. This involved massive government investment, in the form of coaching, research, facilities, sports medicine, struc-

The appearance of Arthur Rowe in the professional Highland Games circuit of the 1960s gave the sport a much-needed boost.

tured competition, food allowances, accommodation and work incentives. The most important of these factors was undoubtedly indirect, in the form of such support systems as coaching, facilities and competition, but there is no doubt that the provision of accommodation, food allowances, work incentives, and even direct financial inducements, went far beyond the IAAF definition of amateur. Alas, although the amateur definition was created by the IAAF, its interpretation has always been left to individual governing bodies. This has left the way clear for totalitarian states, who had already invested heavily in the success of their athletes, to interpret the rules to suit themselves.

In contrast, the capitalist world has taken its own, less orderly, route. Sports scholarships began in American colleges before World War I, and undercover payments to prominent athletes were standard practice in Great Britain and on the Eastern indoor circuit even before the turn of the century. Government intervention, in terms of coaching provision, began in Sweden in 1910 and Great Britain in 1947, but has in all Western countries now reached the point of direct support payments to the athlete.

The rapid development of televised athletics and its subsequent increase in popularity, has created a sponsorship potential which has in turn made star athletes essential to the success of major meetings. That all of the world's leading athletes have at some time been paid by meeting promoters is no longer a matter for conjecture.

It might therefore have been thought, when the world's first professional athletics association, the International Track Association, was formed in 1972, that the time was ripe for a form of 'open' athletics. Alas, the prize money offered by the ITA was vastly inferior to the state subsidies and undercover payments already available to the world's top amateur athletes. The ITA therefore failed to attract the necessary stars which would have made their enterprise viable, and never became much more than a group of ex-college athletes topped up with a handful of athletes at the ends of their careers.

Professional athletics is a myth in that there has never been, since Greek times, a group of full-time professional athletes, although many international athletes are now not far from this situation for large parts of their lives.

The nineteenth century fear of professionalism was a fear of a corrupt world, a fear of dishonesty. If the officials of amateur athletics should fear anything today, it should be a fear of officials who directly involve themselves in evasions of their own rules; of officials who condone these evasions; and of the majority of officials who simply turn a blind eye to this corruption. They should fear, not the mere transfer of money to amateur athletes, but the corrupting atmosphere within which these arrangements take place. There has been much talk about 'open' athletics, without any clear attempt being made to define what responsibilities and disciplines athletes would have to observe within such a system. I would prefer to use the words 'honest athletics', for it matters little whether or not money is given for athletics performances; there is no law of the Medes and Persians which says that the nineteenth century amateur, or some twentieth century variant, is inevitable. Professional athletics, as it now stands, the remnant of a nineteenth century sport, is no more professional in nature than most recreational sport. True professionalism, both in spirit and fact, has long since passed to the top level of amateur athletics. There is nothing wrong in this; the only wrong is the failure to recognize this reality and to relate to it, either by strict enforcement of the amateur rules or by their removal.

Two great sprinters, Valery Borzov (USSR, left) and an unusually tense Pietro Mennea (Italy).

PART II
Running events

4. Sprints

History

Two sprints were included in the Ancient Olympic Games, the *stade* (one length of the stadium) and the *diaulos* (two lengths), the *stade* length at Olympia being 192 m (200 yd). Although no detail of starting commands has been handed down to us, it is known that false starts were punished by whipping. It is also known that starting-gates were used, with a gallows-like husplex, and separate strings channelled back through grooves in the starting sill to the starter. Evidence for the husplex is circumstantial, has little support either from written or artistic sources, but is nevertheless strong.

The evidence of vase-drawings shows that Greek artists had a keen appreciation of the vigour and dynamism of sprinting, even though some artists insisted, for aesthetic reasons, in showing arms and legs out of phase.

Naturally, there is no record of performance available from the ancient Games, but it is unlikely that naked men, running in bare feet on hard, baked earth, could have run much better than 22 sec for the *stade* and 48 sec for the *diaulos*, a race which must have posed great problems for runners converging upon the turning point.

There are early mentions of sprint races in England in the seventeenth century, usually between the servants of the nobility, and there are apocryphal accounts of the speed and jumping ability of the Basques. The first real detail, however, occurs in eighteenth-century Kent, where there are regular reports on running matches, usually measured in 'perches' (4.50 m/5½ yd) rather than yards.

Kentish Post 14 August, 1754

> There will be a match of running in Wye in Harvel Field on Monday next, from East Kent to West Kent, divided by the River Stour; and that a velvet cap, valued at 7s 6d will be run for, forty rods, by any men, that never won the ten pounds at old Wives Lees. To draw lotts and run two and two; the second best to have the entrance money.

These matches were interspersed with running games such as 'prisoner's bases', a rural sport which survived until the middle of the nineteenth century.

The first detailed accounts of sprint matches occur in the late eighteenth century, usually between members of the nobility or their representatives. We hear of a gentleman, Mr Andrew Skewball, running 127 m (140 yd) in an unlikely 12 sec in 1808, and Curley, 'The Brighton Shepherd', running a more acceptable 110 m (120 yd) in 12½ sec in 1805. At this time, races were run, not in stadiums, but on fields or turnpike roads.

The building in England in the late 1840s of the first enclosed running grounds provided homes for both the first 'pedestrian' meetings and for the numerous 'matches' between runners, which had previously taken place on fields and turnpike roads. Previously, as early as the 1820s, the rural games of northern England and Scotland had featured sprints as part of the world's first comprehensive track and field programme.

The creation of the stop-watch in the 1850s made the accurate timing of sprints possible, although many watches were calibrated in eighths or sixteenths. The first great sprinter of this period was the professional runner, 'The American Wonder', George Seward, who was credited with 9.25 sec for 91 m (100 yd) in 1844. The mid-1850s also saw the creation of spiked running shoes, giving sprinters the traction they required on the newly-created cinder tracks.

The greatest sprinter of the nineteenth century was undoubtedly the English professional runner, Harry Hutchens. Hutchens' true worth will never be known as he spent most of his professional career 'running to orders'. However, when the wraps were taken off, as they were in the midwinter gloom of Powderhall in December 1884, Hutchens' quality was clear for all to see. Running from scratch in a 270 m (300 yd) handicap, Hutchens ripped through the field to win in 30 sec, easing up. All contemporary accounts are unanimous that Hutchens was undoubtedly the swiftest runner of the nineteenth century, even if the supporting statistical evidence is slight.

The history of sprinting from the late nineteenth century onwards is essentially amateur in nature and is detailed in the progressive performance lists. Mention must, however, be made of the development of starting rules and techniques. Until the last half of the nineteenth century, many professional sprint matches were decided using 'starts by consent', in which the runners agreed between them on the fairness of the start. Since each runner had right of appeal, the conclusion of such races often took a long time, so a clause in professional contracts was inserted, stipulating 'start by consent, or if no conclusion reached by one hour, start by gun'. In time, the gun start became standard practice.

The 'dab' start, a standing start with the front foot hitting the ground first, was used by professionals until the end of the nineteenth century, as was a conventional standing start from starting holes. In 1887 the Yale University Irish-American coach, Michael Murphy, created the crouch start from holes. This gave both stability in the 'set' position and greater velocity from the gun because of the heavily flexed position of legs working on an almost horizontal trunk, and some variation of Murphy's start has obtained since the end of the nineteenth century.

The fastest 100/200 m runner of the early twentieth century was undoubtedly the white American, Arthur Duffey, who ran 9.6 sec 91m (100 yd) in 1902, and twice ran the distance in an unofficial 9.2 sec in England. In the 400 m (440 yd) sprint (up to World War II mainly non-metric distances were used) the white American, Maxey Long, had run 47.8 sec in 1900 for the first official world record and 47 sec for the distance in the same year on a straight course.

It must be noted that until 1928, all improvements in sprint performances had to be recorded in ⅕ sec (equivalent to an improvement of 2 m/6 ft 6¾ in in the short sprints), records remained relatively static until 1929, when the necessary rule change allowed the negro, Eddie Tolan (USA) to run 9.5 sec for 91 m (100 yd). It will be noted that up to this point world sprinting had been almost

Jesse Owens (USA), the greatest sprinter/jumper in history.

the exclusive province of the white American, though the English sprinter, H. M. Abrahams, had broken the American monopoly in the 100 m in the 1924 Paris Olympics.

1929 saw the first 9.4 sec 91 m (100 yd) run by George Simpson (USA). Simpson's record was not, however, accepted, because he had used starting blocks, which were not to be used in Olympic competition until 1948.

The greatest sprinter of the 1930s was undoubtedly the American negro, Jesse Owens, who, on 25 May 1935, at Ann Arbor, Michigan, broke or equalled six world records within the space of an hour. Owens ran 10.2 sec for 100 m and 20.3 sec for 200 m in 1936 to take world records in both events, and won both sprints in the 1936 Olympics.

The longer sprint had also remained an American monopoly and by 1936 the 400 m record stood at 46.1 sec to the American negro, Archie Williams, to be taken to 46 sec by the German, Rudolf Harbig, in 1939.

Since World War II, with the rapid development of air travel, meetings of the world's great sprinters have not been confined to the Olympics, and it has therefore been possible to effectively compare their competitive records in a way which was not previously possible, except within the closed circuit of American college competition. In competitive terms, the great 100/200 m sprinters of the 1950s were undoubtedly Sime (USA), Morrow (USA), and Jerome (Canada), whilst in the 1960s, Carr (USA), Hary (Germany), Hayes (USA), Hines (USA) and Smith (USA) must be considered the leaders.

The burly American, Bob Hayes, possibly the fastest 100 m runner in history, taking gold at the Tokyo Olympics.

The predominance of the American sprinter declined gradually all through the 1960s, but what was particularly noticeable was the rapid decline of the American white sprinter. Indeed, it is interesting to note that in 1968 all finalists in the 100 m in the Mexico Olympics were coloured and that only three of the sixteen semi-finalists were white.

In 1960, the American grip on the Olympic 100 m was broken by the fast-starting German, Armin Hary, and in the 200 m by the Italian, Livio Berutti, and although in 1964 and 1968 the Americans regained their supremacy, in 1972 it was a Russian, the slick, automatic Valery Borzov, who was to take both Olympic sprints. In 1976, although both Olympic sprint victors (Crawford and Quarrie) were coloured and American-based, they were again not native-born Americans. It would therefore seem that, though negro sprinters are always going to rank high in world sprints, the improved technique and conditioning of European sprinters has at last brought them level.

The 400 m has produced a similar change in the balance of power. In the 1960 Olympics 400 m the German, Kaufmann and the American, Davis hit the tape together in a world record of 44.9 sec, with Kaufmann the victor. Since then the American grip on 400 m has been more firm than in the short sprints, but in 1976 the Cuban, Alberto Juantorena, took Olympic gold in the Montreal Olympics.

The introduction of electrical timekeeping in the 1970s has made it possible to assess the

Scottish sprinter, Allan Wells (752). Nurtured on the traditional programmes of Scottish professional runners, Wells has shown himself to be a world class sprinter.

true speeds accurately, if not the competitive abilities, of sprinters. It is now, for instance, clear that no male sprinter has ever run inside 10 sec for 100 m at ground level, as the major competitions held at altitude indicate a gain of at least 1/10 sec in the 100 m and close to 3/10 sec in the 200 m. Electrical timekeeping has shown that world sprinting is now almost static, with the adjusted performances of Mexico City – i.e., 10.05 sec (9.95), and 20.06 sec (19.83) – still capable of winning gold medals in the 1980 Olympics. Similarly, no international 400 m runner of recent years has shown himself capable of regularly running inside 45 sec, and here we must look back at Lee Evans whose 43.8 sec at Mexico City in 1968 might possibly be worth 44.3 sec at ground level. The picture in world men's sprinting is therefore essentially a still life.

Women

The first official world record for 100 m was achieved by the Polish sprinter, Stanislawa Walasiewicz, who ran 11.7 sec in 1934, taking also the 200 m record a year later in a creditable 23.6 sec.

The United States, lacking a women's college competitive and scholarship structure similar to that obtaining for its male competitors, have never dominated women's sprinting in the same way, though its female coloured athletes has undoubtedly the same natural sprinting talent. The successes of Wilma Rudolph (100 m, 200 m, Rome 1960), Wyomia Tyus (100 m, Tokyo 1964, Mexico City 1968), and the more recent successes of Evelyn Ashford, certainly hint at a rich abundance of talent. The world record for the short sprints has, however, been bandied about between nations as diverse as Poland, Taiwan, Czechoslovakia, and East Germany, and since 1972 has rested in East or West Germany. The GDR has, since the early 1970s, produced a flow of great female sprinters, from Renate Stecher in the early seventies to Marita Koch in the last years of the decade.

The women's world records, standing at 10.88 and 21.71 sec (effectively translating to hand-timed 10.6 and 21.5 sec) are comparable with men's sprinting before World War I, a position which they hold in few other events. As a comparison, the present women's long jump record of 7.09 m (23 ft 3¼ in) was achieved by a male athlete in the 1885–1895) period, the 800 m record (1 min 54.8 sec) during the same period. Women do, therefore, seem to have a particular talent in the sprints, particulary in 100 m, where sheer size is less important.

When, however, we look at the 400 m, the position is quite different. A 400 m record was recognized only in 1957 and it was not until five years later that 54 sec was first

Britain's 'golden girl' of the 1970s, the fine all-round sprinter, Donna Hartley.

Irena Sewinska (left, Poland), the greatest all-round female sprinter of all time, with a career spanning five Olympics.

broken, by Maria Itkina of USSR. The development of the event in recent years has been almost entirely Eastern European in nature. First, the Pole, Irena Szewinska, moved up from the short sprints in 1974 to take the record inside 50 sec with 49.9 sec, and by 1979 the record had been butchered in stages by the East German, Marita Koch, down to 48.56 sec. The present situation is that no athlete, other than Koch, can guarantee a run of inside 50 sec in still conditions, and that any run inside 51 sec will win most events outside of the European Championships or Olympic Games.

Technique

Sprinting is best explained by the equation: stride-length × leg-cadence + endurance. The sprinter's skill lies in his ability to cover track (stride-length) rapidly (cadence), with minimum loss of speed after peak velocity is reached (endurance).

Sprinting is not, like distance running, dependent on a balance between energy-expenditure and oxygen intake. The sprinter runs on short-term energy already stored in his muscles and can run flat out for about 275 m (300 yd) before the build-up of muscular wastes brings him to a grinding halt.

The velocity pattern of a 100 m race is worth looking at, as the point of peak velocity in a 10 sec 100 m runner is about 50 m (54¾ yd). It is followed by about 20 m (21¾ yd) of constant speed and 30 m (32¾ yd) of deceleration. What is therefore being seen in the closing stages of a sprint is not a series of accelerations, for the competitors have reached top speed at 40–50 m (43¾–54¾ yd) but rather a collection of decelerations. There are many sprinters (the American, Houston McTear, is a classic example) who lead easily at 60 m (65½ yd), but fade quickly and are trapped and caught by the fast finishers. Such runners usually dominate indoor competition, but rarely show comprehensive sprint qualities outdoors over 100 m and 200 m distances.

The start

Sprinting has a strong natural element, but one totally artificial aspect is the sprint start, taken from starting blocks. Reaction time (the first muscular response to the gun) is usually between 0.12 and 0.17 sec in an international sprinter (although the 1960 German Olympic champion, Armin Hary, was clocked at inside 0.10 sec), but thereafter it is the force which the sprinter can apply backwards against the ground that is critical to velocity during the acceleration period.

More research has probably been done on starting than on any other aspect of sprint technique, but the results have been modest. This is to a degree because the variables of block angles, joint angles, trunk length, limb relationships and the position of the centre of gravity, are almost infinite and it is therefore quite impossible to exercise the type of controls required to produce good research results. What is known is that most of the work is done from the front block, which should be shallow to give a good pushing angle. The leg angle of the front leg must be no more than 90°, (though it may well be 10° less) to give a long, rangy push from the block. It is also essential to have the sprinter's centre of body weight above or ahead of his front foot so that the forward push can be immediate. Finally, essential to a good start is a full-range push (fig. 1.4) through a straight, low trunk; these rangy pushes continuing from the start through the pick up until peak velocity is reached.

The pick-up

Acceleration during the pick-up is governed by the power and range of the muscles of the legs during these periods of sustained ground contact. Strides lengthen gradually, as the inertia of the body is overcome.

Trunk angles change from the start to the end of the acceleration phase. The sprinter is low at the beginning of this period and is erect by its end, and any attempt to artificially keep the trunk down will result in loss of balance, with the legs unable to 'catch up'.

In the 200 m, world-class sprinters cover the first 100 m round the curve in 10.5–10.7 sec, covering the final 100 m in 9.5–9.8 sec. As in 100 m, this means a deceleration over the final 100 m. Important to the sprinter is a fast, relaxed bend – there is no point in running the bend in 10.3 sec to come out of it tense and lose speed rapidly in the final 100 m. A middle lane (3–5) is an advantage as it

1 Sprint start

2 Sprint action

has a gentler curve, whilst still allowing the sprinter to get the 'feel' of the race by having runners outside him to pull him through. In contrast, the first and second lanes have tight, often tension-producing, curves.

Two hundred metre runners set their blocks at a tangent to the bends in order that their early, acceleration strides may be run on a straight line. This means marginally extra distance, but a smoother, more relaxed pick-up phase.

The production of an automatic, relaxed running action is the aim of the sprinter. The main power unit is the legs, which must drive forward a still, fixed trunk and head, and any bowing of the back, torsion of the trunk, or head wobble will detract from a full-blooded, efficient sprint action. The secondary power unit is the arms, which also act as stabilizers of the trunk. The Russian, Valery Borzov, and the Italian, Mennea, epitomize relaxed, automatic sprinting at its best.

The finish

There are two basic finish techniques. The first is a straight drive through the tape, and this type of finish is perfectly adequate for young athletes. However, international athletes normally use a 'dip' finish, throwing in the trunk in the final stride. Here good timing is essential, for too early a dip means that the sprinter stops his arm drive and decelerates quickly. The dip must therefore be late and perfectly timed.

400 metres

Four hundred metres is a sustained sub-sprint and the technical factors pertaining to sprints are identical. Where the 400 m runner must exercise caution is in his balance of effort between first and second halves of the race. In the early 1950s, several runners, such as the American, Lou Jones, experimented with a first 200 m only 0.3 sec short of their best 200 m sprint times and tended to fade badly over the second part of the race. Recent years have, however, shown that a differential of between 1.3 sec and 2 sec is more likely to produce the best results. The differentials in women's 400 m running seems to be substantially higher; a 48.6 sec run possibly having 'splits' of 23.0 sec and 25.6 sec, and slower runs even higher differentials. It does, therefore, appear that women's tolerance to this type of fatigue is slightly lower than that of men.

Event background

'A tiger's picture is outside, a man's picture is inside': thus goes the Tibetan proverb. The same might well be said for the sprinter relative to the middle-distance runner, for the sprinter's picture is not in his heart and lungs, but rather in his external musculature. The sprinter is fast-reacting, explosive and rangy, and these qualities are not as

Don Quarrie (1, Jamaica) and Hasely Crawford (6, Trinidad and Tobago)

1
6

A relay take-over, downsweep pass

trainable as those in an essentially artificial event such as hammer and pole vault.

The top 100 m sprinters vary immensely in size. For instance, the 1968 Olympic final won by Jim Hines (USA) at 1.83 m (6 ft) had in third place Charlie Green (USA) at 1.73 m (5 ft 8¼ in). Similarly, in the women's final, the winner, Wyomia Tyus (USA) stood at 1.72 m (5 ft 7¾ in) whilst the silver medallist, Barbara Verrell (USA) was only 1.58 m (5 ft 2¾ in) tall. In both male and female sprints the average height of the 200 m runners was significantly taller than that of the 100 m sprinters, and this trend continued in the 400 m runners, who were taller still. In general terms, it would appear that the longer the sprint, the taller the athlete.

Age-range

At one time, sprinting was thought to be the province of the young, but this possibly reflected the American college system, rather than any physiological requirement. At the Mexico Olympics of 1968 the average age of the men's 100 m runners was twenty-four years, seven months and the women's twenty-two years, eight months. Although there were just as many male sprinters over twenty-seven as under twenty-three, over half of the females were under twenty-three, reflecting again, possibly, a social rather than a physiological factor.

Psychological focus

As explained in the technical section, the aim of the sprinter is a relaxed, automatic action, and to this end he must close his mind to all distractions and must treat his race as a totally automatic skill, like a shot put. He must see only the 1.20 m (4 ft) of space down which he has to surge without reserve. All other information, therefore, must be blocked out.

When the gun has released him, the sprinter should be a blur of fluid movement, pouring with range and leg speed.

The situation of the 400 m is slightly different, in that for at least one quarter of the race he is running in a state of fatigue. Particularly critical for him is control in the third 100 m of the race, where he must try to stay in a commanding position before the final drive down the straight.

Training

The training of sprinters is concerned mainly with improving the explosive power and endurance of the legs and in drills which polish and refine running technique. This improvement in technique enables the sprinter to make immediate and effective use of his improving physical condition. The 100/200 m sprinter's training therefore heavily stresses bounding, medium-level weight training, mobility and technique: and the 400 m sprinter necessarily increases the volume and intensity of his training.

Rules

The start

The commands are 'On your marks' and 'Set', followed by the gun. A gap of two seconds between 'Set' and gun is estimated to give the best likelihood of a fast, fair start, but at the Montreal Olympics there were 'holding' times of up to four seconds and few false starts. At major games like the Olympics, starting blocks have sensory mechanisms geared to a minimum reaction time of 0.10 sec. Any runner putting pressure on the blocks inside the 1/10 sec after the report of the gun is, therefore, penalized for a false start. After two false starts, a runner is removed from the race.

The runner must have his hands *behind* the start-line and both feet in contact with the blocks. Both hands must be in contact with the ground.

The German, Annagret Rechter (181), takes gold in the Montreal Olympics 100 m final.

A runner who follows out a competitor who has made a false start is not necessarily adjudged to have committed a false start if, in the opinion of the starter, he was 'triggered off' by the original offender.

The finish

Assuming no runner infringes his lane (and this includes running on the line, an occasional infringement in 200 m races) the other main rules relate to the finish. Here, as in all races, it is the *torso* of the runner which is the deciding factor, rather than his head, arms or legs. In most sprint races a cotton finishing tape helps the judges in their assessment of the finish, but this is only a guide as following or retarding winds may cause the tape to billow. At Olympic and European levels, all finishing is automatic.

Wind speed

For record purposes, following wind speed must not be beyond 2 m/sec (2 yd/sec) taken for ten seconds after the gun in 100 m and for the same time as the runners enter the straight in the 200 m. The tables below show the effect of following or retarding winds, and the estimated effects of running at altitude, showing the importance of diminished air-resistance.

Wind speed (m/sec)	Time with tailwind	Estimated advantage	Time with headwind	Estimated disadvantage
1	10.11 sec	.09 sec	10.30 sec	.10 sec
2	10.04 sec	.16 sec	1.40 sec	.20 sec
3	9.97 sec	.23 sec	10.52 sec	.32 sec
4	9.91 sec	.29 sec	10.65 sec	.45 sec
5	9.87 sec	.33 sec	10.80 sec	.60 sec
10	9.73 sec	.47 sec	11.76 sec	1.56 sec

The effect of following and retarding winds.

	Estimated advantage
100 m	.11 sec
200 m	.20 sec
400 m	.36 sec
800 m	.59 sec

The effect of running at altitude.

5. Relays

History

The modern relay is an American invention, having been created in 1893 by F. B. Ellis and H. L. Geyelin, who eventually created the University of Pennsylvania Relay Carnival. The standard relays are now 4 × 100 m and 4 × 400 m, involving the exchange of a 28–30 cm (10–11 in) long baton within a 20 m (21 yd) exchange zone, but early events involved no batons and simply required the outgoing runner to wait until touched by the incoming one.

The first world 4 × 100 m record of 42.3 sec was set by the German team in the Stockholm Olympics of 1912 and this was shaved by 1/10 sec in 1920 at the Antwerp Olympics by the United States team. The infrequency with which American college teams ran over metric distances meant that the world record between Olympics often remained with well-trained European club teams in the 1912–30 period, but increasing international competition in the post-war period has caused the record to remain with national teams, the exception being a 38.6 sec run by the University of Southern California team in 1967.

Until the Munich Olympics of 1972, the outgoing runner had to work within the 20 m (21 yd) exchange zone; to this was added a 10 m acceleration zone to allow him time to develop speed, although the exchange itself had to take place within the 20 m (21 yd) zone. The world record, to the credit of the United States team, now stands at 38.03 sec, though this is scarcely an adequate reflection of the superb sprinters which their national teams have contained.

Women's sprint relay racing has an even shorter history, the first world record of 46.4 sec being set by the German team in 1936 and the present record standing at 42.09 sec by the East Germans. The United States has never achieved the stranglehold over women's sprint relays that it has over the men's event, and the world record, and with it Olympic success, has been shared by many nations. Over recent years, the strength of the East German team has prevailed and no national team has run within 4/10 sec of the East German's world record time.

4 × 400 m relay

Here the first world record of 3 min 18.2 sec was set by the United States team in 1911, and the world record has only once been outside the United States, in 1952, when it was held for eight years by the brilliant Jamaican quartet of Wint, Laing, McKenley and Rhoden. The thin air of Mexico City and a superb United States team of Matthews, Freeman, James and Evans, brought the record down to 2 min 56.1 sec, where it now rests.

Until 1971, the women's world record was between six teams, but since 1971 it has been

URS

Above: the perfect change. Matching speeds exactly, Judy Vernon (Great Britain) hands off to Andrea Lynch.
Left: Valery Borzov (left) drives out strongly in the 4 x 100 m relay at the Munich Olympics.

in the possession of the powerful East Germans, who now average just under 50 sec per stage.

Technique

The aim of relay racing is to get the baton round the track in the fastest possible time, but this is not simply a matter of four men running fast and passing the baton to each other. Apart from the safety of the pass, it is essential that incoming and outgoing runners' speeds are matched and this means the securing of accurate check-marks.

The check-mark, (usually talcum powder or adhesive tape) is placed at a pre-arranged distance from the beginning of the acceleration zone. As the incoming runner's hips cross the check-mark, the outgoing runner drives out, only putting his hand back on a shout from the incoming runner. In a good exchange this will be in the last one third of the zone, thus ensuring that the outgoing runner is moving at high speed.

3 Relay pass: upsweep

4 Relay pass: downsweep

There are two main methods of exchange, the upsweep and the downsweep (figs. 3 and 4). The upsweep has the advantage that, if the runners are too close (a common fault), a safe exchange can still be made, but has the disadvantage that on each exchange a few inches of 'free distance' (i.e., distance which does not have to be run) is lost. This may mean a loss of about 0.5 m over the whole distance. Another problem with the upsweep is the 'loss' of baton on each exchange.

Most teams use the alternate pass, in that the receiving runner retains the baton in the hand in which he receives it, thus incurring no speed-loss in changing the baton from one hand to another. This usually means left-right-left-right, and means that the outgoing runner must position himself correctly (i.e., on the right when he receives the baton in his left hand) so that the incoming runner has space in which to make the pass.

If a comparison is made between the winning teams in the 1976 Montreal Olympics and the Canadian team, it shows that the differentials between the runners' aggregate 100 m times and their relay times for the USA and GDR teams was only 1.4 sec, compared with 2.24 sec for the Canadian men's team and 1.93 sec for their women's squad. Had those differentials been possessed by either the USA or East German team, then world records of 37.36 sec and 42.07 sec would have resulted.

The positioning of runners is important, first because the distance run with and without the baton varies. The first runner, assuming he runs to within 5 m (5½ yd) of the end of the zone, runs about 115 m (125½ yd), but the second and third runners may run 130 m (142 yd), and the fourth runner 125 m (136 yd). This means that the second and third runners in particular must have good finishing power.

Equally important is baton skill, with the second and third runners, the only team members who have to give *and* take; it is therefore essential that athletes in these positions are skilful baton handlers.

4 × 400 m relay

The long relay poses quite different problems than the 4 × 100 m relay, in that only the first 500 m (550 yd) is run in lanes and this means that all changes are visual ones, two of them taking place in crowded, high-contact conditions. Added to this, the incoming runner arrives in varying stages of fatigue.

The USA and Kenya contend in a crowded 4 x 400 m relay exchange at the Mexico Olympics, 1968.

Moment of victory. Steve Riddick (USA) holds the baton aloft in triumph as the United States of America wins the 4 x 100 m relay at the Montreal Olympics.

Most teams pass with the dominant right hand, taking in the left, and it is essential that the outgoing runner provides a clear display for his tiring incoming team mate. Some runners work on a subjective judgement of the incoming runner's condition; others place a check mark 5 m (5½ yd) from the beginning of the zone. Once the outgoing runner takes the baton, his aim must be to get into a strong position out of the maelstrom of activity that takes place at the changeover, being constantly aware of the runners around him.

The individual clockings of relay runners are almost invariably much faster than their flat times, if only because times are taken from a running start in a crowded situation. There is also the fact that most runners run with greater vigour and dynamism in a team situation.

The positioning of runners is critical. The first stage is run in lanes, using a 500 m (550 yd) 'slogger', and is often a good place to put a less experienced runner. This is because in the lead position he does not have the tactical problems of challenging for pole position in the exchange situation, or the subsequent tactical problems. The runner in the final stage should be the psychologically strongest runner. He should be capable of staying cool under pressure and capable of making up big deficits.

Rules

These are few and simple:

1. The baton must be exchanged within the 20 m (21 yd) zone.
2. If the baton is dropped, then it must be picked up by the runner by whom it has been dropped.

6. Hurdles

History

The earliest record of hurdle-racing is in England in the 1840s, though it is likely that some form of hurdling took place before this time. One hundred and ten metres (120 yds) with 106 cm (3 ft 6 in) hurdles, spaced 9 m (10 yd) apart seems to have been the standard distance from the outset.

Until the end of the nineteenth century, hurdling was firmly based in public schools and the universities of Oxford and Cambridge although hurdle matches for wagers between professionals occasionally took place. The hurdles of the period remained as they had been from earliest times, heavy sheep-hurdles firmly entrenched in grass. The aim of the hurdler was to jump the hurdles in balance, rather than to skim them. The event was therefore light years away from the sprint-hurdles event it was eventually to become.

Credit for the sprint form of hurdling, where the aim is to flow flat over the barriers, making the minimum modifications to sprint form, is usually given to the German Jew, A. C. Kranzlein, in 1898. It is, however, likely that many American college hurdlers were at this period experimenting with a flatter sprint-type flight-path, and that the English hurdler, A. C. Croome, had reached the same technical conclusion over ten years earlier. The Americans had, by the late 1890s, introduced a loose hurdle-top which advanced the cause of driving flat over the barriers. To the United States must go the credit, both for the T-shaped hurdle which replaced the nineteenth-century sheep hurdles and which prevailed until 1935, and for placing hurdle races on cinder tracks rather than on the infield grass where they were normally held in Britain. Both of these changes propelled hurdling towards fluid sprinting rather than mere obstacle avoidance.

The invention by the American coach, Harry Hillman, in 1935, of the weighted L-shaped hurdle completed the technological development of the hurdle. It also advanced the development of hurdles as a sprint event.

110 m hurdles

The Olympic 110 m hurdles event was entirely the province of the United States until 1976, but it was only in the late 1940s that sub 10.6 sec 100 m sprinters came to the fore. Until then, tall 1.90 m (6 ft 3 in), supple, technically excellent medium-speed athletes, such as Earl Thompson (11.3 sec 100 m, 14.4 sec 110 m hurdles) and Forrest Towns (10.9 sec 100 m, 13.7 sec 110 m hurdles) had dominated the event. Harrison Dillard, 1948 Olympic 100 m victor, changed that. Dillard, after eighty-two consecutive hurdles victories, blundered in the 1948 American Olympic trials and failed to qualify for their

Victorian hurdling was more a question of hurdle avoidance than of modified sprinting.

Olympic team. However, he scraped into the 100 m squad by an eyelash and won the Olympic 100 m title in 1948. Dillard, a 10.3 sec 100 m runner, though not a classy technician, returned to the Olympic arena in 1952 in Helsinki to win gold in the 110 m hurdles.

The successors to Dillard were, however, athletes who fused technique to speed, men like the German, Martin Lauer (13.2 sec), the slick American, Lee Calhoun (13.2 sec), the graceful Rod Milburn (13.1 sec) and the skilful French 1976 Olympic victor, Guy Drut (13.0 sec). More recently, the coloured American, Reynaldo Nehemiah (13.0 sec electrical) has linked unparalleled speed (100 m 10.38 sec) to flawless skill.

100 m hurdles (women)

Until 1969, the women's hurdles event was an 80 m one, over 75 cm (2 ft 6 in) hurdles. It is now a test involving ten barriers 85 cm (2 ft 9 in) high. The event has been almost exclu-

Willie Davenport (USA) shows the fluid, horizontal attack of modern hurdling.

sively East European at world level, as can be seen by the performance list.

The women's hurdle does not present to the female sprinter, even taking into account the difference in the average height of men and women, the same problem. The average height of Olympic hurdles finalists is the same as the sprinters, in comparison with the male Olympic hurdlers, who are substantially taller than their sprint counterparts. We are therefore looking at women of only average height, but of great sprinting speed.

The differential between flat 100 m performances and 100 m hurdles performances is, at international level, in the 1–1.3 sec area, in comparison with 1.8–2.3 sec for male hurdlers, stressing the small modifications to running technique which have to be made by female hurdlers. The technique of hurdling is virtually identical, with female hurdlers making less body-dip, because of the lower barrier.

5 Hurdling

Technique

The basis of hurdling is fluid sprinting over barriers, making minimum modifications to sprint technique. Easy to say, but not so easy to do.

Fig. 5 shows the classic hurdle technique. The hurdler 'runs in tall' at the barrier and dips fast with a snappy, bent lead-leg, (fig. 5.2) which straightens in flight.

The rear leg circles *round* the barrier (fig. 5.6) centring on landing so that the hurdler can sprint fluidly into his three stride pattern. Notice, too, the maintenance of 'dip' at peak of flight, in order that the lead foot is not too far ahead of the body on landing.

What cannot be portrayed in any diagram is the horizontal attack, the sheer dynamism of sprint-hurdling, where hurdlers, their legs a high-cadence blur between barriers, run 1.0 sec for the distance between each hurdle.

The run-in to the first hurdle normally takes the hurdler eight strides, but this usually involves considerable modification to the natural running stride, and some hurdlers, notably Munkelt (GDR) have opted for seven strides. This gives a strong, full-blooded, run-in on the first hurdle, but involves a rhythm change as the hurdler has to move to a high cadence between barriers, so it is a swings and roundabouts situation.

Event background

The male high hurdler is usually well above average height, Olympic male finalists normally averaging around 1.87 m (6 ft 1 in)

6 Hurdling: front view

with the ladies closer to the average height of 1.69 m (5 ft 6½ in). Top male hurdlers are also usually long legged, thus making it easier to negotiate the 106 cm (3 ft 6 in) barriers, but this is not true of the female hurdler.

Few male hurdlers are world-class sprinters, though Reynaldo Nehemiah (USA) and Greg Foster (USA) are both capable of running inside an electrical 10.40 and 20.30 sec, thus giving them a considerable advantage in horizontal speed. It is, however, the ability to link this speed with technical efficiency which makes Nehemiah unique, as the gap between him and Foster in sprinting ability is negligible.

Women hurdlers are similarly rarely world-class sprinters, though Ehrhardt (GDR) and Rabsztyn (Poland) have been capable of running inside 11.50 sec for 100 m. Potentially, the fastest of all female hurdlers was the Formosan, Chi Cheng, who ran a hand-timed 11.0 sec 100 m (possibly worth an electrical 11.20 sec) which, with a 1.1 sec differential, could have given her 12.30, 0.18 sec inside the present world record. The long-legged Cheng never, however, achieved the necessary specific skill over the barriers to take her to better than a hand-timed 12.8 sec, giving a modest differential of 1.8 sec.

The psychological focus of the sprint-hurdler is exactly the same as the sprinter, in that the hurdler must focus his attention on a narrow tunnel containing ten barriers, ignoring what is happening on either side of him. The essential difference between hurdling and sprinting is the information bursting in on him from each side as his rivals crash through and across the barriers. Another critical difference is that, unlike the sprinter, the hurdler's delicate balance can be disturbed by even the slightest contact with the hurdles and a serious hit can turn winning into losing in a fraction of a second. Nehemiah (USA) is remarkable in the error-free quality of his hurdling and it was notable that when, in 1979, he made a rare error, he was caught and passed by fellow countryman, Dedy Cooper, in a modest time of 13.49 sec.

The training of a hurdler is similar to that of a sprinter with more stress placed on hip mobility, and running drills giving way to specific hurdles practices. Sheer raw speed is insufficient and has little value unless it is fed into a fluent, efficient technique.

Rules

1. Each hurdle must be cleared. This means that any trailing of leg or foot outside the barrier will involve disqualification.
2. Deliberate knocking down of hurdles will involve disqualification.
3. Any competitor going out of his own lane will be disqualified.

400 m hurdles

When we consider that the 400 m hurdles event was included in the programme of the 1900 Paris Olympics, it is remarkable how scanty the previous history of the event turns out to be. Indeed, the literature of the late nineteenth century hardly refers to the original event, the 440 yd hurdles, though it is certain that 400 m (440 yd) hurdles match-races were held between professional athletes in the middle of the nineteenth century. It is also notable that the first great international club match between New York Athletic Club and London Athletic Club in 1895, at Manhattan, did not include a one lap hurdle event. And yet, in 1860, 'a quarter mile, over twelve flights' was held in the first Oxford University Sports in 1860. All very mysterious.

The first Olympic event in Paris in 1900 was won by the American, Fred Tewkesbury, in a modest 57.6 sec, but in the 1904 St Louis Olympics, Harry L. Hillman, who thirty years later was to invent the modern hurdle, recorded a respectable 53 sec, albeit over 75 cm (2 ft 6 in) hurdles. Five years later, Hillman, manacled to the American coach Lawson Robertson, set up a world 100 yd 'three legged' record of 11 sec, a record which still stands.

By the 1908 Games, the present event, over ten 90 cm (3 ft) hurdles, became standard and the record, as can be seen by the performance lists, has been the almost exclusive property of the United States ever since. The Olympic situation until 1968 was almost identical, with only the British athlete, Lord Burghley (1928) and the Irishman, R. M. Tisdall (1932) breaking American supremacy.

Until relatively recently, the 400 m hurdle event has been the province of only moderate 400 m runners, but the past twenty years has seen the entry of first-class, one-lap runners,

Above: Lord Burghley, 1923. Even here the hurdle still bears a strong resemblance to the original sheep-hurdle. Burghley's technique is, however, a modern one.

Right: John Akii Bua (Uganda), who used alternate lead-legs in the 1972 Olympic final, to add a new technical dimension to the event.

such as Glenn Davis (USA), Gerd Potgeiter (South Africa), David Hemery (Great Britain), John Akii Bua (Uganda), and Edwin Moses (USA), men capable of running the 400 m flat in the 45.0–46.0 sec area. With a differential between flat and hurdles times of 2.0–2.5 sec, this naturally brought the event to the present record of 47.5 sec.

There is little evidence in the early technical history of the event of any great concern with stride patterns, and there is no mention until the South African Gerd Potgeiter, in the late 1950s, of any hurdler using alternate legs. This meant that most hurdlers used fifteen strides between hurdles all the way, with the less well-trained hurdlers previous to 1930 probably dropping to seventeen strides over the final barriers. Potgeiter was the first world-class hurdler to methodically alternate, thus giving himself a fluency denied to those who did not.

This development of the alternate-leg lead requires explanation. Normally, after five or six hurdles, the athlete becomes slightly fatigued, has difficulty in maintaining stride length, and drops down to a pattern involving two more strides between hurdles. This change, which means 'losing' about 4 m (4½ yd), does not relate to the hurdler's natural loss of stride length and he has to make considerable adjustments. The hurdler who has the ability to alternate, to hurdle effectively from both legs, needs to 'lose' only 2 m (2 yd), which can be more easily accommodated.

The stride pattern of John Akii Bua (Uganda) 1972 Olympics hurdles champion, is shown on page 66. Akii Bua dropped from thirteen strides to fourteen strides between hurdles five and seven, then went back to his 'strong' leg from hurdles eight to ten. In contrast, the 1976 Olympic champion, Edwin Moses (USA) ran thirteen strides all the way. Moses noticeably chops his stride in the first five hurdles and it is only in the last five hurdles that his stride length directly relates to the hurdles. It is noticeable, if we compare his touch down times with Akii Bua, that they are almost identical until the final hurdle, where Moses, with greater reserves,

2

has a faster run-in time; 4.9 sec to 5.2 sec. Moses is now reported to be considering technical change, but such a major technical change, unless he has already achieved a good level of technique on his 'weak' leg, would be unwise at this late stage.

Women

The introduction of women's 400 m hurdles in 1974 was delayed by needless experimentation by international 'experts' conducting experiments with an infinity of hurdle spacings. This ignored the fact that, unlike sprint-hurdlers, 400 m hurdlers could construct their own stride patterns and that women would almost certainly plump for the stride plans of male hurdlers capable of running 400 m flat in the 52–56 sec area. This was, in fact, what happened with top female hurdlers opting for a fifteen stride pattern, breaking to seventeen strides at the fifth to seventh hurdles. As with early men's 400 m hurdling, the women's event has still to secure a really brilliant 400 m flat runner in the 50–51 sec territory. The record has, since Krystyna Kacperczyk's (Poland) initial 1974 world record of 56.51 sec, come down to 54.78 sec, achieved by Marina Makeyaua (USSR) in 1979, and is capable of considerable improvement in the immediate future.

Technique

The skill of 400 m hurdling is, in terms of hurdle clearance, identical to high hurdling, though the dip and horizontal attack is naturally less pronounced. The special problem of 400 m hurdling is the fact that the strides in the 35 m (38 yd) between hurdles are not, as in the sprint-hurdles, fixed, but present the hurdler with a limited range of options.

The table below shows the stride plans of three Olympic champions in successive

USA 4 x 400 m relay winning team at the Montreal Olympics: Parks, Newhouse, Brown and Frazier

	Moses			Akii Bua			Hemery		
Hurdle 1	6.0	**20 strides**		6.1	**21 strides**		6.0	**21 strides**	
2	9.8	(3.8)	13 strides (hurdles 2–10)	9.8	(3.7)	13 strides (hurdles 2–5)	9.8	(3.8)	13 strides (hurdles 2–6)
3	13.6	(3.8)		13.6	(3.8)		13.6	(3.8)	
4	17.5	(3.9)		17.4	(3.8)		17.5	(3.9)	
5	21.4	(3.9)		21.3	(3.9)		21.5	(4.0)	
(200m)	(23.1)			(23.0)			(23.3)		
6	25.5	(4.1)		25.4	(4.1)	14 strides (hurdles 6–8)	25.4	(3.9)	
7	29.6	(4.1)		29.5	(4.1)		29.6	(4.2)	15 strides (hurdles 7–10)
8	33.9	(4.3)		33.7	(4.2)		33.9	(4.3)	
9	38.2	(4.3)		38.1	(4.4)	15 strides (hurdles 9–10)	38.3	(4.4)	
10	42.7	(4.5)		42.6	(4.5)		42.8	(4.5)	
(Run in)	(4.9)			(5.2)			(5.8)		
Time	47.64			47.82			48.1		
1st 200m	23.10			23.00			23.30		
2nd 200m	24.50			24.80			24.80		
Differential (2nd 200m – 1st 200m)	1.4			1.8			1.5		

Even without the best possible opposition in the shape of Akii Bua and a fit Pascoe, Moses could have improved slightly on the time he set, for he was a bit higher over the last hurdle than he needed to be.

USA

Annelie Ehrhardt (East Germany)

Ed Moses (USA)

Sebastian Coe (5, Great Britain)

Olympic Games, all recording very similar touch down times, yet all using different stride patterns. Edwin Moses is the only hurdler to possess that mixture of stride length and hurdle skill to take thirteen strides between hurdles from start to finish. Close observation of Moses' first five hurdles shows that he tends to chop rather badly coming into barriers, good evidence that he has sighted his hurdle badly and that his stride length has had to be modified considerably to achieve thirteen strides. This factor of 'sighting', judging space between barriers, is critical to good 400 m hurdling, for bad sighting means loss of rhythm, which in turn means fatigue.

There is, in fact, no 'ideal' stride plan, as the plan has to relate directly to the abilities of the athlete and even to conditions on specific days. Alan Pascoe, possibly one of the event's greatest technicians, frequently ran five hurdles as part of his competitive warm-up in order to decide at which hurdle he would 'change down' from thirteen to fourteen strides, and this was particularly necessary in windy conditions. Pascoe's particular strength lay in the final three barriers, where his balance and control over the earlier part of the race paid off in strong, fluent running and vigorous attack at each hurdle.

Event background

Four hundred metres hurdlers enjoy most of the same physical characteristics as 400 m flat runners, in that they are taller than sprinters (Montreal Olympic finalists average 1.85 m/6 ft) and have some of the characteristics of 110 m high hurdlers, from whose ranks they have often come.

It is possibly significant that all of the Olympic champions since 1968 (Hemery, Akii Bua, Moses) have been high hurdlers in the 13.5–13.7 sec area, though it must be said that the present European record-holder, Harald Schmidt (West Germany) comes from the ranks of the 400 m flat group. The skill-demand of 400 m hurdling is, of course, well within the capability of flat runners and it is likely that a mixture of both groups will continue to dominate the event. Certainly, there is no evidence of dominance by sprint-hurdlers in the women's event, which has so far been led by 400 m flat runners, rather than sprint-hurdlers.

Competition

The four hundred metre hurdler must in one way be like the sprint-hurdler, in that he must see only his own lane and avoid the distractions provided by any runners outside him. The frequent comment by television commentators on a hurdler being 'pulled out' by a competitor outside him has therefore no basis in fact, for any hurdler paying attention to a runner outside him would quickly lose focus. Similarly, when a runner has decided on a stride plan for a particular situation, he must see it through to the end; any doubt, or change of plan, can be lethal.

Training

The training of a 400 m hurdler is almost identical to that of a 400 m runner, although a balance has to be found between running and hurdling, the main emphasis being on hurdling itself. Hurdles training can improve flat running, but the reverse is not always true.

Rules

The rules are identical to high hurdles, though there is more likelihood of hurdlers incurring disqualification by bringing their rear legs outside the barrier on the curve. Left leg lead hurdlers have an advantage on the first curve as they are able to 'hug' the inside and run little danger of bringing their rear leg outside the hurdle.

David Hemery (Great Britain), hurdles technician par excellence. *In his 1968 Mexico 400 m hurdles victory, the hurdles appeared to be spaced for his legs and his legs alone.*

7. Middle distance

History

The only distance run in the Ancient Olympics was the *diaulos,* a race of about 5000 m (5500 yd). There are naturally no statistical records of the race, run barefoot in broiling heat on the rough, hard surface of Olympia, but it is unlikely that much better than 16 min 30 sec was run for the distance. Vase paintings show that Greek artists appreciated the low, economical action of the *diaulos* runners, though the athletes appear to be more heavily muscled than distance runners were likely to have been.

The next record of competitive distance running is in eighteenth-century England, though it is likely that competitions between the servants of the nobility (the running footmen) had taken place at least a century earlier. The most accurately recorded performers were those who competed in match races which started to achieve a high level of public interest in the first years of the twentieth century with the performances of the Scot, Captain Barclay Allardice. Captain Barclay's most famous performance, the walking of a thousand miles in a thousand separate hours, took place in 1809, on Newmarket Heath, for a wager of £10,000. This feat, less an athletic performance than one of sleep denial, marked ten years of successful match races by Captain Barclay, who showed true athletic ability by running 56 sec for a quarter mile and 4 min 56 sec for a mile.

Barclay was the first to lay down precise rules for training, and the 'Barclay method' was to linger until well into the twentieth century.

'His regular exercise may be from twenty-four miles a day. He must rise at five in the morning, run half a mile at the top of his speed uphill, and then walk six miles at a moderate pace, coming in about seven to breakfast, which should consist of beef-steaks or mutton chops under-done, with stale bread and old beer. After breakfast, he must again walk six miles at a moderate pace, and at twelve lie down in bed without his clothes for half an hour. On getting up, he must walk four miles and return by four to dinner which should also be beef-steaks or mutton chops, with beer or bread as at breakfast. Immediately after dinner, he must resume his exercise by running half a mile at the top of his speed, and walking six miles at a moderate pace. He takes no more exercise for that day, but retires to bed about eight, and next morning proceeds in the same manner.

After having gone on in this regular course for three or four weeks, the pedestrian must take a four-mile SWEAT, which is produced by running four miles, in flannel, at the top of his speed. Immediately on returning, a hot liquor is prescribed, in order to promote the perspiration, of which he must drink one English pint. It is termed the SWEATING

LIQUOR, and is composed of the following ingredients, viz. one ounce of caraway-seed; half an ounce of coriander-seed; one ounce of root liquorice; and half an ounce of sugar-candy; mixed with two bottles of cyder, and boiled down to one half. He is then put to bed in his flannels, and being covered with six or eight pairs of blankets, and a feather-bed, must remain in this state from twenty-five to thirty minutes, when he is taken out and rubbed perfectly dry. Being then well wrapt in his great-coat, he walks out gently for two miles, and returns to breakfast, which, on such occasions, should consist of a roasted fowl'.

Match races usually took place on heathland or race-courses, but rural distance running took place at fairs or, as in Kent, at specially-held running competitions between villages.

> '21st July 1753. There will be a match of running in the field called Harvol, in Wye, between the Hill and the Dale; the best of eight or ten parishes of a side. To meet at Robert Questad's at the Kings Head in Wye Town by four o'clock in the afternoon and to be stripped by five – there is a forty-rod tye expected before the match for a large sum of money'.

By the late 1840s, when the first 'running grounds', the precursors of the modern athletics stadium, were built in London and the industrial towns of the north of England, the pages of the sporting press were crammed with challenges of runners of all abilities. In 1849, the greatest English distance runners raced before vast crowds in the United States and it was as a result of these races that in 1861 the Indian runner, Louis (Deerfoot) Bennett came to England to challenge the best English professional distance runners. Deerfoot excelled at distances from six to twelve miles and his twelve mile run of 1 hr 2 min 2.5 sec still stands as a world professional record.

By the middle of the nineteenth century, in the absence of a governing body, no standard distances had been set by professional runners, though the mile was then, as now, the most popular distance.

In 1865 'Crowcatcher' Lang and William Richard ran 4 min 17¼ sec in a famous dead heat, and Lang also earlier ran 4 min 2 sec for a straight mile at Newmarket, the closest English performance to the four-minute mile until that of Roger Bannister almost a century later. Surprisingly, there are few significant records for 800 m (880 yd) or 3 miles, though Jack White (the 'Gateshead Clipper') ran 29 min 50 sec for six miles against Deerfoot. It is fashionable to scoff at records of the pre-amateur period, but there is ample reason to believe that the professional runners of this period were capable of such times, if only because substantial bets depended on the accuracy of timekeeping.

Interest in professional matches was always variable, if only because the public were sceptical of the honesty of the runners and their advisors, and by the 1880s amateur distance runners had caught up with their professional counterparts in all but a handful of events. The most famous of the amateurs was W. G. George, the Wiltshire chemist, who dominated English distance running from 800 m (880 yd) to ten miles. Beset by financial worries, George turned professional in 1885 to take on the equally versatile Scottish professional, William Cummings, over a range of distances. This series of matches resulted in George's famous 4 min 12¾ sec mile in 1885, a record which was to stand until 1915.

By the end of the century, the Americans had begun to show, through the clubs and universities of the East, ability in middle distance running, and in 1895 the American,

The professional marathon 'boom' of 1908–1912. Alfred Shrubb (Great Britain) with the Canadian Indian, Longboat.

Charles Kilpatrick had run 1 min 53.4 sec for 800 m (880 yd). The home of distance running was, however, still undoubtedly Great Britain, and in the period between 1900 and 1908 the English runner, Alf Shrubb, established English and world records at all distances from two miles to ten miles, before turning professional in 1908.

The central difference between the athletics of the pre-1950 period and those of the present day is the parochial nature of competition. In the days before the Industrial Revolution, competition was confined to a county, and with the advent of the railway, national competition became possible, thus enabling local champions to test themselves against each other. However, it was not until the development of jet travel that global athletics, and with it regular competitions between athletes living thousands of miles apart, became possible. The competitive records of this period therefore relate mainly to Olympic Games, the only occasion on which athletes from all five continents came together in competition.

The first great distance athlete of the early twentieth century was the Finn, Hannes Kohlemainen, one of a superb family of distance runners who ran brilliantly at all distances from 3000 m to marathon. Kohlemainen triggered off a Finnish distance running culture which lives to this day. The Flying Finn, Paavo Nurmi, dominated the Olympic Games from 1920 in Antwerp until 1928 in Amsterdam, achieving an unprecedented number of Olympic medals. Nurmi was similar to George, Cummings and Shrubb, running excellently over a wide range of distances from 800 m up to 20,000 m, and would have been likely to win the 1932 Olympic marathon in Los Angeles, had he not been declared a professional just before the Games.

The shorter middle-distances possessed no Nurmi, and Nurmi's 4 min 10.4 sec mile in 1923 lasted until 1931, when it was beaten with 4 min 9.2 sec by Jules Ladoumègue (France). It was 1932 before 1 min 50 sec was broken for 800 m, by the English runner, Tom Hampson, in the final of the Los Angeles Olympics.

The late 1930s saw the emergence of three great middle-distance runners in Glen Cunningham (USA), Jack Lovelock (New Zealand) and Sydney Wooderson (Great Britain). Wooderson, who had sustained an ankle injury just before the 1936 Berlin Olympics, did not contest the Olympic 1500 m final, in which the slim, black-vested Lovelock, tracked all the way by the swarthy Cunningham, slipped from him 300 m from the finish and held superb form all the way to the tape, in a new world record of 3 min 47.6 sec.

The War denied Wooderson two Olympic Games, though in 1938 he ran 1 min 49.2 sec for an 800 m (880 yd) world record in a specially-framed handicap race. A less-known performance was the 1 min 47.8 sec run by the American negro, John Woodruffe, on an oversize indoor track which invalidated it for record purposes. Even more outstanding was the 1 min 46 sec 800 m run in 1939 by the German, Rudolf Harbig, a performance vastly superior to Wooderson's 800 m (880 yd) record. Harbig, a 21.6 sec 200 m runner and holder of the world 400 m record at 46 sec, showed the value of sprint-speed over 800 m, though he never appears to have seriously attempted 1500 m.

The World War II period saw athletics being seriously pursued only in the United States and Sweden; it was in Sweden that Gundar Hägg and Arne Anderson unleashed a flow of brilliant performances during the war period, the most significant of these being Hägg's 4 min 1.4 sec mile, and 13 min 58.2 sec 5000 m. Alas, by the time Hägg and Wooderson came together in 1946 the Englishman's hope of a four-minute mile had gone, lost in the stagnant years of war, though he mustered an excellent 4 min 4.2 sec behind Hägg. Wooderson did, however, give some idea of the greatness which could have been his, by winning the European 5000 m in 1946, thus showing the same competitive range as Nurmi and George.

The 1948 Olympics saw the emergence of a new distance-running star in the Czech, Emil Zatopek. In the final lap of the 5000 m, Zatopek trailed well behind the leader, the Belgian, Gaston Reiff, and looked well beaten. Suddenly, with 300 m (330 yd) to go, the Czech summoned a raging sprint and, charging up the rain-sodden track, was beaten by Reiff by a bare metre at the tape. Zatopek broke the great Finn, Heino, in the 10,000 m and by the end of the London Olympics had established himself as the greatest distance runner in the world. In 1952, he went on to become the first athlete to win 5000 m, 10,000 m, and marathon in a single Olympics, a feat unlikely to be repeated.

Zatopek, in his remorseless lapping of the track, interspersed with jog-rests, was pursuing interval training, which was first formally presented by the German coach, Woldemar Gerschler in his work with Harbig in the late 1930s. Gerschler disavowed credit for interval training, placing it at the door of Lauri Pihkala, the Finnish coach, who in turn confessed to being directly influenced by the early twentieth-century American coach, George W. Orton. Thus we travel back into history, finding that we can rarely be accurate in crediting one particular person with a new technique or training method.

What did Zatopek bring to distance running? First, an iron will, a will expressed in a massive volume of interval training, during which his body soaked up lap after lap of high speed running with short recovery periods. Zatopek's training was not, by modern standards, scientific. It did not have to be, for its sheer volume swamped the light training programmes pursued by most of the runners of that period. However, many runners copied Zatopek, without achieving his competitive success, for above all the Czech was a competitor.

By the early 1950s, the scramble for the Holy Grail, the four-minute mile, was on.

Magic moment. Roger Bannister becomes the first man to achieve a mile in under four minutes, in 1954.

True, the 3 min 43 sec 1500 m runs of Hägg and his countryman, Lennart Strand, did translate (with a modest 17.0 sec added for the final 110 m) to a four-minute mile, but the actual time had not yet been achieved. By 1953, three main contenders had arisen, the clipped front-running Australian, John Landy, the prancing American, Wes Santee, and the English runner, Roger Bannister. Of the three, Landy always looked the most likely to succeed, reeling off a series of sub-4 min 4 sec miles on the sun-baked grass tracks of Australia in the winter of 1953. It was, however, Bannister who, in 1954 at the Iffley Road track, Oxford, was paced by his friends Chris Brasher and Chris Chataway, to 3 min 59.4 sec on a windy April evening.

Landy replied almost immediately with 3 min 58 sec at Turku in Finland, but it was too late. On the only occasion when Landy and Bannister met, at the Vancouver Empire Games of 1954, Bannister trailed Landy until the final straight, when he struck, to win in 3 min 58.7 sec.

It was Bannister's co-conspirator in the breaking of the four-minute mile, Chris Chataway, who was, in 1954, to feature in the other great race of the period, against the Russian 5000 m runner, Vladimir Kuts, who had previously surprised Chataway and Zatopek in the Berne European Games of the same year. In that race, Kuts had simply gone out from the front from the beginning, putting metre after metre between himself and the cautious Chataway. However, in the London–Moscow match of October 1954, Kuts employed different tactics, rocking Chataway with fast laps quite at variance with the theory of even-paced running. Somehow the Englishman hung on, passing the Russian on the line in the most memorable race of modern times.

The races of the 1950s were the last to possess the quality of myth. Landy and Bannister met only once, Kuts and Chataway only a handful of times, and in 1960, when he won the Olympic 1500 m, Herb Elliott had never heard of most of his competitors. With the development of television and cheap jet

travel, athletes were soon to become household figures, men racing one day in Los Angeles, two days later in London. It is possibly for this reason that few present day runners have the charismatic quality of a Nurmi or a Zatopek, or that the great races of today soon become dim memories, quickly overtaken by yet other televised races.

Herb Elliott, unbeaten as a senior athlete over 1500 m and a mile, was soon to be overtaken by a New Zealand athlete, Peter Snell, who had been a surprise victor in the 1960 Olympic 800 m. Elliott had been disciplined on the cruel sandhills of Portsea by the eccentric Australian coach, Percy Cerutty, but Snell (world mile record-holder at 3 min 54.1 sec) who had shown excellent 400 m speed as a junior athlete, was trained on quite different lines by the New Zealand coach, Arthur Lydiard. Lydiard, himself a marathon runner, stressed the need for over-distance training as the endurance platform for ultimate racing speed and his foundation period involved the running of up to one hundred miles a week. Lydiard's methods were to significantly influence all distances up to marathon and he can be considered the major single influence in modern distance training.

It was, however, an American, the highly-strung Jim Ryun, who was to take the world record from the Frenchman, Michel Jazy, (3 min 53.6 sec) down to 3 min 51.1 sec in 1967 and the 800 m (880 yd) (the Americans still stuck grimly to non metric distances) to 1 min 44.9 sec in 1966.

The Soviet Union produced no natural competitive successor of Kuts' calibre and it was the Australian, Ron Clarke, who had earlier in his career 'dropped out' from miling, who was to re-discover his taste for running and was to dominate the 1960s over a range of distances from 3000 m to 25,000 m. Clarke brought the 5000 m down to 13 min 25.8 sec in 1965 and the 10,000 m to 28 min 15.6 sec in 1963, and his capacity for churning out fast times at short notice all over the world has never been equalled. Clarke never, however, showed the ability to peak for big races, though his best chance, in the 1968 Mexico City Olympics, was thwarted by the thin atmosphere.

The recent development of the 800 m has been unusual. Neither Peter Snell, Ralph Doubell (1964 Olympics victor), Wottle (1972 Olympics victor), or John Walker, were blessed with more than competence over the 400 m. The next Olympic champion and record-holder, the Cuban Alberto Juantorena, was, however, essentially a rangy, muscular sprinter, being the only man in history to win both 400 m and 800 m in the same Olympics.

Juantorena is no great tactician, his raking stride making it difficult for him to make the subtle cadence adjustments necessary in fast moving 800 m fields. His 1976 Olympic victory was therefore achieved by keeping out of trouble by getting to the front early and staying there.

The most recent 800 m record-holder, the British runner, Sebastian Coe, is essentially an endurance runner with high (46.8 sec 400 m) basic speed, so the 800 m event still seems to be trembling in the balance between speed and endurance.

Coe's 1979 season, one in which he took world records in 800 m, 1500 m and mile, was a remarkable one, and his 1980 meetings with Steve Ovett are awaited with anticipation. Ovett has come up from 400 m running but has revealed an even greater competitive

Moment of moments in a race of races. Chris Chataway (Great Britain) edges ahead of Kuts (USSR) at the White City in a memorable 5000 m race in 1954.

781
102

Above: Alberto Juantorena (Cuba), the only man to achieve an Olympic 400 m/800 m double.
Left: bitter moments for the great Australian Ron Clarke in the mean air of Mexico City, in the 1968 Olympics.

range than Coe, and in 1978 took on and beat some of Britain's best long distance runners in a half-marathon.

By the late 1960s it had become clear that Kenyan athletes were to become a major international force. Some hint of Kenyan talent had been given by the plucky Maiyoro in the mid 1950s, but it was the silky fluid Keino, the powerful Jipcho, and the technically eccentric steeplechaser, Biwott, who were to bring Kenya to world attention.

The 1972 and 1976 Olympics saw a return to Finnish distance glories of earlier times, with the victories of Lasse Viren. Viren, blessed with excellent basic speed (48 sec 400 m), also showed excellent tactical sense and a rare ability to 'peak' for big competitions. However, although the Kenyans have achieved progressively less in the Olympic arena, they showed through the American-based Henry Rono and Wilson Waigwa, that they were far from spent.

Training for the middle distances is still far from scientific, and many recent improvements have simply come from an increase in the sheer volume of training by athletes whose life styles allow them to devote as much time as they wish to training. More time must now be given to finding more economic methods of training.

Women

Women's middle distance running made a bad start at the Amsterdam Olympics of 1928, when the German, Lina Batschaeur-Radke, led an ashen-faced, rubber-legged field in the 800 m in 2 min 16.8 sec. It may give some flavour of the times that the second finisher was K. Hitomi (Japan), the world's leading long jumper. The desperate condition of several finishers was just what the opponents, male and female, of women's athletics needed, and the 800 m did not appear again in the Olympics until 1964.

The surprise of the Tokyo Olympics, 800 m novice Ann Packer (Great Britain) destroys the field in the final straight to take gold.

The Soviet Union gripped the 800 m event until the early 1960s with Nina Otkalenko and Lyudmila Shevtsova, but it was a British 400 m runner, Ann Packer, who cruised behind a field of specialist 800 m runners at the 1964 Tokyo Olympics and demolished them in the home straight in 2 min 1.1 sec. Packer's potential in the 800 m was undoubtedly well inside 1 min 57 sec but she retired after Tokyo, giving only a hint of what might have been.

The first woman to slip inside 2 min was the German, Hildegard Falck (1 min 58.5 sec) in 1971, and soon 2 min became the standard required of an international competitor. The 1976 Montreal final, which saw the first four runners inside 1 min 56 sec, gave a flavour of the potential of women over this distance.

The present world 1500 m record of the Soviet runner, Tatyana Kazankina, which stands at 3 min 56.0 sec is better than the men's record in 1912, and again indicates the ability of women over the middle distances. Similarly, Lyudmila Bragina's (USSR) run of 8 min 27.2 sec is, in fact, faster than the great Paavo Nurmi ever ran.

However, women are showing even greater potential in the ultra-long distances, and the Norwegian, Greta Waitz's recent New York marathon of 2 hr 27 min 33 sec would have gained victory in every Olympic marathon up to 1952. It is unlikely, alas, that any distance beyond 3000 m will be contested by women in the 1984 Olympics.

Mark Liquori (USA) and the fast-finishing Yifter (Ethiopia) in bitter contention in the 1977 World Cup.

Event background

The physical profile of the distance runner is of a lean, light ectomorph, weighing in the 50–60 kg (110–132 lb) area. Specialist sprint-type 800 m runners of the Juantorena type may be heavily muscled, but from 1500 m to 10,000 m the outward appearance is similar and heart rates of 33–45 are common, the lower heart rates belonging to the runners in the longer distances.

Physiological factors

The psychological profile of the distance runner has probably more in common with a Tour de France cyclist than with a sprinter or jumper. The distance runner tends towards introversion and phlegmatism in contrast to the explosive and volatile nature of the sprinter or field events athlete.

The international middle-distance runner is, above all, a superb piece of machinery for the use of oxygen and the removal of waste products. In this, the female athlete is marginally inferior, in that she has a smaller, weaker heart, and a poorer oxygen transport system. Recent studies do, however, show that the physiological gap between the sexes is probably smaller than has been supposed.

Until recently, it was thought that drugs did not present a problem in middle-distance running. The recent suspensions of world-class runners Totka Petrova (Bulgaria), Natalia Maresescu (Rumania), and Ileana Silai (Rumania), for the ingestion of anabolic steroids does, however, put the whole of middle distance running into question. The anabolics' main value does not lie in weight gain, but rather in improvement in work-rate and this would undoubtedly be of value in distance training.

The strength of the distance runner is internal, in his capacity to supply his muscles with life-giving oxygen. This does not mean that the distance runner does not have to have an efficient running action, for an inefficient action will result in a rapid build-up of waste products. Rather, the phrase reflects the fact that the power of the external musculature is less important for the distance runner than for the sprinter.

Psychological considerations apart, what we see in the great distance runner is a superb piece of machinery for the transport of oxygen and the removal of waste products. When the wastes produced by the muscles become substantially greater than the capacity of the circulatory system to remove them, then the runner must slow up, for he is in a state of extreme oxygen-debt through which no amount of will power can drive him.

The table shows the balance between the aerobic (using oxygen), and anaerobic (without oxygen) systems in a range of running events. As can be seen, 100 m and marathon are at opposite ends of the physiological pole, with 1500 m delicately balanced between the systems. The training of runners therefore relates directly to the physiological demands of the event, in that training for 10,000 m requires a high component of steady running

7 Middle distance

Event (metres)	Total oxygen requirement (litres)	Oxygen intake (litres)	Oxygen debt (litres)	Type of work	Approx. %
100	10	0.5	Total	anaerobic	100%
200	16	1.0	15–17	anaerobic aerobic	95% 5%
400	20	3.0	17	anaerobic aerobic	84% 16%
800	26	9.0	17	anaerobic aerobic	67% 33%
1500	36	19.0	17	anaerobic aerobic	45% 55%
5000	80	63.0	17	anaerobic aerobic	20% 80%
10 000	150	130 +	17	anaerobic aerobic	10% 90%
Marathon	650 +	650 +	17	anaerobic aerobic	2% 98%

The balance between aerobic and anaerobic systems in a range of running events.

training, whilst the speed element must be stressed heavily in 800 m. Speed is, however, vital for two main reasons, even in the longer distances. The first is that when there is any major change in race pace (i.e., a sudden fast lap is thrown in) the speedy runner is capable of responding and staying up, maintaining a reserve in hand. More important, however, is the ability to 'kick' in the closing stages or to stay with fast-kicking runners. Juantorena at 800 m, Ovett at 1500 m, and Yifter and Viren in the longer distances, have shown this quality.

The main characteristic of modern training has been the sheer volume of mileage covered by runners even in the short middle-distances. Before 1960, it was rare for an 800/1500 m expert to be able to compete successfully with specialists in the 5000, 10,000 m events, except after several years of preparation. Now many such runners can smoothly graduate to longer distances and similarly, runners like Viren can go close to an Olympic marathon medal at first attempt.

Tactics

The tactics of distance running have changed little over the years. In 800 m, high first lap speeds make it essential that runners stay in contact with the leaders from the early stages. The slipstreaming effect of running behind another athlete (64 per cent of wind resistance can be avoided by running 1 m behind) makes front running unwise, unless the front-runner has superb pace judgement, outstanding physical qualities, and great strength of will. Few front runners of modern times have achieved success in major games and the runner who can stay with the leaders, reserving a strong finishing 'kick', is always going to be dangerous. Runners who lack finishing power have, however, no choice but to keep the overall pace as high as possible, thus taking the sting from their opponents' finish. Their other alternative is to make a long drive for home, thus exposing themselves to tracking runners over a long period of time. This tactic was excellently deployed by Brendan Foster in winning the

Above: the English cross country season. There, the seeds of endurance are sown for summer successes. Here David Bedford trails.

Right: Brendan Foster (Great Britain)

1974 Rome European 5000 m championship.

The central questions which a runner must ask himself are:

1. Which athletes will never lead, but will always want to come from the back?
2. Which like leading, but lose heart when they have lost the lead?
3. Which runners prefer it fast all the way?
4. Which men favour a short, fast finish?
5. Which runners like a long finishing burst?
6. Which athletes like to break off and establish a big lead?

Central to all tactics is that a runner makes other runners feel uncomfortable and imposes his pattern, his will, upon the race. This precept has been the mark of all great runners from W. G. George, through Nurmi, to Lasse Viren.

GATESHEAD
Debenhams
1

Nationwide
Building Society
35

Left: Samson Kimobwa (Kenya)

Above: Lasse Viren (Finland) defeats a fading field in the 1976 Olympic 5000 m.

8. Marathon

History

It is unlikely that the Greek courier, Pheidippides, ran from Marathon to Athens in 490 BC with news of the Athenian victory over the Persians and the dying words 'Rejoice, we conquer'. Be that as it may, the members of the Much Wenlock Olympian Society sent to Athens in the 1850s a medal for a 'marathon' to be held at the primitive Pan Athenian Games which were then being held on the cobbled streets of the city. Credit for the creation of the modern marathon is, however, usually given to the Frenchman, Michel Bréal, who presented a cup for the first Olympic marathon held in 1896.

The Marathon–Athens distance was found to be 24¾ miles and twenty-four competitors (seventeen of them Greek) set out on the dusty course to the Averoff Stadium. None of the competitors were experienced long-distance runners, the best of them, such as the Australian, Flack, and the Frenchman, Lemursiaux, being 800/1500 m specialists.

Lemursiaux set a blistering pace in the stern afternoon heat and at 14¼ miles had such a commanding lead that the villagers of Karvati attempted to crown him with a victor's garland. Lemursiaux refused, and it was just as well, for he caught cramp on the hill outside Karvati and was passed by Flack. Flack was, in turn, passed by the Greek, Spiridon Loues, at 21¾ miles.

Loues' welcome in the waiting Averoff Stadium was little short of delirious. The two royal Greek princes, George and Constantine, leapt from the royal box and, dwarfing Loues, ran beside him to the finish.

The marathon had been the most dramatic event of the 1896 Games, but it was the 1908 London Olympic marathon which was to bring the event to public consciousness. It was also the occasion which brought marathon to its present 26 mile 385 yd distance, the apocryphal justification being the need to have the race finish in front of the royal box. The race, which commenced in Windsor Great Park, started with a suicidally fast first mile of 5 min 1.4 sec set by the English runners, Price and Lord. Although the Englishmen's pace dropped to 56 min 53 sec by 10 miles, they had shot their bolt by 15 miles (1 hr 28 min 22 sec), when the lead was taken by the South African, Hefferon. By the seventeenth mile, Hefferon was being overhauled by the Italian, Dorando Pietri, and not far from the White City was passed by Pietri.

'It was not until I saw the stadium that the weakness came over me and then, as I had no attendant, I became confused. If I had had my attendant to guide me and give me such aid as I was entitled to, I could have finished without falling again, but they would not allow my attendant to come into the stadium with me'.

London Olympics, 1908. No hint as Dorando Pietri (Italy) cruises through Willesden, of the drama that is to unfold later, in the White City stadium.

Thus Pietri describes what was to be the most dramatic marathon finish in history as Pietri staggered and stumbled the agonizing final 385 yd towards the finish, engulfed in the hysteria of an 80,000 crowd. Pietri was lifted to his feet and supported to the tape by an official, J. M. Andrew, and this resulted in his disqualification. At the prompting of Sir Arthur Conan Doyle, Pietri was later awarded a replica cup similar to that given to the winner, the American, E. C. Hayes.

The 'Dorando' marathon triggered off a professional marathon 'boom' in which Pietri, the Canadian Indian, Longboat, Appleby, Hayes and Shrubb competed in marathons throughout the world, including an indoor series at New York's Madison Square Garden, and an unknown composer called Isador Baline (later Irving Berlin) penned a song entitled 'Dorando'. The professional 'boom', unregulated by an international governing body, ended with Willi Kohlemainen's 2 hr 29 min 30.2 sec at Newark in 1912, a time which has been ignored by most athletics statisticians.

Although the 1912 Stockholm Olympics was to provide the best organized marathon held until that time, it was also to furnish the first death, that of the Portuguese runner, Lazaro. However, the runners of the period had moved far from the untrained optimists of Athens and henceforth marathon competitors were to come from the ranks of hardened 5000 m and 10,000 m runners. Indeed, had he not been at the last moment barred from competing in the 1932 Olympic marathon, the Finn, Paavo Nurmi, could well have run well inside 2 hr 30 min.

The marathon has, however, no official record, because of the immense variation in courses, but it was the Japanese, Kitei Son, who was to be the first to break the 2 hr 30 min barrier in an Olympic marathon at Berlin in 1936. Against this, it must be remembered that Hannes Kohlemainen ran 605 yd over the marathon distance in his narrow (13 sec) victory over the Estonian, Lossman, in winning the 1920 Olympic marathon in 2 hr 32 min 35.8 sec.

The first man to go inside 2 hr 20 min was the unlucky British runner, Jim Peters, who had to give way to the aggressive Czech, Emil Zatopek, in the 1952 Olympic marathon and who later wobbled to defeat in the 1954 Vancouver Empire Games marathon.

The Ethiopian, Abebe Bikila, was to become the first man to win successive Olympic marathons when he won in 1960 and 1964, and it was another Ethiopian, Wolde, who was to take gold in the 1968 Olympic marathon, held in the mean air of Mexico City.

In 1969 the Australian, Derek Clayton, became the first man to average inside 5 min per mile over the distance, recording at Antwerp (shades of Kohlemainen almost fifty years before) 2 hr 8 min 33 sec. Clayton's qualities were never, alas, reflected in the more fragile world of major competitive marathons.

The 1972 Olympic marathon went to the American, Frank Shorter, possibly the most consistent marathon runner of modern times, but Eastern European organization finally broke through in 1976 when the East German, Cierpinski, took gold at the Montreal Olympics.

Marathon – the 26 mile 385 yd ultimate test of the distance runner.

Women's marathon

During the writing of this chapter, it has been announced that the marathon has been included in the women's programme of the 1982 European Games. This contrasts with the 1980 Olympic programme, where the longest distance for women is 1500 m! The Norwegian Greta Waitz's 1979 sub 2 hr 28 min run (at her second marathon attempt) hardly represents the potential of female athletes over distance (and indeed over other distances such as 5000 m and 10,000 m) but the competitive opportunities for women in longer distances are few. Here governing bodies have shown insufficient sensitivity to the quantity and quality of training pursued by female middle-distance runners who are absorbing weekly mileages far in excess of male distance runners previous to 1960. This is symptomatic of the conservatism which has accompanied the development of women's athletics; no such caution was observed by male officials when male athletes tackled distances from 26 miles to 600 miles without the benefit of scientific scrutiny. Indeed, had such investigations been deemed necessary, it is doubtful if the present men's Olympic programme would have been achieved by 1980. So, the time is long overdue for the inclusion of women's distance races in the Olympic programme.

Technique

All distance running is about economy of effort, but the marathon runner, with his low, clipped, frugal stride, epitomizes this economy. The foot lands heel first, the stride is short and rapid. As in race walking, there are no tactical 'bursts' in marathon, as the essence of marathon-running is evenness of effort and any sudden, violent change in pace will invariably cause later suffering. Front runners do not exist, winners usually dragging their challengers with them through a fast overall pace, leaving them struggling somewhere beyond the 20 mile point, or making a sustained drive in the final few miles. All marathon runners are gamblers; they are never sure that their bodies can hold out in the final 4–6 miles beyond the 'wall'.

The 'wall' occurs at 20–22 miles, and is the point at which muscle-glycogen starts to run out. Many novices have run well until this point, then faded or succumbed to cramps in the desert of these final few miles. To this end, most top marathon runners pursue a glycogen-loading programme a week to ten days before a major event. The aim of this programme is to 'trick' the body into laying down extra glycogen reserves. The runner has a hard run a week before competition, then denies himself carbohydrates in 'three days of sugarless hell'. He then pursues a high carbohydrate diet all the way into competition.

This 'loading' programme can only work twice per year, as the body apparently 'learns' that it has been tricked, but this presents the runner with no problem, as he will rarely 'peak' for more than two races per year. It is interesting to note that marathon runners have been found to have two to three times the amount of muscle-glycogen of the untrained person. Perhaps the most exciting recent theory is that the caffeine content of a strong cup of coffee one hour before a marathon could improve a runner's performance 7½ per cent. This is apparently because caffeine causes the body to burn high-powered fuel (glycogen) in preference to the lower-powered free fatty acids.

Any high-sugar food or drink before racing is inadvisable, for this in fact reduces the amount of glucose available, and most runners eat cereal, juice, or some other light, easily-digestible meal before races. During races it is essential to take drinks at 10–15 minute intervals, 250 ml (½ pt) at a time.

A master of marathon, Ron Hill (Great Britain).

Event background

The marathon runner comes from the same physical 'stable' as the 5000 m and 10,000 m runners although since Zatopek only one runner, the American, Frank Shorter, has been a world-class 10,000 m runner concurrent with his marathon success. At the other extreme, 1974 European marathon champion, Ian Thompson, was not even a national level 10,000 m runner, his physiological make-up being suited exclusively to marathon.

The marathon runner is, therefore, small, light and lean, his fat bodyweight being only 5 per cent relative to the sprinter's 10 per cent and the average man's 15 per cent. His pulse is almost invariably in the 30s per minute, even lower than his colleagues in the 10,000.

Rules

The essential rules are:

1. That the race be run on roads, but not on soft ground, with the finish always taking place in a stadium.
2. That courses have a single turning-point, or be composed of a single circuit.
3. A less well-known rule is that a competitor must retire at once if ordered to do so by a member of the medical staff.
4. Refreshments are provided by organizers at 3 miles and thereafter at 3 mile intervals. In addition, sponging points and water-only points are usually provided, between refreshment stations. Competitors taking refreshments at any unofficial points render themselves liable to disqualification.

9. Steeplechase

History

Steeplechase is essentially an enclosed, artificial version of the cross-country 'runs between steeples' common in the nineteenth century. Its appearance at the Oxford University–Cambridge University athletics match of 1864 therefore merely represented the first major meeting in which the 2 mile steeplechase had taken place. 'For many years, the steeplechase was considered as forming the comic part of the entertainment at a meeting, and the managers of sports made huge water jumps which it was impossible for anyone to clear, so that the lookers-on might see runner after runner tumble into a filthy pool and emerge muddy, bleeding, soaked and groaning'. Thus said Montague Shearman in 1900.

Steeplechase, originally a race between church steeples.

6
ANCS
1
7

8 Steeplechase

Only when the 3000 m event became a formal part of the Olympic programme in 1920 (steeplechases of varying distances had been held at the Olympics of 1900, 1904 and 1908), did steeplechase receive the necessary status. From 1920 to 1936 the Olympic event was dominated by the Finns, but it was not until the post-war period that specialist steeplechasers, like Ashenfelter (USA), Brasher (Great Britain), and Krzyskowiak (Poland) appeared.

Surprisingly, records for the event were only first recognized in 1954, at which point Horace Ashenfelter's (USA) time of 8 min 45.4 sec was the best on record. Since then, the event has never secured the regular attention of great runners, and whenever such athletes as Roelants (Belgium), Jipcho (Kenya) and Keino (Kenya) have focused on the event, they have revealed the modest level of performance which still exists.

Steeplechase, therefore, still awaits a fast, technically skilful specialist who will take the world record where it belongs, below 8 min.

Technique

The aim of the steeplechaser is to flow over the barriers, making the minimum interruption to his racing rhythm. He has, therefore, much in common with the 400 m hurdler. The main difference lies in the fact that the steeplechaser does not run in a lane and is not, therefore, given uninterrupted freedom to pursue his running rhythm. The second difference is that the hurdles and water-jump are not, as in 400 m hurdles, evenly spaced.

The steeplechaser is therefore in a 'free' situation, in which he must find himself space in a bustling, jostling field, to run in smoothly on the barriers. His hurdle action is a modified version of the 400 m hurdler; the action is the same, but there is less punch, less horizontal drive.

The water-jump must be crossed by running smoothly to the barrier, placing the strong leg on the rail with spikes on the far side and 'giving' at the knee, thus allowing bodyweight to travel horizontally across the water. A wide split is maintained and the steeplechaser, one foot in water and one outside, runs off his landing towards the next hurdle. The picture of a good steeplechaser is therefore of a smooth, horizontal flow on and off the barrier.

Andy Holden (Great Britain) dips at the hurdle, preserving speed and running rhythm.

Event background

There is no real reason why the steeplechaser should be very different from the distance runner in physical type, as the skill and mobility required in the hurdle-clearance places no excessive demands on the distance runner. As explained in the historical sec-

The 1979 Spartakiade steeplechase. The leading runner is correctly running out of the water, but the second runner appears to have his body weight too far behind his lead foot to be able to run fluidly out of the water.

tion, the event has, as yet, never received sustained attention from any of the really great runners and it is clear that no great value is yet placed upon it by them.

Tactics

Race tactics are similar to all other distance-runs, the only major difference being that the front runner has the advantage of having an uninterrupted view of the barriers. Within packs of runners, the steeplechaser is faced with the constant problem of finding himself space within which to run in at the hurdle in balance.

Rules

The rules are as in runs and hurdles, there being twenty-eight hurdle-clearances and seven water-jumps. From the start to the beginning of the first lap there are no jumps, the hurdles being removed until the competitors have entered the first lap, which gives the pack time to sort itself out.

10. Race walking

History

The period between the seventeenth and nineteenth centuries is replete with stories of walking matches against time and matches between members of the nobility and their servants. The first great pedestrian of modern times was the Scot, Captain Barclay, who in 1809 walked 1,000 miles in 1,000 hours on Newmarket Heath.

The first really great walker of modern times was not Barclay but rather the late nineteenth-century professional, William Perkins, who walked a mile in 6 min 23 sec at Lillie Bridge in 1874. Perkins, the fairness of whose form was never questioned, held at one time all professional records up to 20 miles (2 hr 39 min 57 sec) and must be considered the greatest walker of the nineteenth century.

The last part of the nineteenth century saw the Six Day Races sponsored by Sir Edward Astley for his Championship Belt. These were held on the 200 m (220 yd) tan track of the Agricultural Hall, Islington, and ended with George Littlewood's magnificent walk of 623 miles, a distance which was never beaten.

From 1908, when George Larner (Great Britain), won both the two mile and 10,000 m walk at the London Olympics, the story of walking is essentially an amateur one. In 1912, the Olympic walk moved up to 10,000 m, in 1920 3,000 m was added, but dropped for good in 1924. It was not until 1932 in Los Angeles that 50 km became the Olympic distance, and in 1956 the 20 km distance was added. This situation obtained until 1976 when the 50 km walk was, under heavy protest, removed from the programme.

The development of walking has therefore been an erratic one, when compared with other standard athletics events. Although the early leaders, such as Larner and Ross, were British the main development of the event took place in Europe, and particularly in the 1920s in the Italians Valente, Callegari and Pavesi. The war period was dominated by neutral Sweden, but the immediate post-war period has been almost exclusively East European in nature. As in other events, they analysed the technique and the conditioning methods required to produce both good technique and competitive performance. They soon, therefore, produced a stream of great walkers and only recently has the West broken through in the shape of Bernd Kannenberg (Germany) and a cluster of Mexican walkers, such as Daniel Bautista.

Technique

Mastery of technique is essential to perform the act of walking. A walker's action is simply an explosive, high-frequency version of ordinary walking, and his speed, like that of the sprinter, relates directly to his length of

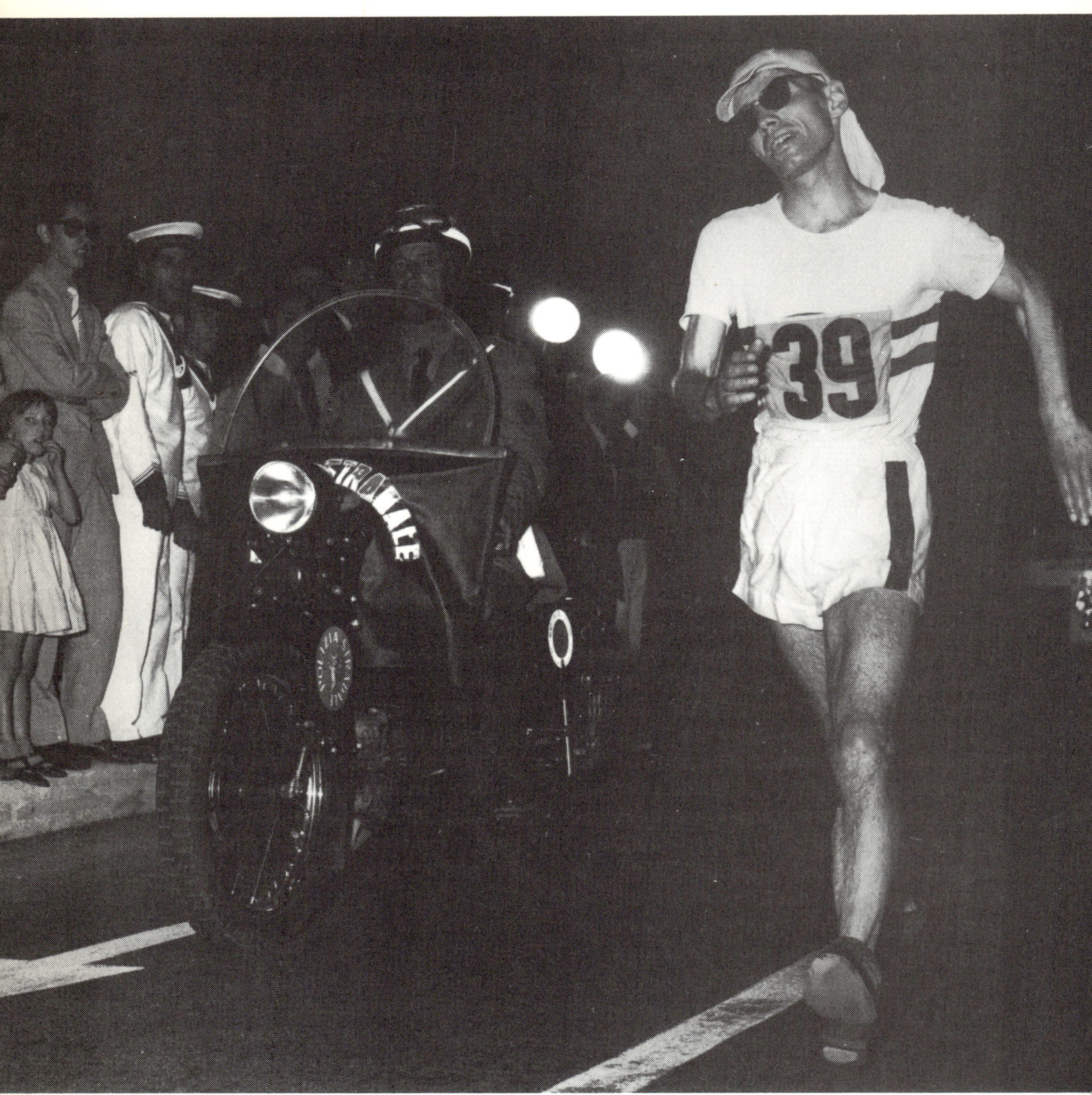

Britain's 'Mighty Mouse', Don Thompson, grinds his way to victory in the 1960 Rome Olympics 50 km walk.

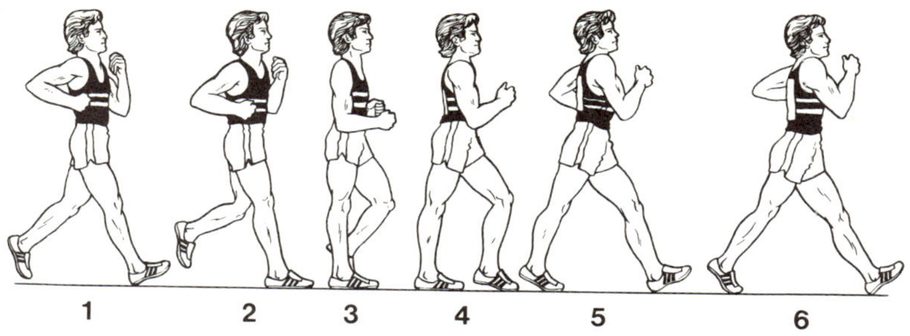

9 Race walking

stride multiplied by his stride cadence. His problem is that, in doing this, he must maintain ground-contact at all times.

The action of a top-class walker is marked by excellent range of movement (fig. 9). This means that on each stride, ankle, knee and hip are fully extended. It also means that the hip rotates to ensure an even longer stride; this produces the hip wobble so characteristic of race-walking but so unlike even the fast walking of the pedestrian.

The forward leg is virtually straight on landing and will straighten almost immediately after contact, before it supports bodyweight. It then moves from support to driving as the rear leg swings through low.

The arms balance the legs (fig. 9.5) by working strongly across the body, and the upper-body development of the walker is therefore pronounced compared with that of the distance runners. Indeed, at least one top walker, Kannenberg, had previous experience in weightlifting. As in sprinting, it is essential that there is no rotation of the trunk and the arms, therefore their action balance and nullify the rotational elements of the leg action.

The impression given in race-walking is a low, flowing movement across the ground, and good technique is essential, not only to operate within the rules, but also to cover long distances efficiently.

Event background

Race-walking, unlike running, involves big increases in energy for any sudden increase in speed. Tactical bursts or sprint-finishes are therefore not part of race-walking's vocabulary. There is also, of course, the problem that any big speed increase may result in the walker 'lifting'.

Race-strategies fall into two main categories:

Strategies aimed at winning the race

1. A fast overall race-pace, which the walker is capable of maintaining from start to finish. The hope is that challengers will gradually fade away during the race.
2. A 'killing' fast early pace to separate the walker from the rest of his competitors, before settling down to his own, slower pace.
3. Staying with the leader or leading group, before breaking away for victory.

Strategies aimed at achieving the best possible time

1. Settling down to a pre-arranged pace, ignoring the other walkers.
2. Hanging on to a slightly faster walker for as long as possible.

Whatever the walker's strategic aims, the international walker will always have tried out various strategies in lesser, minor races

372

so that he has had ample experience of them. Central to all tactics is good pace-judgement for, like middle-distance running, even-pace effort is the most economic method of using energy.

Physical types

The race walker is psychologically and physiologically similar to the marathon runner, in that he possesses the same light, lean body, and his pulse beats in the same low sub-40 beats per minute area. The essential difference lies in the upper body, where the walker's pumping arm-action requires and develops much greater muscularity. Race-walking, like distance running, is an endurance skill, because of its technical demands.

Rules

'Walking is progression by steps so taken that unbroken contact with the ground is maintained. At each step, the advancing foot of the walker must make contact with the ground before the rear foot leaves the ground. During the period of each step when a foot is on the ground the leg must be straightened (i.e., not bent at the knee) at least for one moment, and in particular, the supporting leg must be straight in the vertical upright position'.

Bernd Kannenberg (West Germany) shows both the form and the quality of physique required of the modern international walker.

The above quotation is more comprehensive than the conventional 'unbroken contact' definition and precludes bent-knee scuttling (sometimes called 'creeping') which might involve unbroken contact.

In races above 50 km, feeding-stations are provided by the organizers at 10 km and thereafter at 5 km intervals. The walkers are permitted to take their own refreshments, but these must be consumed only at the refreshment stations.

Disqualification occurs if, in the opinion of two judges (one of whom must be the Chief Judge), a competitor's action is unfair. An alternative option is the decision of three judges other than the Chief Judge. A walker can also be cautioned during the race if he looks in danger of going outside the definition of walking. He is not entitled to a second caution.

PART III
Jumping events

*t: Mexico City, 1968. Bob Beamon leaps
› the twenty-first century with a jump of
0 m (29 ft 2½ in).*

Top: Dwight Stones (USA)
Above: Sara Simeoni (Italy)

259

The origins of competitive jumping are far from clear. The ancient Olympics (776 BC–390 AD) had only one jump, the long jump, the rules of which are uncertain, and which occurred only in the pentathlon. There is no evidence that the Greeks practised any other form of jumping, and although there are mentions of jumping in medieval times, we must look to the eighteenth century before we come to any specific mention of these events in any competitive sense.

In Sir Thomas Elyot's *The Boke Named the Gouvernour* (1531), Elyot refers to running, jumping and throwing as excellent exercise for a gentleman. The woodcut of Robert Dover's Cotswold Olympick Games shows jumping (albeit down a surprisingly steep hill), but there are no direct references to either rules or distances until the beginning of the nineteenth century. This is possibly because, until the development of the railway system in the second quarter of the nineteenth century, most rural sports were of a strictly local nature. This meant not only local rules, but specifically local events. The record books of the late nineteenth century list dozens of separate jumping events, the techniques and rules of most of which are lost to us. Many of these were undoubtedly simply stunts created by professional jumpers for the purposes of betting in jumping matches.

There were, however, some survivors. The hitch and kick, for instance, which was confined to the border areas of Scotland, was taken to the United States by Scottish immigrants. It made contact with the documented period of athletics history when the great Irish-American high jumper, Michael Sweeney, competed in the professional Highland Games of the East Coast and jumped 2.90 m (9 ft 4 in), which still stands as a 'world record', if only because no one else has attempted it for the last seventy years.

Similarly, the hop, hop and jump, which is still an option in certain Scottish professional Highland Games, made its first and last appearance in the Athens Olympics of 1896. It was used by the winner, Connolly, who cleared a modest 13.45 m (44 ft 11¾ in). 'Disgusting,' shouted the Greek prince who was judging the event. Connolly paled. Fortunately, it was only the Prince's English that was at fault, because Connolly's technique was allowed, albeit for the last time in the Olympics.

The origins of the modern jumps are, therefore, essentially Celtic rather than Classic, and the college athletics programmes which Baron de Coubertin witnessed in his

Charles Kokoyo (Kenya)

pre-Olympic visits to the United States were a direct reflection of the Highland Games programmes carried there in the early nineteenth century by immigrant Scots.

The development of the Olympic movement and the creation of the International Athletics Federation in 1912, saw the death of the infinity of jumps which had enriched and often bewildered the nineteenth century. It is, however, interesting to note that even as late as the IAAF Convention of 1912, several countries were formally advocating the retention of the standing jumps, three spring jumps, and a 'gymnastic' vault. The IAAF Conference of 1913 decided that the standard jumping events were to be high jump, long jump, pole vault, and triple jump, and the multitude of nineteenth-century jumping events gradually sank into oblivion.

Berlin Olympics, 1936. Cornelius Johnson (USA) becomes the last athlete to win an Olympic title using the western roll technique.

11. High jump

History

'No documentation, no history' is a problem which bedevils all sports historians. It is, for instance, certain that competitive high jumping took place before the early nineteenth century, but no account of any competitions exists. The first recorded high jumping is in the professional Lowland Games of Scotland in the early 1820s, when heights in the 1.60–1.70 m (5 ft 4 in–5 ft 7 in) range were recorded, together with standing high jumps (from a two-footed take-off) in the 1.30–1.40 m (4 ft 3 in–4 ft 5½ in) area.

Most high jumping in the first half of the twentieth century was by the professional athletes of Scotland and Northern England. No landing-areas and no agreed rules existed and so the Scot, Tivendale's 1.85 m (6 ft 1 in) and the great Scottish all-rounder, Donald Dinnie's 1.80 m (5 ft 11 in) clearances cannot therefore be compared with the first recorded 1.83 m (6ft) clearance by M. C. Brooks of Oxford in 1876. Brooks' best clearance of 1.87 m (6 ft 2½ in) stood until eclipsed by the tiny American W. Byrd Page, with 1.94 m (6 ft 4½ in) in 1891.

The clearance techniques of this period fall into three categories. The first was the scissors, the second a rough side-on jump, the precursor of the western roll, and the third (used by Brooks) a frontal back lay-out. All were relatively uneconomic jumps, (with the scissors the least economic), but all were strongly influenced by the need to land on the feet because of the poor condition of the shallow sand-pits which were coming into use in the last quarter of the century.

The first major technical advance was the eastern cut-off, whose greatest exponent (if not its inventor) was the Irish American, M. F. Sweeney. The cut-off was essentially a modified scissors jump, where the jumper, instead of sitting upright in mid-flight (resulting in low hips) lay flat at the peak of flight, almost looking through his own legs. In the first international amateur match of the nineteenth century, the New York AC versus London AC at Manhattan Island in 1895, Sweeney astounded the English visitors by clearing 1.97 m (6 ft 5⅝ in) to set a new world record.

M. F. Horine (USA), who took the record to 2 m (6 ft 7 in) in 1912 is credited with the invention of the western roll, in which, taking off from his inside foot, the jumper presented the side of his body to the bar, thus achieving a simple economic lay-out.

The next great American jumper, Harold Osborn, modified and refined the western roll in the 1920s, but his number of marginal clearances resulted in claims that he was 'holding' the cross-bar on the pegs, and in consequence of this, the rules were changed. Until that time the cross-bar supports had pointed outwards, but the rules were changed so that they pointed inwards.

The next technical change was the straddle, though no jumper has claimed credit for its creation. Here the jumper (fig. 11) lies face down to the cross-bar, thus producing an even more economic lay-out than the western roll. The only limiting factor at this time was the rule which prohibited 'diving'; i.e., the jumper leading the hips with his head and trunk over the cross-bar. When this rule was abolished in 1938 the way was clear for even more economic straddle clearances.

Until the early 1950s the high jump record had been held exclusively by American athletes, and in 1952 the world record had been held for eleven years by the American, Lester Steers. The entry of the USSR into the Olympic movement in 1952 resulted in a detailed analysis of existing techniques. Russion sports specialists decided that flight technique, which had dominated the thinking of athletes and coaches since the late nineteenth century, was relatively unimportant. What was important was the approach-run and take-off. The Russians therefore created a fast, highly-stereotyped (fig. 12) approach-run and take-off, and soon produced a flood of great jumpers, starting with Yuriy Stepanov, who took the world record in 1957, after the American straddler, Charles Dumas, had been the first to clear the magic 2.14 m (7 ft) with 2.15 m (7 ft 0½ in) in 1956.

The Russians also showed creative technical imagination in their development, in the mid 1950s, of the built up take-off. This gave the jumper considerable extra take-off leverage, and new IAAF rules were brought in to limit present maximum sole-thickness to 13 mm.

Greatest of them all, Valeriy Brumel (USSR), rotates his rear leg round the bar for a world record of 2.26 m (7 ft 5 in) in 1962. Note the sand/sawdust landing area.

Using the curve of the eastern cut-off jumper and a back lay-out clearance, Dick Fosbury leaps to victory and immortality in the 1968 Mexico Olympics.

Classic Russian high jumping reached its peak in 1960, when Valeriy Brumel took the Olympic title in Rome. Brumel repeated his Olympic victory in 1964 and took the world record on to 2.28 m (7 ft 5¾ in) but a tragic motorcycle accident ended his career.

By 1960, the western roll and eastern cut-off had virtually vanished from the international arena and the straddle reigned supreme. However, in the winter of 1967–68 news came from the United States of a young American jumper, Dick Fosbury, who had unwittingly linked the curved run of the eastern cut-off (1895) with the back lay-out technique of M. C. Brooks (1876). The chance fusion of forgotten techniques produced the Fosbury flop, which, being essentially a modified scissors jump, introduced a simplicity to high jumping which the more complex Russian straddle did not possess.

Fosbury took the 1968 Olympic title with a magnificent display of competitive jumping, and by 1972, over 50 per cent of the world's top jumpers were using his technique. Although the 1972 Olympic title was won by a classic Russian straddler, Tarmak, the 1976 title went to a flopper, the young Pole, Wzola. The two techniques are now split fairly evenly on the men's side, with Eastern European jumpers opting, conservatively, for the straddle, and the rest of the world almost exclusively for the flop.

The existence of the flop was heavily dependent on the development of built-up

Rosi Ackermann, a classic straddler (East Germany).

foam landing-areas. In the early 1960s, primitive versions of foam landing-areas were created (until that time built-up sand and sawdust had obtained), but by the late 1960s these had reached a high level of sophistication, thus enabling the flop to develop with safety.

High jump has, therefore, come from a period (1850–1952) of trial and error, with the main stress on flight technique, into a period (1952–1968) of technical stereotyping, with the main emphasis on approach-run and take-off. The last ten years have seen trial and error return in the shape of the Fosbury flop, which has in its turn been analysed and re-structured.

Technique

The techniques of high jump have now divided into two, the Fosbury flop and the straddle, in contrast to the 1948 Olympics where five separate techniques could be seen.

The *flop* (fig. 10) usually involves a total of eight to twelve strides, the first strides being straight and the final three to four strides being on a curve. This is in contrast to Fosbury and his first imitators, who ran the whole approach-run on a curve.

10 High jump: Fosbury flop

The take-off point of international jumpers is usually about 1 m (1 yd) directly out from the jumping stand, though this varies according to the speed of the jumper, with the faster jumpers taking off further away and the slower jumpers closer in. The aim is to get the high point of the jump at the centre of the bar, its lowest point.

Speed is a vital factor in the Fosbury flop. Broadly speaking, the greater the controlled speed, the greater the height cleared, as the stretch placed on the muscles of the take-off leg produces an explosive, vertical recoil.

The jumper's aim is to *drive straight up* (fig. 10.5), for only then will he achieve the maximum centre-of-gravity height at the peak of his flight, and the curved run of the flop helps him to place bodyweight where he wants it, over his take-off foot.

The flopper has two other means of driving himself vertically at take-off. The first is the swing up of the free thigh (fig. 10.6), and the second is the swing up of both arms. Both of these actions give lift and raise the centre of gravity at take-off. The drive of the free thigh also helps his spin round the bar.

In flight, his aim is to gain maximum lay-out advantage at the peak of flight. This means a stretched, draped position on the bar.

The final problem is the clearance of the trailing legs. This is achieved by 'piking' to speed up rotation and flip the legs clear.

Although the straddle has experienced only minor modifications over the years, the flop has produced many hybrid versions, some of which have embodied a full-blooded use of both arms and straight free leg, in mimicry of the straddle.

The *straddle technique* (fig. 11) is more complex in the structure of its approach-run and take-off, and has a high degree of artificiality.

During the last three strides (fig. 11.2), the jumper settles on to his heels, still holding approach-run speed. The penultimate stride is long, with the arms drawn back (fig. 11.3).

At take-off, both arms and free leg are swung high, aiding the drive of the take-off leg (fig. 11.5). As in the flop, there is a powerful, vertical thrust, aided by the sweep of arms and free leg.

11 High jump: straddle

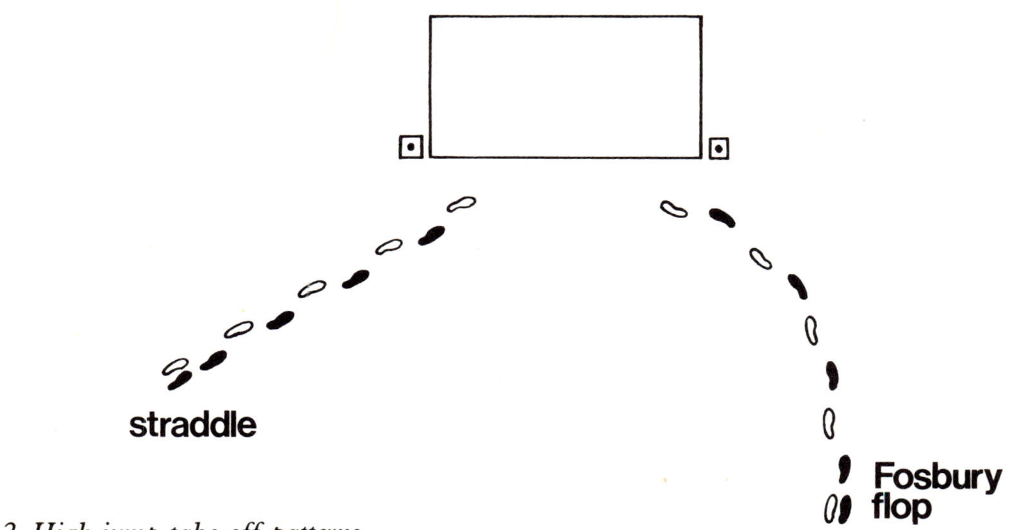

12 High jump take-off patterns

Men		height	height achieved	differ-ential	efficiency rating	**Women**		height	height achieved	differ-ential	efficiency rating
Franklin Jacobs	USA	1.73	2.32	59	182.3	Rosemarie Ackermann	GDR	1.76	2.00	24	112.6
Ron Livers	USA	1.75	2.24	49	164.2	Michiyo Inaoka	JAP	1.62	1.85	23	97.2
Kazunori Koshikawa	JAP	1.72	2.21	49	160.3	Maggie Woods	CAN	1.58	1.80	22	91.6
Juan Carrasco	SPA	1.70	2.18	48	155.7	Ann-Marie Pira	BEL	1.71	1.92	21	101.6
Mike Lattany	USA	1.71	2.19	48	154.9	Yordanka Blagoyeva	BUL	1.74	1.94	20	102.3
Ni Chih-chin	CPR	1.84	2.29	45	167.1	Joni Huntley	USA	1.73	1.93	20	101.4
Mike Cawthorn	USA	1.59	2.03	44	134.6	Marie Mracnova	CSR	1.72	1.92	20	100.4
Rory Kotinek	USA	1.85	2.29	44	166.1	Hiroe Ishida	JAP	1.59	1.79	20	88.7
Valeriy Brumel	SU	1.84	2.28	44	164.9	Sara Simeoni	ITA	1.78	1.97	19	104.0
Rolf Beilschmidt	GDR	1.88	2.31	43	167.7	Heidi de Kock	RSA	1.66	1.85	19	92.9

An efficiency rating has been calculated for each athlete; the idea is to give almost equal rating to the size of the athlete and the differential achieved. The formula is: height (in metres) x differential (in cm) + height (in metres) x height achieved (in metres) x 20.

In flight, the jumper delays his rear leg and curls himself around the bar (fig. 11.7), to achieve an economic lay-out position. His final problem is to clear his rear leg, and this he does by rotating it outwards, to land on his back.

A magnificent Fosbury arch by 1976 Olympic champion Wzola (Poland).

Event background

The world-class high jumper is lean and light and normally above 1.85 m (6 ft 1 in) in height. Against this, one of the world's leading jumpers, the American, Franklin Jacobs, is only 1.73 m (5 ft 8 in) tall. The table shows a recent study of height *vis-à-vis* height cleared, and it can be seen that the five leading differentials are held by small men in the 1.70–1.75 m (5 ft 5½ in–5 ft 6½ in) range.

Competitions are not, alas, decided by differentials, but by height actually cleared, and the tall, long-legged athlete of above 1.83 m (6 ft) is the prototype of the successful high jumper.

High jump shares with pole vault the characteristic of indefiniteness, in that, as long as he makes a successful clearance, the competition continues. The high jumper always faces an exact challenge, unlike the long jumper, who only realizes his performance after it has been measured. The competitive focus of the high jumper is intense, particularly when he faces a height which he has never before cleared. He must 'feel' and 'see' himself clear of the cross-bar even before he starts his approach-run.

Another competitive factor of importance is the number of jumps taken, for if there is a tie, then the first clearance at the previous height wins. If there is still a tie, then the total number of failures is the deciding factor, and if the leaders are still locked, the total number of jumps decides. Against this, if conditions are bad, it is often wise for the jumper to keep warm and keep a 'feel' for the bar by jumping at every height, once he has started. Otherwise, on a cold, slippery runway he may find it difficult to clear even a modest height.

The training of high jumpers contains a high element of bounding, mobility and running for floppers, whilst the slower, Eastern European straddlers also add a considerable measure of weight training. Central to all high jump training is, of course, regular grooving-in of high jump technique.

Rules

1. A competitor fails:
   (a) If he dislodges the bar.
   (b) If he touches the ground beyond the plane of the upright without first clearing the bar.
2. Three consecutive failures result in disqualification.

	1.78 m	1.82 m	1.85 m	1.88 m	1.90 m	1.92 m	1.94 m	Total failures	Total jumps	possible
A	—	XO	O	XO	—	XXO	XXX	4	8	2
B	O	O	O	X—	XO	XXO	XXX	4	9	3
C	O	O	X—	O	XXO	XXO	XXX	5	—	4
D	O	—	—	XXO	XXO	XO	XXX	—	—	1

O = Cleared X = Failed — = Did not jump

A, B, C and D cleared 1.92 m and failed at 1.94 m.

The rule regarding ties comes into operation, and as 'D' cleared 1.92 m at his second attempt, the others taking three, he is declared the winner.

The other three will tie and the judges add up the total number of failures, up to and including the height last cleared, i.e. 1.92 m.

'C' has more failures than 'A' or 'B', and is therefore awarded fourth place. 'A' and 'B' still tie and the judges add up the total number of jumps up to and including the height last cleared, i.e., 1.92 m. 'A' being awarded second place.

If the tie still remains:

(i) If it concerns the first place, the competitors tying shall have one more jump at the height at which they failed, and if no decision is reached, the bar shall be lowered or raised to the heights which shall be announced; they shall then attempt one jump at each height until the tie is decided. Competitors so tying must jump on each occasion when deciding the tie.

(ii) If it concerns any other place, the competitors shall be awarded the same place in the competition.

12. Long jump

History

The Greek Olympic long jump took place only in the pentathlon, not then a highly-regarded event, which at that time consisted of sprint, discus, long jump, javelin and wrestling.

The main account of Greek long jumping lies in vases, which all show jumpers using halteres (jumping weights). The halteres found have varied from 1.35–7.70 kg (3 lb to 17 lb) in weight and it is likely that the heavier weights were used for strength training rather than for jumping.

Although there are written accounts describing jumpers 'making the bater (take-off board) ring' in a manner similar to the powerful 'strike' of the modern long jumper, there is no certainty that the Greek long jump was anything like a modern long jump, as no rules have been handed down to us. The professional jumpers of the nineteenth century frequently used weights, which they released in mid-flight (thus changing mass), but there is not a single vase drawing showing haltere-release, and if we assume that the Greeks retained their halteres in flight, there would be little advantage in using them in a conventional running long jump, as the weights would have slowed up their approach-run. More likely is a series of flowing two-footed spring jumps, (fig. 00) where the swing of the halteres would have added to the distance of each jump.

The greatest recorded jump of all time was the 8.95 m (29 ft 7 in) of John Howard of Chester. Chester's jump was, however, made from a beat-board using 3.60 kg (8 lb) dumb-bells. Although Howard's feat is closer to us than those of the Greeks, there are no accurate accounts of his technique.

The major limiting factor in the primitive rural games of nineteenth-century Britain was the lack of soft landing-areas, and this meant that the majority of jumps were ground-to-ground jumps in the 6 m (19 ft 8¼ in) area, distances which in no way reflected the abilities of, admittedly untrained, jumpers. The best professional jump, without weights, handed down to us is the 7.20 m (23 ft 6 in) of Ben Hart (Mountain Stag) in the middle of the nineteenth century.

The amateur jumpers of the late nineteenth century at first followed the professional practice of jumping from no fixed mark, but by 1900 the present 20 cm (8 in) take-off board was established and the first world record holder was the Irish-American, Peter O'Connor, in 1901.

O'Connor's technique was simple.

'Well y'see, I have a mark so far back, and another mark beyond that. I hit the first mark easy like, then I run harder for the near one: and when I'm after hitting that, I go for all that's in me, and about four steps from the take-off I shut my eyes and put my trust in God'.

It is not until the 1920s that the 'hang' flight technique is mentioned, and soon after, the hitch-kick, which was at that time called 'the running in the air' technique, is mentioned in coaching literature.

The first man to break the 7.93 m (26 ft) barrier was the Haitian, Silvio Cator in 1928, but the strength of long jumping has always lain in the fast, springy American negro jumpers. Jesse Owens epitomized this group, and his 8.13 m (26 ft 8¼ in) jump in 1935 (made from a grass approach at the end of an hour in which he had already broken or equalled five world records), stood for twenty-five years. Owens stressed the need for running speed (he had run a 10.2 sec 100 m) and it should also be noted that he had jumped close on 2 m (6 ft 6¾ in) in the high jump and competed for the United States in the preliminary rounds of the basketball tournament in the 1936 Olympics.

American supremacy in long jumping was maintained in the Olympic Games by Willie Steele (1948), Jerome Biddle (1952), Greg Bell (1956), and Ralph Boston (1960), but was broken by the Welshman, Lynn Davies, in 1964, on a rain-sodden Tokyo runway. Davies epitomized a new type of long jumper, relying less on natural speed and spring and more on a heavy conditioning programme, with stress on weight training.

Long jumping possesses a high natural element and the entry of the Communist nations to the world athletic scene in the early 1950s had less impact than it was to have in the more technical triple jump event. Nevertheless, the USSR produced Igor Ter-Ovanesyen, a worthy challenger to Davies, in Boston in the 1960s.

Superb stylist, 1969 Olympic champion and world record holder, Ralph Boston (USA).

The crucial need for natural spring and speed was clearly shown in one magic moment in the thin air of Mexico City at the Olympic Games of 1968. Attacking the board with incredible speed, the American, Bob Beamon, launched himself into the twenty-first century to clear 8.90 m (29 ft 2½ in), a performance which is unlikely to be surpassed at ground level.

The post-Beamon period has been an anti-climax, with few world-class jumpers able to guarantee a jump of much better than 8 m (26 ft 3 in) even on the fast, consistent, synthetic runways of the 1970s. The American, Arnie Robinson, 8.35 m (27 ft 5 in) in 1976, the Yugoslav, Nened Stekič, 8.45 m (27 ft 9 in), and the Frenchman, George Rousseau, 8.26 m (27 ft 2 in) in 1976, have shown themselves capable of regular jumps around 8.10 m (26 ft 7 in), but with the possible exception of the American, Larry Myricks, 8.52 m (27 ft 11½), there is as yet no new Beamon on the horizon.

Women

Women's long jump was held back by the social factors which restrained the development of women's athletics as a whole. To these were added the medical and paramedical prophets of doom who counselled against any form of jumping, rationalizing their views by drawing heavily from science and pseudo-science. For instance, the hitch-kick came in for censure, one argument being that it would displace the uterus. Happily, female athletes ignored the 'experts' and jumped on, their uteri secure.

The first jumper of real calibre to develop was the Dutch girl, Fanny Blankers-Keon 6.25 m (20 ft 6 in), the 'Jesse Owens' of her generation. Blankers-Koen, who possessed great speed (11.5 sec 100 m) and spring (1.71 m/5 ft 7½ in high jump) lost some of her best years during the German Occupation of Hol-

13 Long jump

land, but achieved four gold medals in the 1948 London Olympics. Such was her all-round ability, she did not compete in either long or high jumps, in both of which events she held the world records! The world record progressed slowly till 1964, when the Russian, Tatyana Schelkanova (6.70 m/21 ft 11¾ in) and the British all-rounder, Mary Rand (6.76 m/22 ft 2¼ in) took the record to a respectable level. Since then the record has edged gradually towards 7 m (23 ft), and like the men's event, has shown only modest response to modern training methods. The record stands at the moment of writing to the credit of the Russian, Vilna Bardauskiene, at 7.09 m (23 ft 3¼ in).

Technique

The technique of long jumping is basically simple. The event is essentially a fast run flowing into a high jump, ending with the feet as far as possible in front of the body without the jumper falling back.

First, let us look at the approach-run.

Approach-run

Most international class jumpers take twenty-one to twenty-four strides, resulting in approach-runs of 40–45 m (44–50 yd). Their aim is to hit the board at the maximum controlled speed, in perfect balance. The advent of synthetic runways in the late 1960s has meant that accurate approach-runs are more easily achieved, but variable winds and minor variations in the jumpers' stride length add a 'spatial' factor to the long jump approach. This means that the jumper must be able to judge space at speed as he comes closer to the board (the earlier the better), so that he can make a series of minor stride-adjustments rather than massive last-ditch modifications.

The jumper reaches top speed three to four strides from the board, his aim being to hold this speed into take-off, and it is in this area that even many top class jumpers fail.

Take-off

The aim of the jumper is to reach the board at speed and in balance, securing at least 15 cm (6 in) of board with his take-off foot. He has only ¹⁄₁₀ sec in which to apply vertical and horizontal force to his body, which must be upright at take-off (fig. 13.5). The jumper, who has involuntarily 'settled' in order to prepare to jump, lifts powerfully. It must be remembered that speed must never be sacrificed for 'lift', as the ratio of the horizontal to the vertical is 2 : 1.

Mary Rand (Great Britain), whose 6.76 m (22 ft 2¼ in) on the rain-sodden runway at the Tokyo Olympics was possibly the greatest female long jump in history.

11
12
13
14
15
16
17

Above: Angela Voigt (East Germany), one of a new breed of finely-conditioned East German jumpers.
Right: Bob Seagren (USA)

Flight technique

Once a jumper is in flight, he cannot change the path of his centre of gravity any more than an inanimated object, such as a cannon-ball, can change its flight path. What he *can* do is to secure himself an advantageous landing position, by making clockwise movements with his legs (fig. 13.7–14), as in the two and a half hitch-kick technique. This slows up the tendency of his body to rotate forward, which would mean that his point of contact would be too early. On landing, the jumper bends his knees quickly, in order to speed up his rotation over his heels.

Event background

The long jumper is a speed-spring athlete, with the accent on speed, and the world's top male jumpers are capable of electrically-timed 100 m in the 10.40–10.60 sec region, with the ladies running in the 11.50–11.90 sec region. It can be seen that the ladies appear to be further from top class female sprinters than the men are from their male counterparts.

High-jumping ability appears to be of relatively small importance in long jump, though most top male jumpers can produce good high jumps, and the occasional jumper, such as the diminutive Ron Livers (USA), a world-class one. Few female jumpers appear to have above average high-jumping ability, though Mary Rand (Great Britain) was an international-class jumper in the 1960s. Most, like ex-world record-holder, Heidi Rosendahl (11.3 sec 100 m), rely on running speed.

Height appears to be a significant factor in long jump and the average height of the Mexico Olympics long jump finalists was 1.83 m (6 ft), relative to the 1.87 m (6 ft 2 in) of the high jumpers, and the 1.75 m (5 ft 8½ in) of the 100 m sprinters, with the same general pattern in the women's event.

Though long jump has not the technical complexity of such events as pole vault or hammer, there are few athletes who can surge at 24 mph down the runway and smack a 20 cm (8 in) board in balance, applying effective vertical forces in $^1/_{10}$ sec, and proceed to execute a skilful flight technique.

The long jumper operates at the highest speed of all jumpers and has to apply maximum force at take-off. This means that he must ever be sensitive, like the pole vaulter and triple jumper, to changes in wind-strength both before and during his approach-run, which contains a high component of spatial awareness.

The training of the long jumper relates more closely to that of the triple jumper than that of the high jumper, because of the high speed component. It therefore stresses sprinting, bounding, and weight training, with the priority on the first two factors.

The creation in the late 1960s of synthetic runways has undoubtedly led to improvements in performance, yet long jump has remained surprisingly static. Indeed, it is impossible to imagine any other event in which the stars of thirty to forty years ago (Owens, Steele, Bell) could return and, without any improvement in performance, cope comfortably at world level. The conclusion must be that the event has, like the short sprints, a high natural element and is therefore, to a degree, resistant to modern training methods.

Geoff Capes (Great Britain)

Rules

1. The jump is measured from the furthest back point of landing, back to the take-off line, at right angles to that line.
2. A 'foul' occurs if the jumper:
   (a) Employs any form of somersaulting.
   (b) Uses weights.
   (c) Walks back through the pit.
   (d) Takes off from the area on each side of the board.
   (e) Touches the ground beyond the take-off line so as to leave a visible mark on the material beyond the board.
3. The material used to mark the area beyond the board is usually plasticine raised to a level of 30°. The board itself is made of wood measuring 1.21–1.22 m (4 ft) long and 20 cm (8 in) wide.
4. Wind speeds in excess of 2 m/sec invalidate jumps for record purposes.
5. In the event of a tie, the jumper with the next best jump wins.

13. Triple jump

History

Triple jump is an event which has often been criticized because it is not 'natural'. When measured against this criterion, neither, of course, are hurdles, pole vault, hammer, javelin and discus. In his most primitive state, man in any case probably ran, climbed and scrambled over objects rather than jumped over them. Most athletics events are, as they now stand, unnatural, if by that we mean they are not tests which man might have faced in his natural state. The only test to which athletics events have been subjected is popularity, and the formal recognition of this popularity took place in 1913 when the International Amateur Athletic Federation recognized triple jump as a part of the international programme.

Triple jump emerged from the mass of nineteenth-century jumping events, a programme dictated mainly by the money matches of professional jumpers, who were usually specialists in specific jumps.

The best triple jump of the nineteenth century professional jumpers is the 14.95 m (49 ft 9 in) by Hogg of Hawick. This jump is well documented, as are many of Hogg's other jumps, and there is little doubt that he was capable of this distance.

The early history of triple jumping is essentially Celtic, and it was the Irish-American, Dan Ahearne, who was the first man to break 15.25 m (50 ft) with, in 1911, 15.50 m (50 ft 11 in). Early jumpers gave little attention to technique and Ahearne's hop-step-jump distances were 6.09 m (19 ft 11½ in) hop (measured board to toe), 3.40 m (11 ft 3 in) step (measured toe to toe), and 5.99 m (19 ft 8 in) jump (measured toe to furthest back point). Ahearne's tiny step phase was typical of this period, for the event was not yet a true triple jump.

The springy Japanese, such as Oda, Nambu and Tajima, who dominated the late 1920s and early 1930s, brought both speed and technique to the natural efforts of their predecessors. The Japanese were substantially faster than the jumpers of their period, but they also brought a unique balance to the phases, producing long bounding steps and active landings from one phase to the next.

World War II saw the end of a Japanese supremacy which had culminated in the 1932 and 1936 Olympic victories of Oda and Tajima. The post-war world was to belong to totalitarian nations of the communist bloc who developed stereotyped techniques and training methods which brought to the fore such great jumpers as Leonid Sherbakov, Vitold Kreer, and Josef Schmidt. Two separate schools of jumping developed.

El supremo of triple jump, Viktor Saneyev (USSR), the only jumper to win three successive Olympic titles.

ZEISS DISTANCE
West Germany

14 Triple jump

The first was the classic Russian school typified by Kreer and Sherbakov. These relatively slow – 11.4–11.6 sec 100 m – jumpers used long, high hops and steps, using the swing of free leg and both arms (double arm swing) to aid distance in each phase.

The Poles, in contrast, stressed running speed and employed low flat hops and steps, with the hop and jump phases equal. Thus the Poles used a 10:8:10 ratio and the Russians 11:7:9, to gain a given distance.

The Polish school triumphed in the 1960 and 1964 Olympics through Schmidt, but in 1968, in the thin air of Mexico City, the fast (10.5 sec 100 m) Russian, Victor Sanayev won and repeated his Olympic victory in 1972 and 1976. The combination of speed and Russian technique therefore triumphed, and Sanayev's lead has been followed by almost all of the world's jumpers, including the Americans (whose natural jumping talents have still to be accurately reflected at world level), and the Cubans, of whom the Russian-coached Pedro Perez has been the most successful.

Technique

Like long jump, triple jump is essentially a speed event, and the triple jump approach-run is almost identical to that of the long jump, in that the jumper aims to hit the board in balance at speed.

The hop

Where the events differ is at take-off. The triple jumper cannot make a high, flat-out jump at take-off because a hop of such a height would make it impossible for him to complete a long step and jump. Thus, even at international level, triple jumpers rarely jump much more than 6.50 m (21 ft 4 in) in their hop. The hop therefore consists of a flat, controlled drive out from the take-off board.

The technical image at which the triple jumper aims, is of having his legs making powerful, rangy movements under an upright trunk.

In hop flight the triple jumper prepares for landing by splitting his thighs wide, to ensure an active 'plant' of his hopping foot (fig. 14.4).

The hop landing is a powerful 'drive out' assisted by the swing of his free leg and both arms. It is this combination of the drive of the hopping leg and the swing of free leg and arms which gives distances up to 5.20 m (17 ft) in the step phase.

Step

In fig. 14.7 the massive, bounding step of the modern triple jumper can be clearly seen. Again, in flight, there is preparation for landing as the arms are drawn back (fig. 14.9), and the lower leg is planted firmly ahead of the body.

The jump

The jump is as in long jump, though it must be noted that the triple jumper, because of the intermediate landings, is losing speed more quickly than the long jumper. The jumper is therefore using a simple 'sail' technique

Event background

World-class triple jumpers, at 1.83 m (6 ft), tend to be the same height as long jumpers. The technical and physical demands of the event tend to produce success in the mid-to-late twenties, though the world record in 1971 of the eighteen-year-old Cuban, Pedro Perez, shows that distance, if not competitive success, can be gained at an early age.

Up to take-off, the triple jumper has the same problems as the long jumper. Thereafter, two successive landings, which on both occasions mean the absorption of forces constituting two and a half times body weight, present him with particular problems. The section on technique describes the methods which the jumper uses to deal with this situation, but behind this is a weight training and bounding programme which enables the triple jumper to secure the strength and leg resilience to absorb landing shocks of this magnitude. The triple jumper can therefore be separated from the long jumper by this essential difference in leg and back strength and leg resilience.

Before the advent of synthetic runways in the late-1960s, triple jump could well have been called 'cripple jump', as hard, rutted, board-to-pit areas caused many heel bruises and ankle sprains. Now, because of the quality of modern runways and the introduction of protective heel-cups, such injuries are rare.

Rules

The central rules relating to measurement are as in long jump. There are, however, certain specific rules:

1. That the hop be made from the take-off foot back on to the same foot, and that the step be made to the opposite foot.
2. That if the jumper touches the ground with the 'sleeping' leg the jump as a whole shall be considered a failure.

This last rule is probably a vestige of the days when all manner of multiple jumps were used; by putting his 'sleeping' leg on the ground, the jumper could conceivably produce the force for another jump. In practice, the jumper occasionally 'scuffs' the ground at the end of the hop, a technical error which is of no practical advantage to him, but which results in a 'foul' being given.

João de Oliveira (Brazil), who took the world record to a massive 17.89 m (58 ft 8½ in) in the thin air of Mexico City in 1975.

14. Pole vault

History

The first records of pole vaulting are in the early 1840s, when the event was usually called 'the high jump with pole', and was featured in professional Scottish and northern meetings. There is some evidence that poles were used to clear walls and ditches in rural areas, but no clear bridge has been established between this practice and competitive pole vaulting. Most historians have placed the origins of modern vaulting in the Ulverston area of northern England in the early 1840s, but there is good evidence that the Scots took the event with them to the United States in the early 1850s, so it is likely that pole vault existed at the same time, in the early nineteenth century, in the rural areas of northern England and Scotland in their local professional games, without any apparent interchange of competitors or any agreement on rules.

Until the beginning of the twentieth century, vaulters, using steel-pronged ash poles, simply planted the pole in the ground in front of the cross-bar and swung over on to unprepared ground on the other side. The most successful of the amateur vaulters was the Ulverston athlete, Tom Ray, who in 1888 cleared 3.40 m (11 ft 8 in) using what became known as the 'climbing' method. Ray simply pulled himself up, hand over hand, as the pole reached the vertical position. He took this method to the United States, where he

Early indoor athletics, at the Agricultural Hall, Islington in 1871. Note the existence of a primitive 'trough' and landing area.

The final years of the stiff pole; Breitman (France) in a Great Britain versus France match, 1953.

became the first (and last) Englishman to win an American title. Ray's 'climbing' method, which had never, in any case, been widely used, was later banned.

In the early twentieth century, with the advent of the take-off trough, cinder runways and sand landing-areas, the technique of pole vaulting stabilized. It consisted of:

1. A fast approach-run and plant.
2. A 'hang' behind the pole.
3. A swing and tuck.
4. A pull and push.

The speed of the approach-run was improved by the advent of the light, springy, bamboo pole in the first years of the twentieth century.

The event was, like high jump, dominated from the first by American college athletes, with the American, Marc Wright, the first to break 4 m (13 ft 1½ in) in 1912, and Bill Sefton, 4.50 m (14 ft 11 in) in 1937. No athlete dominated the 1900–40 period, but in 1939–44, the American, Cornelius Warmerdam, took bamboo vaulting to its limits with over fifty clearances of 4.60 m (15 ft 1 in) or over, taking the world record to 4.77 m (15 ft 7¾ in) in 1942.

The early 1950s saw the development of light, durable, steel poles, but no major change in technique was required. This period was dominated by the American vaulter, Bob (The Vaulting Vicar) Richards, who took gold in both the 1952 and 1956 Olympics, and ended with the last rigid-pole Olympic victory by the American, Don Bragg, in Rome.

The word 'rigid' requires explanation. In the early 1960s a flexible, fibre-glass pole was introduced in the United States. This had the advantage, because of its flexibility, of allowing vaulters to achieve higher grip heights. Thus the grip of the 'rigid' era of a maximum of 4 m (3 ft 9 in), changed to grips more than 50 cm (19¾ in) higher. Since fibre-glass also had excellent recoil properties, the world record, which had never looked like reaching 5 m (16 ft 6 in) by 1970, had by that time climbed to 5.45 m (17 ft 10½ in).

Initially, the massive bend of the fibre-glass pole gave the impression of a fundamental change in the technique of pole vaulting. However, further analysis showed that the basic principle of keeping the body low at the beginning of the vault and lifting it late and fast, had not changed.

The first great fibre-glass vaulters were the Americans, John Uelses and John Pennel, but in an era of improved communications, Europeans were not long in catching up and soon European vaulters were challenging the Americans, and the American grip on the event was broken in Munich in 1972 by the East German, Wolfgang Nordwig.

The 1964–80 period has seen a massive improvement in the quality of landing-areas and this has made possible full-blooded clearance techniques at the top of the vault and safe landings on the back. The technological change in the nature of poles has, therefore, been matched by necessary changes in the nature of landing-areas.

The technique of vaulting seems to have stabilized and we can only look for improvement to developments in vaulting poles or a superbly gifted athlete. Only then will the world record approach the magic 6 m (19 ft 8¼ in.)

Technique

The height cleared is limited first by the height on the pole at which the vaulter can place his hands and still raise the pole to the vertical position. This overlaps with the height above his hands which the vaulter can achieve; top vaulters can clear over 1 m (3 ft 3½ in) above their grip height.

Wladislaw Kozakiewicz (Poland) demonstrates the powerful drive needed at take-off.

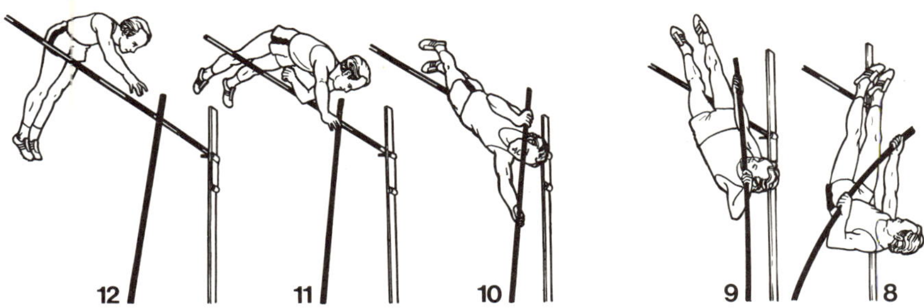

15 Pole vault

International vaulters have approach-runs similar to long jumpers, covering 40–50 m (44–55 yd) before the 'plant' of the pole into the take-off box. Fig. 15.1 shows the pole 'carry', with pole-tip carried high, thus minimizing the strain which a low pole-carry would have upon the vaulter's arms and shoulders.

As in long jump, accuracy is essential, because small errors at take-off can be magnified in flight. The vaulter must judge space whilst holding speed and balance into take-off.

As can be seen in fig. 15.2, the take-off foot is directly below the top hand, with a big angle between vaulter and pole. This ensures that the speed of the vaulter is applied directly into the pole through his fixed left arm (we will assume a left foot take-off); it is essential that force is applied directly through the pole to achieve both maximum bend and upward pole velocity.

The vaulter adds to the speed of his take-off by a vigorous drive of his take-off leg (similar to that in long jump) with a strong free thigh pick up (fig. 15.3). A good vault is made at take-off and expressed in flight, and from the moment of take-off a vaulter knows if he is in strong, dynamic balance, ready to make smooth co-ordinated movements in flight.

Fig. 15.4 shows the situation immediately after take-off. The vaulter stays low, keeping his left arm fixed and plenty of space between himself and the bulging pole. Then comes the swing (fig. 15.5) as the vaulter begins to swing back towards his straightening pole, maximizing its lifting potential. Fig. 16 shows this position from the front, showing also the sideways movement of the pole.

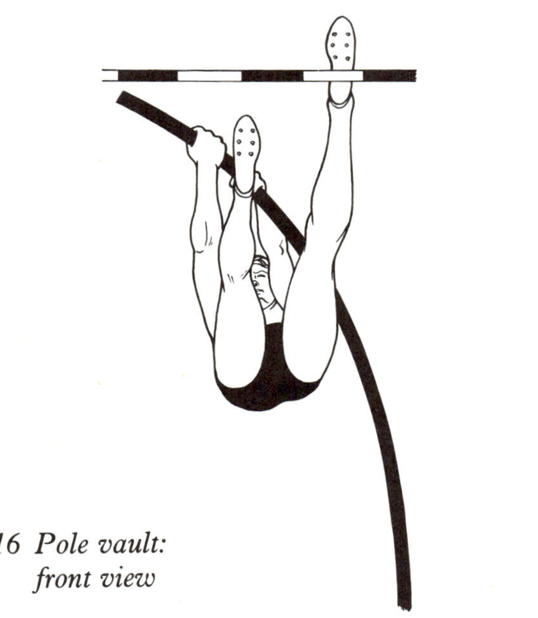

16 Pole vault: front view

This tuck position is followed by a flowing pull-push phase (fig. 15.8) in which the hips rise vertically above the hands (fig. 15.10).

The aim now is to avoid the cross-bar and it is at this late point that many vaults are lost by bad timing or lack of 'feel' for the position of the bar. The vaulter aims to lift the hands late, as any rushed movement might throw his chest down on to the bar.

Event background

World-class vaulters have an average height of 1.83 m (6 ft), the same height as world-class long jumpers, and bearing in mind the need to hold high on the pole, this is understandable. Their running speeds are, however, about 0.3 sec slower, averaging around an electrical 10.9 sec 100 m. Vaulting seems to be a sport which is best started in early youth; no world-class vaulter is likely to have started much later than eighteen years of age and the average starting-age at world level is only fourteen.

Modern vaulters have effective push-offs (deducting the 20 cm/18 in lost in placing the pole in the take-off trough) of about 1 m (3 ft 3½ in), and the major factor limiting improvement is the height of grip, which in turn is limited by take-off speed and pole resilience.

The vaulter usually has excellent gymnastic qualities and often spends much of his training time performing gymnastics and trampolining, both of which aid him in securing the necessary 'feel' for flight positions.

Competition

Most vaulters are sparing with their vaults, wishing to conserve energy and realizing that competitions are often decided, like high jump, on count back, and this often results in vaulters coming in too high and 'fouling out' at their opening height.

Vaulting is highly susceptible to wind conditions and vaulters will always try to wait until wind conditions are favourable before starting their run.

Rules

Rules are basically as high jump, the central difference being in the fact that the vault-stands can be placed 46 cm (18 in) in front of or behind the front of the take-off trough. Note too, that if the pole comes through with the vault, without dislodging the cross-bar, this counts as a clearance. If it dislodges the cross-bar then the vault is adjudged a failure.

Overleaf: denied victory because of an IAAF ruling on poles, Bob Seagren vaults at the Munich Olympics on a borrowed pole.

PART IV
Throwing events

The history of throws is a mixture of Celtic and Classic, in that javelin and discus come directly from the Ancient Games, where they were part of the pentathlon programme, while shot and hammer are of Celtic origin. All throwing events derive from the use of work (hammer), military (javelin), or natural (discus and shot) materials by men during their leisure. Many events have vanished into the mists of history. There are medieval accounts of throwing 'the barre' or 'axletree', and in the nineteenth century the Scots and Irish tossed ringweights both for height and distance, and light 2.5 kg (5½ lb) balls for distance alone. The throwing of the 'barre' surfaced briefly in 1956 when the Spanish thrower, Erasquin, who had pursued the event in Spanish rural sports, adapted it to javelin throwing and launched a conventional javelin to close on 100 m. The rotational javelin technique, which differed totally from the linear methods used up to that time, was banned immediately before the Melbourne Olympics because of the danger to spectators and officials.

From the infinity of throws of varying weights, with and without 'follow' (the follow-through beyond the stop-board), came in 1913, with the creation of a standard programme by the IAAF, the four events we now accept as the standard international throwing events. Shot and hammer, with their Celtic antecedents, were 7.25 kg (16 lb) in weight, with 2.15 m (7 ft) circles, whilst discus, 2 kg (4½ lb) and javelin 800 g (1¾ lb) followed metric weights and dimensions.

All throws follow certain basic principles. First, there is a 'run' which gives linear acceleration (shot and javelin) or rotational acceleration (discus and hammer) to the body-implement system. This puts the thrower in a strong pre-tensed delivery position, ready to make use of the speed already gained and the potential of his previous muscular pre-tension. From then until implement-release, the problem is one of skill, resting on the ability of the thrower to use first the heavy, slow-moving muscles of the legs and back, progressively transferring responsibility to weaker, fast-moving muscles in the arms.

The early history of shot and hammer was essentially Celtic, passing to Irish-Americans. Discus, surprisingly, was in the same period quickly grasped by East Coast Americans. By the 1920s the centre of gravity of shot and discus lay firmly in the warmth of the Californian coast, but hammer and javelin, events which were banned in many areas of the United States, withered and the main development of these events was to take place in Europe.

Tessa Sanderson (Great Britain) about to pull the javelin explosively over a long range.

Hartmut Briesenick (East Germany) sets himself for a strong drive across the shot circle.

The 1940s saw the introduction of progressive weight training as a means of increasing explosive power, and with it the disappearance of the relatively light (Fonville, Nemeth, Fitch) throwers of the previous period. Henceforth, no world-class shot putter, discus or hammer thrower, could be much less than 100 kg (220 lb) and the average of the top six Olympic shot putters was, in 1976, to be a massive 125 kg (275 lb). The women's events showed a similar development, and in 1976 in Montreal the average weight of the shot putters (90.3 kg or 199 lb) was higher than several male world record-holders of the pre-war period.

This process was quickened in the period from 1952 onwards, when the USSR returned to the Olympics, bringing with her an unprecedented development in research into, and coaching of, throwing techniques. More recently, it has been East Germany which has dominated all women's throws and all men's throws except javelin, and it is becoming clear that the United States college system and its weak post-college structure is no longer capable of matching the organization of Eastern Europe.

Another major and less savoury factor in the improvement of throwing standards (and one which will be referred to in specific sections), has been the introduction in the early 1960s of anabolic steroids. This has had a significant effect in all throws and the table below shows the changes in body-weight which have taken place since the 1960 Olympics. It can be seen that, although average heights have remained constant, average body weights have gone up by almost 20 kg (44 lb) in the men's events and 7 kg (15½ lb) in the women's. The steroids have enabled the quantity and quality of training to rise massively and this has been reflected in an equally massive surge in throwing standards.

Rules

The rules for throws are very similar in nature and for this reason they have been brought together.

1. Shot and hammer are thrown from a 2.15 m (7 ft) circle, with the shot circle fronted by a stop-board. The discus is thrown from a 2.50 m (8 ft 2½ in) diameter circle.
2. In all circular throws the competitors must retreat from the rear half of the circle.
3. Any infringement of the rim (or in the case of the shot put, the stop-board) is a 'foul'.
4. No competitor should leave the circle until the implement has touched the ground.
5. Measurements are always made from the furthest back mark made by the implement, back through the centre of the circle, distances being read over the front rim.
6. In javelin, similar general rules obtain, the areas to the side of the runway also being forbidden to the thrower after his throw, distances being measured over the scratch line, the tape being taken to a point 8 m (8¾ yd) beyond it.

	Rome 1960				Tokyo 1964				Mexico 1968				Munich 1972				Montreal 1976			
	Height		Weight		Height		Weight		Height		Weight		Height		Weight		Height		Weight	
	m	ft	kg	lb	m	ft	kg	lb	m	ft	kg	lb	m	ft	kg	lb	m	ft	kg	lb
Men																				
Shot	1.90	6′2¾″	107.5	237	1.91	6′ 3″	108	238	1.93	6′ 4″	119	262	1.93	6′ 4″	124.3	273	1.92	6′ 3½″	125	275
Discus	1.86	6′ 1¼″	99	218	1.91	6′ 3″	104.5	230	1.92	6′ 3½″	111.2	245	1.91	6′ 3¼″	109.6	241	1.93	6′ 4″	116.8	257
Hammer	1.84	6′ 0½″	96	212	1.83	6′ 0″	98.5	217	1.84	6′ 0½″	100.8	222	1.87	6′ 1½″	107.3	236	1.88	6′ 2″	114.4	252
Women																				
Shot	1.73	5′ 8½″	83	183	1.76	5′ 9″	86	190	1.76	5′ 9″	85	187	1.74	5′ 8½″	85.2	187.4	1.78	5′ 10″	90.3	199
Discus	1.76	5′ 9¼″	81	179	1.76	5′ 9″	84.5	186	1.77	5′ 9½″	83	183	1.75	5′ 8¾″	83	183	1.76	5′ 9¼″	88.6	195

Changes in the average body-weights of throwers between 1960 and 1976.

15. Shot put

History

There are references to shot putting in the Irish *Book of Leinster* (thirteenth century BC), and in *Havelock the Dane* (AD 1275), and similar references in the medieval period, but accurately-recorded competitive shot putting has its origins in mid-nineteenth century Scotland and Ireland. Of these, the Scottish experience in Highland and Lowland Games is most accurately recorded. Here there are two types of throw, usually of stones. In the lowlands, putting from a circle or square with follow-through, was common, whilst in the Highlands no such follow-through was permitted. As the nineteenth century came to a close, the Highland method, using a 7.25 kg (16 lb) steel ball from a 2.15 m (7 ft) square or circle, became standard, both in amateur and professional athletics.

The Highland Games were from the beginning professional, in that they offered money prizes, prizes which were quite substantial in the economic climate of rural communities. Soon, aided by a growing railway system, what had been local sports became national in nature and a small touring group of athletes developed in the May–September period. Of these athletes, the most famous was the great all-rounder, Donald Dinnie, the greatest all-round athlete of the nineteenth century. In the early 1870s the Scots, who had already exported large sections of their population in the Highland Clearances of the late eighteenth and early nineteenth century, started to export their Games champions and Dinnie and his contemporaries carried the Scottish Games all over the United States and the Empire.

Dinnie's best put of 15 m (49 ft 6 in) was by far the best of the nineteenth century, but there were many puts in the 14 m (46 ft) area in the Games of the 1870–1900 period.

The English amateur movement of the late nineteenth century, possessing no direct links with the rural sports of Scotland and Ireland, was running-based and only in the United States, where on the East Coast the influence of Scottish and Irish immigrants had been strong, was shot put pursued, and it was from these sources that many of the early amateur putters, such as Pat McDonald and Ralph Rose, were to come. From the early twentieth century, as the amateur movement grew, the professional games, lacking central organization and international competition, remained static in performance. The performances of the 1920s were, therefore, little different from those of half a century earlier.

The first put over 15.25 m (50 ft) was the Irish-American, Pat McDonald, but his technique and indeed that of those who followed, breaking 16 m (52 ft 6 in) and 17 m (55 ft 9 in), was essentially the same side-on

Ralph Rose (USA) one of the last of the early twentieth century putters in the 'Irish Whele' tradition, soon to be replaced by leaner, faster throwers.

hop as had been used by the nineteenth-century putters of Scotland and Ireland. All that had changed was the quality of training and the increasing population from whom throwers were being drawn.

The story of shot putting in the early twentieth century was mainly told on the East Coast of the United States, but increasingly the centre of gravity of the event moved westwards to the warm West Coast from 1920 onwards.

The shot putters of the 1920–50 period were, in the main, light men in the 85–95 kg (187–209 lb) area and, to modern eyes, look more like decathletes than shot putters. Of these, the fast American negro, Charles Fonville (94 kg 195 lb) was the most characteristic, but Fonville was to be the last of the small putters and no athlete less than 102 kg (224 lb) was thereafter destined to hold the world record. Indeed, by 1976 the average weight of Olympic *women* shot putters was at 90 kg (198 lb).

It was from a second generation Irish-American, Parry O'Brien, that the first major technical change was to come. Release-velocity in shot putting, like any other throwing event, is heavily dependent on the range through which muscular force is applied. The circle itself produces certain constraints and O'Brien stretched these to their limits by taking the shot outside the circle, thus increasing impulse time. More important, by achieving a deeper, stronger throwing position, O'Brien increased the range over which the powerful leg and back muscles could apply force to the shot. The O'Brien technique, with modifications, has been the technique which has brought shot putting to its present level.

O'Brien, a superb competitor, won gold in both 1952 and 1956 Olympics, and in 1960 another massive American, Bill Neider (included late in the United States team because of injury to his team-mate Davis) took the Olympic gold, to be followed in 1964 by Dallas Long and in 1968 by Randy Matson.

The 1960s saw a shadow fall upon shot put, and indeed ultimately upon the whole range of power events. This was due to the anabolic steroids, originally used for the development of strength and bulk by weight lifters and body builders. Shot putters, because of their use of weight training,

Randy Matson (USA), Olympic champion in 1968, probably the greatest of the American school of putters, later to be overshadowed by the East Europeans.

became absorbed in the culture of weight lifting and copied what were, at that time, legal methods of gaining stength and work capacity. Soon, the use of anabolic steroids became widespread and this was reflected, not only in performance, but in the body weight of competitors, as can be seen in the table on page 141. Drug controls set up by the IAAF have been relatively ineffective because the steroids are essentially training drugs and can be clear of the system within three weeks of testing. More recent methods, using diuretics to 'flush out' steroids, have enabled athletes to continue to take these drugs to within a few days of competition.

Present performances do not, therefore, reflect the true evolution of event performance and the 22.85 m (75 ft) professional performance of Brian Oldfield, using a rotational technique, was done without even the scrutiny of the amateur authorites. While it would be invidious to suggest any particular performance, it would be fair to say that if those who took anabolics were removed, the record books would have to be substantially revised.

Women

The first official women's record holder was the lean, angular German, Gisela Mauermeyer, with 14.38 m (47 ft 2¼ in) in 1934, but the record since the post-war period has been held mainly by Soviet or East German athletes, with the exception of a short period in 1976 when the Bulgarian, Ivanka Kristova, briefly held the record, and 1976–77 when the Czech, Helena Fibingerova, took the record to its present position. The 1950s were dominated by the Soviet athlete, Galina Zybina, (1952 Olympic gold), the 1960s by her colleagues, Tamara Press (1960, 1964 Olympic gold), and Nadyezhda Chizhova (1972 Olympic gold).

Tamara Press (USSR) the greatest shot/discus exponent of modern times.

The event, heavily influenced by anabolic steriods, has now become an Eastern European monopoly and the point has been reached where some Western nations, unable to field athletes who can do much more than barely reach Olympic qualifying standards, have stopped entering athletes in the event.

17 Shot put: short shift, long base technique

18 Shot put: rotational technique

Technique

As explained in the introduction, there are three basic phases in all throws, the 'run' which gives initial linear speed, which in shot is called the 'glide', the delivery position, and the delivery itself. In shot the glide gives 8–16 per cent of the total velocity of the implement, with most throwers closer to 10 per cent. Thus, a 21 m (69 ft) thrower could launch the shot around 19 m (62 ft 3 in) from a standing position.

Two variations of the basic O'Brien technique can be seen in the delivery positions of modern putters. The most conventional has the shot tucked behind the right foot, which is based at the circle centre and which points either parallel to the diameter line or slightly towards the back of the circle. The right hip is driven in and there is a late lift, well over the left foot.

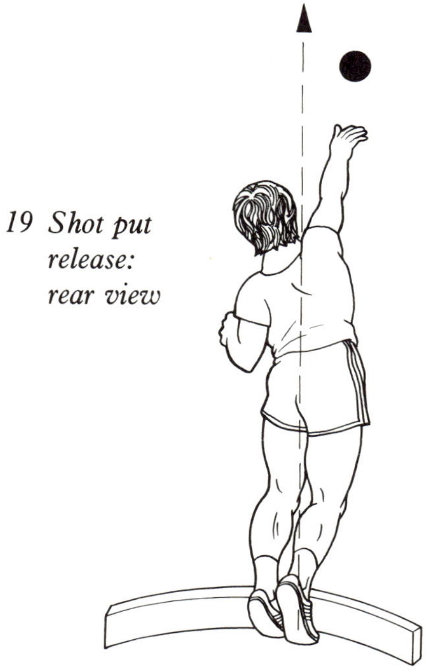

19 Shot put release: rear view

The major variation, used by many East Germans, is the short shift, long base technique, in which the right foot does not reach the circle-centre (fig. 17). The putter drives horizontally through his long, stretched base, lifting late with the release point only just beyond the stop-board. This keeps the shot moving horizontally, rather than shifting its drive to the vertical, but requires considerable leg and back strength.

The most recent innovation has been the rotational technique, shown at its best by the American, Brian Oldfield, and the Russian, Aleksandr Baryshnikov, and illustrated in fig. 18. Here the problem is that, though the technique gives greater continuity on landing for delivery, the timing is fine and few rotational putters put consistently well. It is, therefore, unlikely that the rotational technique will attract more than a handful of putters; it can in no way be considered as an alternative technique of the same nature as the Fosbury flop in high jump.

Like discus and hammer, the limitations of the circle cut down the technical options possible and it is unlikely that we will see any major technical breakthrough in the event.

Event background

The physique of the world-class putter is, for a man, the 120–125 kg (262–275 lb) area, and for a woman, the 86–90 kg (190–199 lb) area. At around 1.92 m (6 ft 3½) and 1.80 m (5 ft 10 in) both men and women are well above average height, and putters are at the extreme end of the physical range.

It is a common belief that putters are slow and cumbersome, but this is far from true, and athletes like Geoff Capes excel in a range of sports from soccer to basketball. The shot

putter is usually exceptionally quick and can usually stay with sprinters over 30 m (32 yd). What we see, therefore, in the circle at the Olympics are great, skilful cats, capable of co-ordinating their explosive force over a long range.

As in other throws, the shot putter faces the complex task of applying massive forces in a fraction of a second. In major competitions, the tendency for the putter is always to tighten up and 'rush' his movements. This consequently first cuts down the impulse given to the shot, and second, because of muscular tension, seriously decreases the muscular force applied to it.

Thus, there have been many occasions when putters broke the Olympic record in warm-up puts, only to fall far short of it in the competition itself. Other field events, such as the jumps (and even to a degree the javelin) permit modifications to be made in the approach-run. The shot, in its clipped dig across a cramped circle by a tall, bulky man, does not allow such adjustments to be made and does not in its delivery allow for the flight adjustments possible to a vertical jumper who has only to leave the cross-bar quivering on the pegs to be allowed to tackle the next height. So, paradoxically, the biggest, most powerful men have to perform fine, explosive skills, within the limited confines of a 2.15 m (7 ft) circle.

It is not uncommon for major competitions to be won with big first-round puts, and it is indeed rare for them to be won in the final rounds. The big first-round put tends to lay pressure on the other putters who, instead of staying calm and loose, telescope their movements and achieve mediocre distances or 'fouls'. It is always, therefore, the aim and the dream of the international shot putter to begin with the magic 'big one'.

The explosiveness of the event is directly reflected in the training methods, which include general (squat, clean and jerk) and specific (bench press, inclined bench press) exercises, in the 80–100 per cent area. In periods of competition, these exercises are tapered off in extent, but not in quality.

Shot putters also use bounding and sprinting as part of their training, and in such events as standing long jump and standing triple jump, can often rival sprinters and jumpers.

As in all other events, the development of specific skill is central, as power is of no value if it cannot be channelled effectively into the shot. Thus, there is never a separation between skill and physical conditioning, as increasing fitness must always be blended into a developing technique.

Udo Beyer (East Germany), victor at the Montreal Olympics, is a fine example of the technically excellent East German putters.

16. Discus

'Discobolus' by Myron, a magnificent sculpture which poses more questions than it answers about the techniques of the ancient Greeks.

History

Discus, like javelin, is of classical origin, though in the Olympic programme it featured only in pentathlon. The word 'discus' means literally 'thing for throwing' and discoi from 1–4 kg (2¼–8¾ lb) have been unearthed by archaeologists. What is unclear is the techniques used in the Greek period. Myron's 'Discobolus' presents more problems than it solves. Is it a standing right to left throw or left to right? Or is it merely an idealized version of the wind-up to a turning throw? We do not know and the literature of the period is of no help to us.

When the event was revived in the 1896 Athens Olympics the throw was made from a standing position, from a pedestal called the balbis. It was also made throwing with the right foot placed forward, and with a follow through. The 'free style' turning throw, at first made from a 2.15 m (7 ft) diameter circle was at first held as a parallel discus competition, in the 1908 Olympics, but the uncertain link with Greek throwing was broken in 1913, when the present method, using a 2.50 m (8 ft 2 in) diameter circle was adopted by the IAAF. Nevertheless, the first official world record 47.58 m (156 ft 1 in) was made by the American, James Duncan in 1912, from a 2.15 m (7 ft) diameter cinder circle.

The technical development of the event after 1913 is far from clear. Many authorities claim that the technique used in the pre-War

Champion of champions, Al Oerter (USA), four times Olympic discus winner.

period was a walking pivot on the left foot, yet the author has film of the 1908 and 1912 Olympics showing athletes performing primitive jump turns from a side-on starting position. Since one of these athletes was a decathlete, Jim Thorpe, it is clear that the running side-on turn must have been fairly common during that period.

Phil Fox of Stanford University was possibly the first leading athlete to use the full circle by starting his turn from a back-facing position; 'By taking the step almost to the edge of the rim with the left foot to the rear of the circle, you have more distance to travel in' was his statement at a clinic in 1941.

Until 1941, when the portly Italian, Adolfo Consolini, took the record with 53.34 m (175 ft), the world record had been the almost exclusive property of the United States. Robert Fitch (USA) regained the record in 1946 with 54.93 m (180 ft 3 in) and was wrongly credited as the first thrower to use the back-facing technique, in which the thrower uses the whole diameter of the circle to make his 'running rotation' across the circle. Such technical changes are usually credited to champions or record-holders simply because these are the athletes who are fully exposed to the media, but they are just as likely to have been made by lesser athletes.

The first thrower over 60 m (198 ft) was the American, Jay Silvester, in 1961, and in 1962, Al Oerter, the only athlete to win four consecutive Olympic gold medals in the same event, took the record to 61.10 m (200 ft 5 in). Since 1962, only Bruch (Sweden), Van Reenan (South Africa), Danek (Czechoslovakia), and the present record-holder, Wolfgang Schmidt (GDR), have prised the record from American hands.

The technical development of discus is now relatively static, dividing itself, like shot, into two main camps. This relates to the use of the pinned, braced left leg, with no follow through (practised mainly by the East Germans) and the 'stroke away' technique performed by most other throwers.

118

20 Discus

Women

The first official world record-holder was the angular German, Gisela Mauermeyer, with 48.31 m (158 ft 6 in) in 1936. The world record has never left Europe and Liesel Westermann (Germany) is the only Western European since Mauermeyer to hold the record, which now stands at 70.72 m (232 ft) to Evelyn Jahl (GDR). The greatest thrower of the 1950s was the Soviet athlete, Nina Dumbadze who was, in the 1960s, succeeded by her countrywoman, Tamara Press, and in the 1970s by another Soviet thrower, Faina Melnyk. The event, like shot put, is ideally suited to heavily-muscled East Europeans, and it is unlikely that the world record or Olympic gold medals are now ever likely to travel westwards. Indeed, many Western countries are now, as in shot, unwilling or unable to fulfil their permitted quotas of athletes in the Olympic and European Games in these events.

Technique

Fig. 20 shows the modern technique in discus. It is a 'running rotation' and 40–60 per cent of the speed of the discus is gained from the turn.

The thrower faces the back of the circle and takes one or two wind-up swings, going into the turn with the weight well over the left foot (fig. 20.4) in a torque position. This is followed by a drive across the circle from the toe of the left foot, with the discus trailing, and the right leg swept out.

The aim at the end of the turn is to land on the back of the right foot with hips ahead of shoulders (fig. 20.7) and discus trailing the shoulders. To facilitate this, the right knee is swept in to bring hips ahead of shoulders on landing.

The drive-in of the right leg and hip then begins, against the resistance of the left leg, ending with the arm coming out long and loose. At this point there are two variations. East German throwers tend to keep the left leg braced, whilst most other throwers 'pull away' the left leg as they launch the discus. This left leg brace has been the source of considerable discussion as it is believed to cause lower back injuries.

Event background

Discus throwers, as can be seen in the table on page 141 tend to be as tall as shot putters, but lighter, possibly because of the great need for mobility in the waist and hips. There has, as in the other throws, been a considerable rise in the average weights of Olympic throwers since 1960.

Discus training tends to be similar to shot training, in terms of the use of heavy weights, but there is a greater emphasis on mobility as cramped, short-range movements are of no value in discus. Shot-discus combinations at world level are becoming

Faina Melnik (USSR) in perfect dynamic balance at the back of the circle.

USA
FINNAIR

increasingly rare, and although discus throwers are more than competent shot putters (and vice versa), both events are becoming increasingly specialized.

The discus thrower, operating like the hammer thrower, within the confines of a 40° sector in a delicately balanced rotational event, often has similar problems in placing his implement within sector lines. Similarly, as in the other throws, there is often a tendency to tighten up, and this is particularly noticeable in Olympic qualifying rounds, where world class throwers often have difficulty in achieving modest qualifying standards.

The effect of wind on discus is similar to that on javelin, in that a moderate head-wind is distinctly advantageous, while a head-wind quartering from the right can produce considerable improvements. The left-handed thrower is almost always at a disadvantage when throwing conditions are at their most favourable.

Left: Matt Wilkins (USA), explosive and technically excellent.
Below: John Powell (USA) illustrates the high degree of flexibility of the discus thrower.

17. Hammer

Above: a fanciful woodcut of Henry VIII throwing the hammer, at that time an unmodified sledge-hammer.
Right: Faina Melnyk (USSR)

History

Hammer, like shot, is Celtic in origin, although there are records of English hammer-throwing competitions (alas, recording fatalities) as early as the sixteenth century.

1566, 'Alexander Gyfford, aged twenty-eight, husbandman of Drydrayton, Cambs., pardoned for having by misadventure on 4th June, feloniously struck John Gyfford, a spectator, aged 8, at a game of 'throwing the coulter' at Drydrayton, so that he died there the same day'.

There is little doubt that 'the throwing of the sledge' pre-dates the first recorded Scottish competitions of the 1820s, though competitions were undoubtedly local in nature with varying rules. Scottish throwers of the 1850s threw wood-shafted working hammers from 4–7 kg (8¾–15½ lb), single- and double-handed, with and without turns. There were, therefore, numerous 'champions' each specializing in one or other method and challenges flew thick and fast between them.

By the 1870s, Scottish professional hammer throwing had been reduced to two standing throws 7.25 and 9.98 kg (16 lb and 22 lb) with a hickory or ash-shafted hammer, and occasional distance throws with 12.70 and 25.40 kg (28 lb and 56 lb) ring-weights. The greatest of these throwers was Donald Dinnie, who threw 43 m (141 ft 1½ in) using

TICS

Ruth Fuchs (East Germany)

a shaft so long that a trench had to be dug in front of him to permit swings. Dinnie was undoubtedly capable of over 38 m (124 ft 9 in) with a standard hammer and is credited with the invention, in the 1860s, of the 'round the head' technique which superseded the primitive standing, pendular technique which had previously prevailed.

The professionals of the late nineteenth century, because of the cramped and crowded nature of most Highland Games

Aleksey Spiridonov (USSR), one of the great Russian throwers of the 1970s, pumps the right knee in, with the hammer hanging on long arms.

21 Hammer

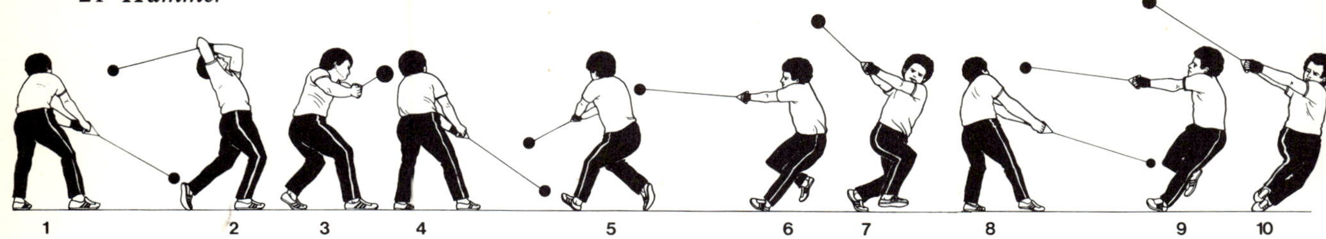

sites, settled for the standing throw with the 7.25 kg (16 lb) hammer, and rotational throws only with the heavier, short-handled implements. The amateurs, competing in larger stadia, opted for the turning event, and by the early years of the twentieth century, after experiments with different types of shafts (including, in the USA, grapevines), settled for a wire 'shaft' ending in a handle within the confines of a 2.15 m (7 ft) diameter circle. This period was dominated by the East Coast Irish-American 'whales', John Flanagan, Matt McGrath, and Pat Ryan, usually using two 'jump' turns before release.

The Irish-American period ended in 1932 with the Olympic victory of the Southern Irish thrower, Pat O'Callaghan, an explosive athlete capable of close on 2 m (6 ft 6¾ in) in high jump. The 1936 Olympics saw the triumph of smooth-turning Germans, Hein and Blask who, under the influence of their coach Sepp Christmann, retained left foot contact at all times during three turns on the cinder surface of the circle.

Although the 1948 Olympic hammer event was won by the lean Imre Nemeth (whose son Miklos was later to win the 1976 Olympic javelin), it was to be the Hungarians, led by the 1952 Olympic victor, Csermak, who were to dominate world throwing with the Russians, until the early 1960s, though a second-generation Irish-American, Harold Connolly, was to win the 1960 Olympic title.

A period of Russian domination (Klim, Bondarchuk, Spiridonov) followed and has only recently been broken by East and West German throwers, such as Karl Hans Riehm and Walter Schmidt. The event has seen massive technical changes, including the four-turn throw, a device to increase hammer velocity, and these have been matched by similar changes in the safety cage from which throwers compete, the result being that the area within which the thrower effectively operates has been narrowed. Increased distances and the uncertain nature of the event have now prompted studies in the possible shortening of the length of the hammer-wire, and in an increase in the weight of the hammer-head, both with the aim of shortening the distance which the hammer can be thrown.

Technique

Because it is suspended on a wire, the hammer is the only missile which is thrown at a release angle of 45°. The hammer thrower, unlike other throwers, gains most of his final velocity from the turns, gaining 80–85 per cent from this source.

The modern thrower takes two initial swings in which he gains hammer speed and sets up the body-hammer relationship which he wishes to progressively develop during his three to four turns. Four turns (the first is virtually on the spot) is more suitable for the smaller thrower, but there is a danger of developing more speed than can be controlled.

In hammer, arms are always straight and passive, (fig. 21.7), because the further the hammer-head is from the turning-axis the greater its velocity. Any bending of the arms simply kills the velocity of the hammer-head.

In the single-support phase (on the turning heel of the left foot) the thrower aims to get the right hip in ahead of the hammer, landing on the toe of the right foot. It is in this high-torque, double-support phase that the hammer is given its big accelerative impulse. It is then that there is a big displacement between hips and shoulders (fig. 21.8). This displacement increases on each turn, until the thrower reaches the strongly wound-up delivery position (fig. 21.17). There his aim is to lift the hammer explosively from a firm, balanced base. Fig. 21.18 shows clearly both the power and the balance of the statuesque Russian-style delivery.

Event background

The increasing size of hammer throwers since the 1960 Olympics can be seen in the table on page 141, but it must be observed that the event's demands on speed and balance would seem to limit the possibilities of success for behemoths above 125 kg (275 lb), and the 1976 Olympic victor, Yuriy Sedhy, was only 1.86 m (6 ft 1¼ in) tall and 113 kg (252 lb) in weight, lighter that the average weight of the finalists as a group. It cannot, however, be ignored that the 1964 finalists averaged only 96 kg (211¾ lb) relative to the 114.4 kg (252¼ lb) average of the Montreal group. Hammer throwers, because of the technical complexity of their event, have always tended to be older than other throwers and the average age of the Montreal finalists was twenty-eight years and four months.

Training for hammer is heavily based on weights, particularly for legs and back (squat, clean and jerk), but like other rotational throws, there is need for great overall mobility to increase the range of pull on the hammer. As in all throws, explosive power is vital and bounding and sprinting form an important part of the training routine.

Hammer throwers, like discus throwers, have a major limitation, in that they have to operate within the confines of a 40° sector. They also have the problem of a protective cage which makes the true throwing angles available to them even smaller.

The technical/competitive problems in hammer are the same as in shot and discus, although, as in discus, circle-surface conditions can play a major part in deciding competitions. The problem is, as always, to fuse into four balanced, constantly accelerating turns, all the training of many years in a controlled, explosive throw. Hammer is an event trembling on a razor's edge and even the world's greatest throwers can be seen spinning helplessly like novices, or launching the implement wildly into the safety net. The hammer thrower must have the strength of an elephant and the grace of a ballet dancer.

18. Javelin

History

Javelin, like discus, was not a specialist throwing event in the Ancient Olympics but was, rather, a part of the pentathlon. The Greek javelin (of which none have survived) was likely to have been made of ash, and in addition to the normal grip, possessed an amentum, a loop by which greater leverage could be exerted on the implement. This method of improving missile velocity can still be found in the primitive tribes all over the world, usually taking the form of a handle linked to a barrel within which the javelin is placed. Indeed, in the early nineteenth century, Napoleon instituted studies into the Greek amentum as a possible weapon of war.

Vase drawings indicate that the Greek throwing technique was probably close to the modern technique, in that it consisted of a run, a withdrawal, a setting-up stride, and a final throwing position. There is, alas, no record of performance, but it is unlikely that barefooted Greek pentathletes, throwing whippy, wooden javelins on rough, broken ground, would have been able to throw much in excess of 60 m (196 ft 11 in).

The weight of the men's javelin was, from the first, set at 800 g (1¾ lb), and the ladies' at 600 g (1⅓ lb), and the first official world record holder with 62.32 m (204 ft 5 in) was the Swede, Eric Lemming, Olympic victor in 1908 and 1912. In the early years of the event, aggregate-throwing was common and in the 1912 Olympics, Julius Saaristo (Finland) achieved a world record of 61 m (200 ft) with his right hand and 48.42 m (159 ft) with his left, for a total of 109.42 m (359 ft).

These victories by a Swede and a Finn reflected accurately the dominance of the Scandinavian nations in this event, and no non-Scandinavian was to win the Olympic event until the German, Gerhard Stöck (also third in shot put) won in Berlin in 1936. Stöck, reduced to a meagre 43 kg (94¾ lb) in weight, was later winched by helicopter out of beleaguered Stalingrad, and in the post-war era became one of the leaders of German sport.

The 1930s, dominated by the Finns, Matti Jarvinen and his countryman, Yrjö Nikkanen, ended with a 78.70 m (258 ft 2 in) world record by the latter, which was to stand until 1953, when the American, Dick Held, took the spear out to 80.41 m (263 ft 10 in). By the 1950s, the ash javelin had been replaced by a steel implement, but Held and his brother, Bud, went further by improving the aerodynamic qualities of the implement.

Top right: James Lusis (USSR), the 'godfather' of modern javelin throwing. Right: a single massive first-round throw brought Olympic victory for Miklos Nemeth (Hungary) in the 1976 Games.

22 Javelin

The cigar-shaped, distance-rated, Held-type javelin became the model for the modern javelin.

A few months before the 1956 Melbourne Olympics, the Spaniards, Salcedo and Erasquin, using a technique based on the ancient event 'throwing the bar', involving a soaped javelin held along the under-arm and a rotational technique, slung the spear to over 90 m (295 ft 5 in), and within weeks the ageing discus thrower, Adolfo Consolini, had launched it to close on 100 m (330 ft) using this same technique.

So far so good, but soon it was realized that throwers using the Spanish technique had no certainty about the javelin's ultimate destination. There was a series of hasty telephone calls amongst top IAAF officials and as a result of these, the rotational technique was banned.

The 1950s were dominated by the agile Pole, Janusz Sidlo, who never, alas, won an Olympic gold medal. Olympic gold medals were, however, spread widely with Young (USA 1952), Danielson (Norway, 1956) and Tsybulenko (USSR, 1960) achieving Olympic victory.

Lusis (USSR), who achieved success in Mexico City in 1968, dominated the 1960s just as Sidlo had the 1950s and possessed the same all-round athleticism as the Pole.

In Munich, in 1972, it was, however, the German, Klaus Wolfermann, who squeezed past Lusis by a mere 2 cm, with an Olympic record of 94.48 m (296 ft 10 in).

The period until 1972 had seen no vast technical changes. Rather, it was the improvement in specific physical conditioning and the smoothing out of the existing technique which had produced improvement. It was noticeable, however, that most throwers were now bringing the javelin *round* as well as back (fig. 22.6) during the withdrawal phase. This brought into fuller play the powerful rotational muscles of the trunk, but, in turn, demanded finer timing. It was this technique which was expressed by the Hungarian, Miklos Nemeth, in a vicious winning first-round throw of 94.58 m (310 ft 4 in) in the Montreal Olympics.

Women

The first official world record was the 46.74 m (153 ft 4 in) by the American, Nan Gindele in 1932, but it was the remarkable all-rounder, Mildred 'Babe' Didrikson (also first in hurdles and second in high jump) who was to win gold in the Los Angeles Olympics, before going on to become the greatest female golfer of her period. The record stayed in Europe until 1958, with Olympic victory going to Eastern European throwers from their first entry in 1952.

Since the early 1970s the event has been dominated by the powerful, technically excellent East German, Ruth Fuchs, who now holds the world record at 69.52 m (228 ft 1 in). However, Fuchs has recently been challenged by the British girl, Tessa Sanderson and the American, Kathy Schmidt.

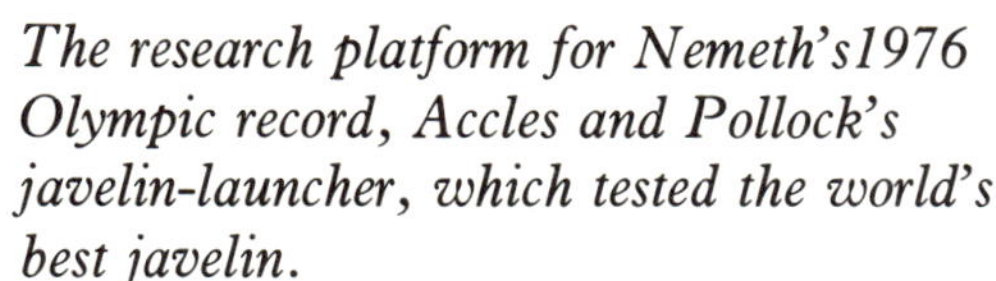

The research platform for Nemeth's1976 Olympic record, Accles and Pollock's javelin-launcher, which tested the world's best javelin.

23 Javelin throw: rear view

Technique

The basic technique of javelin throwing has changed little since the development by the Helds of distance-rated javelins in the early 1950s. Most throwers, wearing spiked boots, use a 5-step rhythm, consisting of three for withdrawal (left, right, left), cross-step (right), throw (left), as shown in fig. 22.

A minority of throwers use a drop-swing withdrawal (Lusis was the most prominent thrower to use this technique) but the vast majority withdraw over the shoulder.

Most throwers now use some form of trunk rotation in their withdrawal, but the main differences between throwers can be seen in the positioning of the right foot in the throwing stride. Few throwers now use the running frontal approach of Lusis, but right foot angles vary from 90° to the frontal, the angle relating directly to the strength, speed and mobility of the thrower. Similarly, some throwers (Kinnunen of Finland is an example) land toe first, securing a quicker hip drive, but most land heel first. Length of base is another variable, relating again to the strength and mobility of the thrower.

Event background

The physical types involved in javelin are quite different from any of the other throwing groups. Javelin is a speed/mobility/elastic strength event and this is reflected in the smaller, lighter men and women who excel at it. The average heights of finalists at Montreal – 1.85 m (6 ft 0¾ in) for men and 1.72 m (5 ft 7½ in) for women – and weights of 68 kg (152 lb) and 100 kg (220 lb), reveal a physique closer to the pentathlete/decathlete than that of the throwing group. It should, however, be mentioned that the average weight of male finalists was 10 kg (22 lb) up on Munich.

Javelin training does not, therefore, lay such stress on the heavy lifting activities of the other three throws, but lays strong emphasis on bounding, ball throwing, mobility, and speed training. This relates directly to the fact that the javelin must be launched at speed from the run and that even the slower-moving muscles of the legs and hips must be able to work quickly to provide an effective impulse.

Above: Ruth Fuchs (East Germany) cocked for the launch of the javelin.
Right: Hannu Siitonen (Finland) lands toe first, primed to drive the right hip in.

Javelin has, unlike shot and hammer, an 'open' element, in that the thrower must often modify the angle of attack of his javelin relative to wind conditions. This means a flatter angle into a strong wind and a slightly greater elevation with a following one. All of this can, of course, be negated by the slightest error in timing at the moment of launch, or by variations in wind conditions during the flight of the javelin. Javelin is therefore a fragile event, and an opening throw like that of Miklos Nemeth in the first round of the Montreal Olympics, with his javelin catching the wind exactly and Nemeth timing his throw perfectly, usually ends all competition for first place.

PART V
Decathlon and pentathlon

Decathlon and pentathlon usually tend to be private events, rather like amateur dramatic performances which are attended only by interested friends and relatives. However, once every four years, the greatest all-round athletes in the world appear in the Olympic Games before a live audience of close on 80,000 people and a television audience of close on one billion, and it is therefore no surprise that the public is often unable to fully evaluate and appreciate their performances.

There is, alas, good evidence that the Greeks placed a relatively low value upon the all-round athlete, for the average prize value for pentathlon at their games was about one sixth of that of the pancratium event.

The Greek pentathlon consisted of javelin, discus, long jump, sprint (192.4 m/200 yd) and wrestling. There were, of course, no points tables, and it is likely that the event took the form of a five-set tennis match. If two athletes won two events each, they would compete in the wrestling; if four won an event each, a 'semi-final' was held. All of this is, of course, supposition, for no rules for pentathlon have been handed down to us.

One poetic record, however, remains. The poet, Bacchylydes, comments on the qualities of Automedes in the Nemean pentathlon:

> He shone among the other pentathletes as the bright moon in the middle of the month dims the radiance of the stars; even thus he showed his lovely body to the great ring of watching Greeks, as he threw the round discus and hurled the shaft of black-leaved elder from his grasp to the steep heights of heaven, and roused the cheers of the spectators by his lithe movements in the wrestling at the end.

The concept of the all-round athlete had its birth, if not its roots, in 1851 at the Much Wenlock Olympics, with a pentathlon consisting of high jump, long jump, shot put 16.35 kg (36 lbs), 800 m (880 yd), and 16.76 m (55 ft) rope climb. In 1880, a similar event was held at the German National Gymnastics Championships, when a triathlon (stone throw, pole vault, long jump) was held, the event being decided on a place basis.

Daley Thompson (Great Britain), possibly the greatest all-round athlete of his generation.

19. Decathlon

In 1884, the Amateur Athletic Union of the United States held the first decathlon, which comprised 91.44 m (100 yd), shot, high jump, 800 m (880 yd) walk, 7.25 kg(16 lb) hammer, pole vault, 100 m (120 yd) hurdles, 25.40 kg (56 lb) weight, long jump, and one mile. All of this took place on a single day. The AAU created for this event the first decathlon scoring tables, based on 1,000 points for the existing world record in each event.

The first time the present decathlon was held was in 1911 in Germany. This was a one day event, with the present programme and sequence, i.e., 100 m, long jump, shot put, high jump, 400 m, 110 m hurdles, discus, pole vault, javelin, and 1500 m. There is no proof that the Germans used scoring tables.

1912 saw the first Olympic decathlon, (though a 'pentathlum' had been held at the St Louis Olympics of 1904 and at the Intercalated Athens Olympics of 1906) at the suggestion of the Swedish official, General Balck. This was a three-day event for which the Swedes created the first scoring tables, and was accompanied by a pentathlon (long jump, javelin, 200 m, discus, 1,500 m). Both events were won by one of the greatest athletes of the twentieth century, the Crow Indian, Jim Thorpe. Alas, Thorpe lost his medals in 1913, when it was revealed that he had accepted money during his summer holidays, playing semi-professional baseball.

The first official world record was established by the Estonian, Klumberg, in 1920, with 6236 points (it will noted that Thorpe's earlier score was 6756 points), but it was another Scandinavian, Helge Lovland, who was to take the 1920 Olympic title with a modest 5921 points. Here the author must observe that, though there have been five separate sets of scoring tables since 1912 (1912, 1920, 1934, 1950, 1962) all scores in this chapter have been transposed to 1962 tables.

1948. The seventeen-year-old Bob Mathias (USA) becomes the youngest winner of the Olympic decathlon title.

The second American to win the Olympic title was the high jumper, Harold Osborn, in 1924, but in 1928 the Scandinavians struck back when the title was won by Paavo Yrjola. From then on, decathlon became an American monopoly with Olympic victories from 1932 to 1964, when the West German, Willie Holdorf, broke the American grip on the event.

The Americans replied in Mexico in 1968 with a victory by Bill Toomey, but fell in Munich in 1972 to the well-drilled Russian, Nikolay Avilov. The Russian had, however, to give way in the 1976 Montreal Games to the overwhelming all-round strength of the American, Bruce Jenner, who took the title with a new world record of 8618 points.

Decathlon has come a long way since the simple unsophisticated days of Jim Thorpe, when an athlete could substitute spikes for football boots and win an Olympic gold medal. Decathletes are now specialists, carefully balancing their training programmes to squeeze points from the scoring tables, and well merit the title of superstars of track and field athletics.

Points	100 m	Long jump	Shot put	High jump	400 m	110 m hurdles	Discus	Pole vault	Javelin	1500 m
500	12.5 sec	5.54 m 18 ft 2 in	10.55 m 34 ft 7¼ in	1.60 m 5 ft 3 in	57.9 sec	19.2 sec	31.14 m 102 ft 2 in	2.90 m 9 ft 6¼ in	40.59 m 133 ft 2 in	4 min 44.0 sec
600	12.0 sec	5.98 m 19 ft 7½ in	12.01 m 39 ft 4¾ in	1.71 m 5 ft 7½ in	55.1 sec	17.8 sec	35.77 m 117 ft 4 in	3.24 m 10 ft 7½ in	47.56 m 156 ft 1 in	4 min 28.4 sec
700	11.5 sec	6.43 m 21 ft 1 in	13.55 m 44 ft 5½ in	1.82 m 5 ft 11½ in	52.5 sec	16.6 sec	40.72 m 133 ft 7 in	3.60 m 11 ft 9¾ in	55.09 m 180 ft 9 in	4 min 14.5 sec
800	11.1 sec	6.90 m 22 ft 7½ in	15.19 m 49 ft 10 in	1.93 m 6 ft 4 in	50.2 sec	15.5 sec	45.99 m 150 ft 10 in	3.97 m 13 ft 0¼ in	63.17 m 207 ft 3 in	4 min 02.0 sec
900	10.7 sec	7.39 m 24 ft 3 in	16.92 m 55 ft 6 in	2.05 m 6 ft 8¾ in	48.0 sec	14.6 sec	51.58 m 169 ft 2 in	4.36 m 14 ft 3½ in	71.81 m 235 ft 7 in	3 min 50.6 sec
1000	10.3 sec	7.90 m 25 ft 11 in	18.75 m 61 ft 6¼ in	2.17 m 7 ft 1½ in	46.0 sec	13.7 sec	57.50 m 188 ft 7 in	4.78 m 15 ft 8 in	81.00 m 265 ft 9 in	3 min 40.2 sec

Decathlon points guide.

Event	1912	1920	1934	1950	1962
100 m	10.8 sec	10.6 sec	10.5 sec	10.7 sec	10.2 sec
Long jump	7.44 m 24 ft 5 in	7.60 m 24 ft 11½ in	7.68 m 25 ft 2½ in	7.58 m 24 ft 10½ ft	7.90 m 25 ft 11 in
Shot put	14.80 m 48 ft 6¾ in	15.34 m 50 ft 4 in	15.70 m 51 ft 6 in	16.00 m 52 ft 6 in	18.75 m 61 ft 6¼ in
High jump	1.90 m 6 ft 2¾ in	1.93 m 6 ft 4 in	1.96 m 6 ft 5¼ in	1.96 m 6 ft 5¼ in	2.17 m 7 ft 1½ in
400 m	48.4 sec	48.2 sec	48.1 sec	48.1 sec	46.0 sec
110 m hurdles	15.0 sec	15.0 sec	14.6 sec	14.3 sec	13.7 sec
Discus	41.47 m 136 ft 0½ in	45.21 m 148 ft 4 in	49.00 m 160 ft 9 in	51.21 m 168 ft. 0 in	57.51 m 188 ft 8 in
Pole vault	3.71 m 12 ft 2 in	3.95 m 12 ft 11½ in	4.20 m 13 ft 9½ in	4.42 m 14 ft 6 in	4.79 m 15 ft 8½ in
Javelin	54.83 m 179 ft 10½ in	61.00 m 200 ft 1½ in	69.98 m 229 ft 7 in	70.40 m 230 ft 11½ in	81.00 m 265 ft 9 in
1500 m	4 min 3.4 sec	3 min 56.8 sec	3 min 54.0 sec	3 min 55.0 sec	3 min 40.2 sec

The improvement in decathlon performances.

Event background

Decathletes have what might best be called indeterminate physiques, in that they are taller and heavier than sprinters, smaller than jumpers, substantially heavier than middle distance runners, and considerably lighter than throwers.

The event demands speed, strength and skill, with endurance making only one appearance in the form of the 1500 m, and the decathlete more closely approximates to the jumper-sprinter than any other event-type.

Below is a break-down of events, excluding the 1500 m, which is invariably the decathletes' weakest event:

	Runs 100 m 400 m 110 m hurdles	**Jumps** long jump pole vault high jump	**Throws** shot discus javelin
Top six in Montreal Olympics	2537 points 33.2%	2685 points 35.1%	2425 points 31.7%

As can be seen, there is a surprisingly even balance, with the tendency towards jumping and running.

The ideal decathlete needs to be about 1.86 m (6 ft 1 in) tall and 84 kg (185 lb) in weight. An ideal age is less easy to assess. Certainly, recent Olympic champions, such as Jenner and Avilov, have had at least one Olympics for experience before reaching decathlon maturity. The recent successes of the young British decathlete, Daley Thompson (twenty years old), may bring us back to the days of Bob Mathias, who achieved his first Olympic victory in 1948 at seventeen and his second in 1952 at the ripe age of twenty-one.

1976. Bruce Jenner (USA) makes his way through the Olympic 1500 m decathlon field.

The decathlon is a tightrope walked ten times and is possibly the most fragile of athletics events. The decathlete's aim is to exercise initial caution in the throws and long jump, scoring close to a 'par' performance in his first attempts. His nightmare is two 'fouls' followed by an inhibited, disastrous, third attempt.

Similarly, in high jump and pole vault, the decathlete has to again exercise caution by coming in early at a modest height to make a score, and also to make any last-minute technical adjustments. Many decathletes have come to grief in the pole vault by coming in too high, making a couple of minor errors, and failing twice at their opening height. In his final attempt, his whole decathlon crumbling in ruins, a height which was normally easily cleared often looks and proves to be impossible to the decathlete.

The decathlon is, therefore, in its technical events, essentially a test of character and nerve, and here it must be remembered that in long jump and the three throws the decathlete has only three attempts.

The 110 m hurdles also presents particular problems. They are usually faced early in the morning of the second day, and stand before the decathlete shining with morning dew. The decathlete, barely awake, knows well that one hurdle-hit can be disastrous and is always relieved when he hits tape, the ten-hurdle ordeal over.

The final event, the 1500 m, is an event feared by all decathletes, for it is faced with the fatigue of nine events in their bodies and is also the event for which they have least physical aptitude. It is particularly feared when the position is close at the end of nine events, for then the potential winners know that they will have to dig deep, into unknown territory, in order to achieve success. My most treasured memory in this category is of the Russian, Litvinov, in the 1972 Olympics, going from sixth to second with an aggressive 1500 m run.

The aim in decathlon is not to anticipate the future but rather to forget the past and to live in the present. The focus must therefore always be on the event in progress.

The atmosphere which suffuses decathlon is one of friendship, for decathletes spend more time with each other than athletes in any other event. They share common problems, having little expertise in particular events, and in this sharing, friendships bloom. In the end, all athletics is a series of personal tests and nowhere is this shown more clearly than in decathlon.

Rules

1. The ten events of decathlon must be held on two consecutive days, in the following order:
   Day 1 100 m; long jump; shot put; high jump; 400 m
   Day 2 110 m hurdles; discus; pole vault; javelin; 1500 m
2. In all the running events, three false starts must occur before disqualification.
3. Only three attempts are permitted in long jump and the three throws.
4. All heats are drawn by lot. In the 1500 m, at least one heat must be drawn from the leading competitors at the end of the ninth event.
5. In the rare event of a tie in the final points total, the winner will be the athlete who has the highest number of points in the greatest number of events.
6. Any decathlete failing to make a trial in any one of the ten events shall not be allowed to continue in the decathlon.

20. Women's pentathlon

Men's decathlon, though it is biased towards strength and speed, is an excellent all-round test of athletic ability. Women's pentathlon does, however, still bear the imprint of cautious administrators and does not yet reflect the all-round fitness of the modern female athlete.

The first pentathlon consisted of 100 m, high jump, long jump, discus, and 800 m, and the first unofficial record of 2548 points was achieved by a Russian, Elena Vasilieva, in 1927. In 1928 a second version (100 m, javelin, long jump, discus, and 800 m) was created and produced a score of 3567 points from another Russian, Ella Mitsis, in 1940, while the first version produced a 3938 point score in 1947 from yet another Russian, Aleksandra Chudina.

The switch to 80 m hurdles produced the pentathlon which obtained until 1975; i.e., 80 m hurdles, shot put, high jump, long jump, and 200 m. The event was heavily biassed towards speed and spring and totally lacked an endurance component.

The pentathlon was, from the beginning, dominated by Eastern European athletes, who managed, like Irina Press, to produce outstanding performances in the speed-spring events and still produce excellent shot puts, in comparison with Britain's long jump world record holder, Mary Rand, whose shot putting performances never matched her achievements in the other four events.

Pentathlon made its first Olympic appearance in 1964 when Irina Press (who had achieved gold in the 1960 Olympic hurdles)

	100 m hurdles	Shot put	High jump	Long jump	200 m
600 points	16.48 sec	10.16 m 33 ft 4 in	1.39 m 4 ft 6¾ in	4.69 m 15 ft 4¾ in	2 min 36.9 sec
700 points	15.45 sec	11.69 m 38 ft 4½ in	1.48 m 4 ft 10¼ in	5.10 m 16 ft 8¾ in	2 min 27.5 sec
800 points	14.54 sec	13.34 m 43 ft 9¼ in	1.57 m 5 ft 2 in	5.53 m 18 ft 1¾ in	2 min 19.2 sec
900 points	13.73 sec	15.09 m 49 ft 6 in	1.67 m 5 ft 5¾ m	5.97 m 19 ft 7 in	2 min 11.8 sec
1000 points	13.01 sec	16.95 m 55 ft 7½ in	1.77 m 5 ft 9¾ m	6.44 m 21 ft 1¾ in	2 min 5.1 sec

Pentathlon points guide.

Mary Peters (Great Britain)

Bruce Jenner (USA)

was victorious. In 1968, it was the East German, Burglinde Pollak, who was to achieve Olympic victory in an event which now featured the 100 m hurdles. The 1972 Olympic pentathlon was desperately close, with the British pentathlete, Mary Peters, holding on in the final event, the 200 m, to stave off the challenge of the West German, Heidi Rosendahl, to achieve an Olympic and world record of 4801 points.

The final Olympic pentathlon of this series was also breathlessly close with the East German girls, Sigrun Siegl and Christine Laser, achieving exactly the same score at 4745 points, the gold medal going to Siegl because she had higher scores in more events.

The powerful Irina Press (USSR) launches herself at the barriers in the Tokyo Olympic pentathlon.

Points	100 m hurdles	Shot put	High jump	Long jump	200 m		Year
(69) 4384 Heidemarie Rosendahl	13.7 sec w	13.93 m	1.59 m	6.24 m	24.8 sec	47 WG Leverkusen	1969
(69) 4414 Heidemarie Rosendahl	13.6 sec W	13.26 m	1.65 m	6.21 m	24.8 sec	47 WG Heidelberg	1969
(69) 4426 Meta Antenen	13.5 sec	11.28 m	1.71 m	6.49 m	24.8 sec	49 SWZ Liestal	1969
(69) 4476 Liesel Prokop	13.9 sec	14.51 m	1.72 m	6.07 m	24.9 sec	41 AUT Leoben	1969
(69) 4540 Heidemarie Rosendahl	13.7 sec	13.95 m	1.64 m	6.33 m	23.9 sec w	47 WG Leverkusen	1969
(79) 4727 Liesel Prokop	13.5 sec	14.95 m	1.75 m	6.62 m w	24.6 sec	41 AUT Vienna	1969
(69) 4775 Burglinde Pollak	13.3 sec w	15.57 m	1.75 m	6.20 m	23.8 sec	51 EG Erfurt	1970
(69) 4801 Mary Peters	13.29 sec	16.20 m	1.82 m	5.98 m	24.08 sec	39 GB Munich	1972
(69) 4831 Burglinde Pollak	13.21 sec	15.40 m	1.74 m	6.45 m	23.70 sec	51 EG Sofia	1973
(69) 4932 Burglinde Pollak	13.21 sec	15.85 m	1.78 m	6.47 m	23.35 sec	51 EG Bonn	1973

Abbreviations: W wind over 4 m/sec; w wind over 2/sec. Key: (69) 1954 scoring system with 100 m hurdles.

The improvement in women's pentathlon performances.

Burglinde Pollak (East Germany), who possessed a rare blend of hurdling and shot putting skill.

In 1976, the 200 m was replaced by the 800 m to provide an endurance factor. This meant an immediate drop of approximately 100 points as sprinter-jumpers adjusted to the endurance event, but the transition has been a surprisingly smooth one, with Tchachenko (USSR), the present world record-holder, running a 2 min 10.6 sec 800 m.

In 1976, the IAAF Congress Women's Committee proposed that from 1981 a heptathlon be introduced, consisting of the following events:

Day 1 100 m hurdles; shot put; high jump; 200 m

Day 2 Long jump; javelin; 800 m

The heptathlon has excellent balance, involving as it does speed, power, and endurance, and is now a fit partner to the men's decathlon as a test of all-round ability.

Event background

It was thought by many experts that the introduction of the 800 m might lead to a change in the physical type most suitable for pentathlon. This has not proved to be so. What has happened is that the world's existing pentathletes, such as Diane Jones (Canada), Tchachenko (USSR) and Pollak (GDR), simply modified their training programmes to accommodate the endurance element. World scores are now according approximately to the pre-800 m period.

The problem in pentathlon is to balance the explosive power required for four events against the endurance required for the 800 m. Fortunately, 800 m does not require the heart-lung endurance of the men's 1500 m, and the world's top pentathletes have therefore effectively accommodated the change.

Montreal statistics show that the top pentathlete should be 1.75 m (5 ft 8½ in) or above, and weigh about 68 kg (150 lb). The height is needed for high and long jump and the weight to put the shot above 15 m (49 ft 3 in). The event is still heavily biassed (as in decathlon) towards the sprinter-jumper.

The qualities of competitive temperament required by the pentathlete are identical with that of the decathlete. A phlegmatic, composed, well-organized attitude is essential; there is no room in a multi-event for the erratic or volatile.

Rules

The rules are as in decathlon, with the leading group of competitors after four events, contesting the 800 m.

Right: Ed Moses (USA) the first 400 m hurdler to use thirteen strides between hurdles over the full distance.

PART VI
Progressive world record lists

The overall position relative to the development of athletics records is clouded by the drug issue, for the present record lists would have to be substantially re-written if drug offenders were to be removed.

In general terms, it looks as if men's 100–200 m is virtually static, though there is still some 'slack' in the women's events, particularly in the 400 m. The 800–1500 m area has still some slack and we should see a 1.40 min 800 m and 3.30 min 1500 m by 1988, with even more substantial improvements (1.52 and 3.52 min) in the women's events. The 5000 m and 10,000 m events will also improve substantially (13.00 and 26.30 min) and the marathon should come down to 2 hr 4 min and the women's marathon to 2 hr 24 min.

The men's hurdles are close to their absolute limit and I doubt if we shall see 12.80 sec, with 12.30 sec in the corresponding women's event. The men's 400 m hurdles are likely to come below 47 sec, whilst the women's event, if tackled by an athlete capable of inside 51 sec for the flat 400 m, should come down to inside 54 sec.

In the throws, I see the shot and discus as likely to remain relatively static with both sexes, with marginal improvements in hammer. Javelin, because of possible improvements in the aerodynamics of the implement itself, is still capable of an improvement to close on 100 m.

Improvements in long and triple jumps will be conditional upon regular international competitions at altitude, where it has been shown that massive jumps are possible. It is unlikely that Bob Beamon's 8.90 m (29 ft 2½ in) long jump will be beaten at ground level in this century, though the world triple jump record could well go to close on 18 m (59 ft) even at ground level. It is, however, significant that of the seven world triple jump records since 1956, four were recorded at altitude. The women's long jump record now stands at a respectable 7.09 m (23 ft 3¼ in), and it is possible that 7.20 m (23 ft 7½ in) will be achieved by 1988.

Rod Milburn (USA) winning the 110 m hurdle final at the 1972 Munich Olympics, and setting a world record of 13.2 sec.

Although the Fosbury flop has thickened up the quality of international high jumping, the world record has been held only once by a flopper, Dwight Stones, and has improved by only 5 cm since 1963. It is therefore doubtful if we shall see much more than a 3 cm improvement in the next eight years. The women's world record has improved by 13 cm since the eastern cut-off jumper, Iolanda Balas' 1.91 m (6 ft 3¼ in) in 1961, and has been brought to 2.01 m (6 ft 7 in) by the flopper Sara Simeoni. The flop has made much more impact on women's high jumping than on the men's event, but performances are likely to flatten out and I look to no more the 2.06 m (6 ft 9½ in) by 1988.

The main factor in pole vault is technological rather than technical, and it is difficult to see the record going much beyond 5.85 m (19 ft) with the present poles, by 1988.

Although track and field athletics is looked upon as a world sport, its development is still uneven, and if we look at a selection of different countries and attempt to assess their present evolutional point to a factor of ten, we can see this difference. For instance, in Africa and South America women's athletics has hardly developed and significant social changes will have to occur before they will.

	Men		Women		Govt.
	track	field	track	field	aid
GDR	9	10	10	10	10
USSR	9	10	10	10	9
France	8	8	5	4	7
Kenya	8	4	3	2	4
China	6	6	4	4	6
USA	9	10	6	5	2
Brazil	6	7	3	2	2
Cuba	7	7	6	7	8
Great Britain	9	7	8	6	5

National development chart (worked out to a factor of 10).

Even in Kenya, where distance running has reached a high point, field events are still far behind. Only in Communist societies, such as the USSR and East Germany, can any real balance be said to exist between the sexes and between track and field events, and these are the only countries in which the sport can be said to have reached maturity.

The world of track and field athletics therefore directly reflects the economics of a world still mainly dominated by the United States and Europe. The increasing economic strength of the Arab world will not be reflected in improved athletics performance for many years, for there is no way in which nations, with the ethnic and cultural disadvantages of the Arab nations, can speedily come to world level in a sport which makes, in so many of its events, a demand for height and weight.

Timing

Since August 1976, for races up to and including 400 m, only performances timed by an approved, fully automatic electrical timing device are accepted as world records.

The inaugural record list of events up to and including 400 m, timed by fully automatic electrical timing devices, was established as at 1st January 1975. Up to the Montreal Congress, this list existed side by side with the hand-timed list for these performances. The electrical list contained performances which were the best recorded up to that date. Several other performances (including marks made at distances over 400 m) were also taken by fully automatic electrical timing devices. These have been indicated by the suffix 'a', and the time (two digits after decimal point only) is shown in parentheses after the venue. In cases where the hand time was not corrected after comparison with the fully automatic electric time, the suffix 'b' has been employed.

Abbreviations

AFG Afghanistan
ALB Albania
ALG Algeria
AHO Netherlands Antilles
ANT Antigua
ARG Argentina
ARS Saudi Arabia
AUS Australia
AUT Austria
BAH Bahamas
BAN Bangladesh
BAR Barbados
BEL Belgium
BEN Benin
BER Bermuda
BHR Bahrain
BIZ Belize
BIR Burma
BOL Bolivia
BOT Botswana
BRA Brazil
BRU Brunei
BUL Bulgaria
BUR Burundi
BVI Br. Virgin Islands
CAE Cen: African Empire
CAN Canada
CGO Congo
CHA Tchad
CHI Chile
CIV Ivory Coast
CKI Cook Islands
CMR Cameroons
COL Colombia
CPR People's Rep. of China
CRC Costa Rica
CUB Cuba
DEN Denmark
DOM Dominican Republic
ECU Ecuador
EGY Egypt
ESP Spain
EST Estonia
ETH Ethiopia
FIJ Fiji
FIN Finland
FRA France
GAB Gabon
GAM Gambia
GBR Great Britain
GDR German Democratic Rep.
GER Germany
GHA Ghana
GIB Gibraltar
GRE Greece
GRN Grenada
GUA Guatemala
GUI Guinea
GUY Guyana
HAI Haiti
HOL Netherlands
HKG Hong Kong
HON Honduras
HUN Hungary
INA Indonesia
IND India
IRL Ireland
IRN Iran
IRQ Iraq
ISL Iceland
ISR Israel
ISV Virgin Islands
ITA Italy
JAM Jamaica
JOR Jordan
JPN Japan
KEN Kenya
KHM Khmer
KOR Korea
KUW Kuwait
LAO Laos
LAT Latvia
LBA Libya
LBR Liberia
LES Lesotho
LIB Lebanon
LIE Liechtenstein
LUX Luxembourg
MAD Madagascar
MAL Malaysia
MAR Morocco
MAU Mauritius
MAW Malawi
MEX Mexico
MGL Mongolia
MLI Mali
MLT Malta
MON Montserrat
MTA Mauritania
NAU Nauru
NCA Nicaragua
NEP Nepal
NGR Nigeria
NHB New Hebrides
NIG Niger
NOR Norway
NZL New Zealand
NGY Pápua New Guinea
PAK Pakistan
PAN Panama
PAR Paraguay
PER Peru
PHI Philippines
POL Poland
POR Portugal
PRK D. P. R. Korea
PUR Puerto Rico
QAT Qatar
ROC Republic of China
ROM Rumania
RSA South Africa
RWA Rwanda
SAL El Salvador
SEN Senegal
SIN Singapore
SLE Sierra Leone
SMR San Marino
SOM Somalia
SRI Sri Lanka
STV Saint Vincent
SUD Sudan
SUI Switzerland
SUR Surinam
SWE Sweden
SWA Swaziland
SYR Syria
TAN Tanzania
TCH Czechoslovakia
THA Thailand
TOG Togo
TON Tonga
TRI Trinidad & Tobago
TUN Tunisia
TUR Turkey
UAE United Arab Emirates
UGA Uganda
USSR Soviet Union
URU Uruguay
USA United States
VEN Venezuela
VNM Vietnam
VOL Upper Volta
WSA Western Samoa
YUG Yugoslavia
ZAI Zaire
ZAM Zambia

Men

100 Metres

10.6	Donald Lippincott	USA	6.7.1912	Stockholm	
10.6	Jackson Scholz	USA	16.9.1920	Stockholm	
10.4	Charles Paddock	USA	23.4.1921	Redlands, Calif.	
10.4	Eddie Tolan	USA	8.8.1929	Stockholm	
10.4	Eddie Tolan	USA	25.8.1929	Copenhagen	
10.3	Percy Williams	CAN	9.8.1930	Toronto	
10.3	Eddie Tolan	USA	1.8.1932	Los Angeles	
10.3	Ralph Metcalfe	USA	12.8.1933	Budapest	
10.3	Eulace Peacock	USA	6.8.1934	Oslo	
10.3	Christiaan Berger	HOL	26.8.1934	Amsterdam	
10.3	Ralph Metcalfe	USA	15.9.1934	Osaka, Japan	
10.3	Ralph Metcalfe	USA	23.9.1934	Dairen, Manchuria	
10.3	Takayoshi Yoshioka	JAP	15.6.1935	Tokyo	
10.2	Jesse Owens	USA	20.6.1936	Chicago	
10.2	Harold Davis	USA	6.6.1941	Compton, Calif.	
10.2	Lloyd La Beach	PAN	15.5.1948	Fresno, Calif.	
10.2	Barney Ewell	USA	9.7.1948	Evanston, Illinois	
10.2	McDonald Bailey	GBR	25.8.1951	Belgrade	
10.2	Heinz Fütterer	GER	31.10.1954	Yokohama, Japan	
10.2	Bobby Morrow	USA	19.5.1956	Houston, Tex.	
10.2	Ira Murchison	USA	1.6.1956	Compton, Calif.	
10.2	Bobby Morrow	USA	22.6.1956	Bakersfield, Calif.	
10.2	Ira Murchison	USA	29.6.1956	Los Angeles	
10.2	Bobby Morrow	USA	29.6.1956	Los Angeles	
10.1	Willie Williams	USA	3.8.1956	Berlin	
10.1	Ira Murchison	USA	4.8.1956	Berlin	
10.1	Leamon King	USA	20.10.1956	Ontario, Calif.	
10.1	Leamon King	USA	27.10.1956	Santa Ana, Calif.	
10.1	Ray Norton	USA	18.4.1959	San José, Calif.	
10.0b	Armin Hary	GER	21.6.1960	Zurich	(.25)
10.0	Harry Jerome	CAN	15.7.1960	Saskatoon	
10.0	Horacio Esteves	VEN	15.8.1964	Caracas	
10.0b	Bob Hayes	USA	15.10.1964	Tokyo	(.03)
10.0	Jim Hines	USA	27.5.1967	Modesto, Calif.	
10.0	Enrique Figuerola	CUB	17.6.1967	Budapest	
10.0	Paul Nash	RSA	2.4.1968	Krugersdorp	
10.0	Oliver Ford	USA	31.5.1968	Albuquerque, N. Mex.	
10.0b	Charlie Greene	USA	20.6.1968	Sacramento, Calif.	(.10)
10.0	Roger Bambuck	FRA	20.6.1968	Sacramento, Calif.	
9.9b	Jim Hines	USA	20.6.1968	Sacramento, Calif.	(.03)
9.9b	Ronnie Ray Smith	USA	20.6.1968	Sacramento, Calif.	(.14)
9.9b	Charlie Greene	USA	20.6.1968	Sacramento, Calif.	(.10)
9.9b	Jim Hines	USA	14.10.1968	Mexico City	(.95)
9.9b	Eddie Hart	USA	1.7.1972	Eugene, Oregon	
9.9	Reynaud Robinson	USA	1.7.1972	Eugene, Oregon	
9.9	Steve Williams	USA	21.6.1974	Los Angeles	
9.9	Silvio Leonard	CUB	5.6.1975	Ostrava, Czechoslovakia	
9.9	Steve Williams	USA	16.7 1975	Siena, Italy	
9.9	Steve Williams	USA	22.8.1975	Berlin	
9.9	Steve Williams	USA	27.3.1976	Gainesville, Fla.	
9.9	Harvey Glance	USA	3.4.1976	Columbia, SC	
9.9	Harvey Glance	USA	1.5.1976	Baton Rouge, La.	
9.9	Don Quarrie	JAM	22.5.1976	Modesto, Calif.	
9.95	Jim Hines	USA	14.10.1968	Mexico City	

200 Metres Turn

20.6	Andy Stanfield	USA	26.5.1951	Philadelphia	
20.6	Andy Stanfield	USA	28.6.1952	Los Angeles	
20.6	Thane Baker	USA	23.6.1956	Bakersfield, Calif.	
20.6b	Bobby Morrow	USA	27.11.1956	Melbourne	(.75)
20.6	Manfred Germar	GER	1.10.1958	Wuppertal	
20.6	Ray Norton	USA	19.3.1960	Berkeley, Calif.	
20.6	Ray Norton	USA	30.4.1960	Philadelphia	
20.5	Peter Radford	GBR	28.5.1960	Wolverhampton	
20.5	Stone Johnson	USA	2.7.1960	Palo Alto, Calif.	
20.5	Ray Norton	USA	2.7.1960	Palo Alto, Calif.	
20.5b	Livio Berruti	ITA	3.9.1960	Rome	(.)
20.5b	Livio Berruti	ITA	3.9.1960	Rome	(.62)
20.5	Paul Drayton	USA	23.6.1962	Walnut, Calif.	
20.3	Henry Carr	USA	23.3.1963	Tempe, Arizona	
20.2	Henry Carr	USA	4.4.1964	Tempe, Arizona	
20.0	Tommie Smith	USA	11.6.1966	Sacramento, Calif.	
19.8a	Tommie Smith	USA	16.10.1968	Mexico City	(.83)
19.8b	Donald Quarrie	JAM	3.8.1971	Cali, Colombia	(.86)
19.8	Donald Quarrie	JAM	7.6.1975	Eugene, Oregon	

19.83	Tommie Smith	USA	16.10.1968	Mexico City
19.72	Pietro Mennea	ITA	12.9.1979	Mexico City

400 Metres

47.8	Maxie Long	USA	29.9.1900	New York	
47.4	Ted Meredith	USA	27.5.1916	Cambridge, Mass.	
47.0	Emerson Spencer	USA	12.5.1928	Palo Alto, Calif.	
46.4	Ben Eastman	USA	26.3.1932	Palo Alto, Calif.	
46.2	Bill Carr	USA	5.8.1932	Los Angeles	
46.1	Archie Williams	USA	19.6.1936	Chicago	
46.0	Rudolf Harbig	GER	12.8.1939	Frankfurt/Main	
46.0	Graver Klemmer	USA	29.6.1941	Philadelphia	
46.0	Herb McKenley	JAM	5.6.1948	Berkeley, Calif.	
45.9	Herb McKenley	JAM	2.7.1948	Milwaukee, Wis.	
45.8	George Rhoden	JAM	22.8.1950	Eskilstuna, Sweden	
45.4	Lou Jones	USA	18.3.1955	Mexico City	
45.2	Lou Jones	USA	30.6.1956	Los Angeles	
44.9b	Otis Davis	USA	6.9.1960	Rome	(.07)
44.9b	Carl Kaufmann	GER	6.9.1960	Rome	(.08)
44.9	Adolph Plummer	USA	25.5.1963	Tempe, Arizona	
44.9	Mike Larrabee	USA	12.9.1964	Los Angeles	
44.5	Tommie Smith	USA	20.5.1967	San José, Calif.	
44.1b	Larry James	USA	14.9.1968	S. Lake Tahoe, Calif.	(.19)
43.8b	Lee Evans	USA	18.10.1968	Mexico City	(.86)

43.86	Lee Evans	USA	18.10.1968	Mexico City

800 Metres

1:51.9	Ted Meredith	USA	8.7.1912	Stockholm
1:51.6	Otto Peltzer	GER	3.7.1926	London
1:50.6	Séra Martin	FRA	14.7.1928	Paris
1:49.8	Tom Hampson	GBR	2.8.1932	Los Angeles
1:49.8	Ben Eastman	USA	16.6.1934	Princeton, N. J.
1:49.7	Glenn Cunningham	USA	20.8.1936	Stockholm

1:49.6	Elroy Robinson	USA	11.7.1937	New York	
1:48.4	Sydney Wooderson	GBR	20.8.1938	Motspur Park	
1:46.6	Rudolf Harbig	GER	15.7.1939	Milan	
1:45.7	Roger Moens	BEL	3.8.1955	Oslo	
1:44.3	Peter Snell	NZL	3.2.1962	Christchurch	
1:44.3b	Ralph Doubell	AUS	15.10.1968	Mexico City	(.40)
1:44.3	David Wottle	USA	1.7.1972	Eugene, Oregon	
1:43.7	Marcello Fiasconaro	ITA	27.6.1973	Milan	
1:43.5a	Alberto Juantorena	CUB	25.7.1976	Montreal	(.50)
1:43.4a	Alberto Juantorena	CUB	21.8.1977	Sofia	(.44)
1:42.4a	Sebastian Coe	GBR	5.7.1979	Oslo	(.33)

1500 Metres

3:55.8	Abel Kiviat	USA	8.6.1912	Cambridge, Mass.	
3:54.7	John Zander	SWE	5.8.1917	Stockholm	
3:52.6	Paavo Nurmi	FIN	19.6.1924	Helsinki	
3:51.0	Otto Peltzer	GER	11.9.1926	Berlin	
3:49.2	Jules Ladoumègue	FRA	5.10.1930	Paris	
3:49.2	Luigi Beccali	ITA	9.9.1933	Turin	
3:49.0	Luigi Beccali	ITA	17.9.1933	Milan	
3:48.8	Bill Bonthron	USA	30.6.1934	Milwaukee, Wis.	
3:47.8	Jack Lovelock	NZL	6.8.1936	Berlin	
3:47.6	Gunder Hägg	SWE	10.8.1941	Stockholm	
3:45.8	Gunder Hägg	SWE	17.7.1942	Stockholm	
3:45.0	Arne Andersson	SWE	17.8.1943	Gothenburg	
3:43.0	Gunder Hägg	SWE	7.7.1944	Gothenburg	
3:43.0	Lennart Strand	SWE	15.7.1947	Malmö	
3:43.0	Werner Lueg	GER	29.6.1952	Berlin	
3:42.8	Wes Santee	USA	4.6.1954	Compton, Calif.	
3:41.8	John Landy	AUS	21.6.1954	Turku, Finland	
3:40.8	Sándor Iharos	HUN	28.7.1955	Helsinki	
3:40.8	Lásló Tábori	HUN	6.9.1955	Oslo	
3:40.8	Gunnar Nielsen	DEN	6.9.1955	Oslo	
3:40.6	István Rózsavölgyi	HUN	3.8.1956	Tata	
3:40.2	Olavi Salsola	FIN	11.7.1957	Turku	
3:40.2	Olavi Salonen	FIN	11.7.1957	Turku	
3:38.1	Stanislav Jungwirth	TCH	12.7.1957	Stará Boleslav	
3:36.0	Herb Elliott	AUS	28.8.1958	Gothenburg, Sweden	
3:35.6	Herb Elliott	AUS	6.9.1960	Rome	
3:33.1	Jim Ryun	USA	8.7.1967	Los Angeles	
3:32.2a	Filbert Bayi	TAN	2.2.1974	Christchurch	(.16)
3:32.1a	Sebastian Coe	GBR	15.8.1979	Zurich	(.03)

1 Mile

4:14.4	John Paul Jones	USA	31.5.1913	Cambridge, Mass.
4:12.6	Norman Taber	USA	16.7.1915	Cambridge, Mass.
4:10.4	Paavo Nurmi	FIN	23.8.1923	Stockholm
4:09.2	Jules Ladoumègue	FRA	4.10.1931	Paris
4:07.6	Jack Lovelock	NZL	15.7.1933	Princeton, N. J.
4:06.8	Glenn Cunningham	USA	16.6.1934	Princeton, N. J.
4:06.4	Sydney Wooderson	GBR	28.8.1937	Motspur Park
4:06.2	Gunder Hägg	SWE	1.7.1942	Gothenburg, Sweden
4:06.2	Arne Andersson	SWE	10.7.1942	Stockholm
4:04.6	Gunder Hägg	SWE	4.9.1942	Stockholm
4:02.6	Arne Andersson	SWE	1.7.1943	Gothenburg
4:01.6	Arne Andersson	SWE	18.7.1944	Malmö
4:01.4	Gunder Hägg	SWE	17.7.1945	Malmö

1 Mile (continued)

3:59.4	Roger Bannister	GBR	6.5.1954	Oxford
3:58.0	John Landy	AUS	21.6.1954	Turku, Finland
3:57.2	Derek Ibbotson	GBR	19.7.1957	London
3:54.5	Herb Elliott	AUS	6.8.1958	Dublin
3:54.4	Peter Snell	NZL	27.1.1962	Wanganui
3:54.1	Peter Snell	NZL	17.11.1964	Auckland
3:53.6	Michel Jazy	FRA	9.6.1965	Rennes
3:51.3	Jim Ryun	USA	17.7.1966	Berkeley, Calif.
3:51.1	Jim Ryun	USA	23.6.1967	Bakersfield, Calif.
3:51.0	Filbert Bayi	TAN	17.5.1975	Kingston, Jamaica
3:49.4	John Walker	NZL	12.8.1975	Gothenburg, Sweden
3:49.0a	Sebastian Coe	GBR	17.7.1979	Oslo

5000 Metres

14:36.6	Hannes Kolehmainen	FIN	10.7.1912	Stockholm	
14:35.4	Paavo Nurmi	FIN	12.9.1922	Stockholm	
14:28.2	Paavo Nurmi	FIN	19.6.1924	Helsinki	
14:17.0	Lauri Lehtinen	FIN	19.6.1932	Helsinki	
14:08.8	Taisto Mäki	FIN	16.6.1939	Helsinki	
13:58.2	Gunder Hägg	SWE	20.9.1942	Gothenburg	
13:57.2	Emil Zátopek	TCH	30.5.1954	Paris	
13:56.6	Vladimir Kuts	USSR	29.8.1954	Berne	
13:51.6	Chris Chataway	GBR	13.10.1954	London	
13:51.2	Vladimir Kuts	USSR	23.10.1954	Prague	
13:50.8	Sándor Iharos	HUN	10.9.1955	Budapest	
13:46.8	Vladimir Kuts	USSR	18.9.1955	Belgrade	
13:40.6	Sándor Iharos	HUN	23.10.1955	Budapest	
13:36.8	Gordon Pirie	GBR	19.6.1956	Bergen, Norway	
13:35.0	Vladimir Kuts	USSR	13.10.1957	Rome	
13:34.8	Ron Clarke	AUS	16.1.1965	Hobart	
13:33.6	Ron Clarke	AUS	1.2.1965	Auckland	
13:25.8	Ron Clarke	AUS	4.6.1965	Los Angeles	
13:24.2	Kipchoge Keino	KEN	30.11.1965	Auckland	
13:16.6	Ron Clarke	AUS	5.7.1966	Stockholm	
13:16.4	Lasse Viren	FIN	14.9.1972	Helsinki	
13:13.0	Emiel Puttemans	BEL	20.9.1972	Brussels	
13:12.9a	Dick Quax	NZL	5.7.1977	Stockholm	(.86)
13:08.4	Henry Rono	KEN	8.4.1978	Berkeley	

10,000 Metres

30:58.8	Jean Bouin	FRA	16.11.1911	Paris
30:40.2	Paavo Nurmi	FIN	22.6.1921	Stockholm
30:35.4	Ville Ritola	FIN	25.5.1924	Helsinki
30:23.2	Ville Ritola	FIN	6.7.1924	Paris
30:06.2	Paavo Nurmi	FIN	31.8.1924	Kuopio
30:05.6	Ilmari Salminen	FIN	18.7.1937	Kouvola
30:02.0	Taisto Mäki	FIN	29.9.1938	Tampere
29:52.6	Taisto Mäki	FIN	17.9.1939	Helsinki
29:35.4	Viljo Heino	FIN	25.8.1944	Helsinki
29:28.2	Emil Zátopek	TCH	11.6.1949	Ostrava
29:27.2	Viljo Heino	FIN	1.9.1949	Kouvola
29:21.2	Emil Zátopek	TCH	22.10.1949	Ostrava
29:02.6	Emil Zátopek	TCH	4.8.1950	Turku, Finland
29:01.6	Emil Zátopek	TCH	1.11.1953	Stará Boleslav
28:54.2	Emil Zátopek	TCH	1.6.1954	Brussels

28:42.8	Sándor Iharos	HUN	15.7.1956	Budapest	
28:30.4	Vladimir Kuts	USSR	11.9.1956	Moscow	
28:18.8	Pyotr Bolotnikov	USSR	15.10.1960	Kiev	
28:18.2	Pyotr Bolotnikov	USSR	11.8.1962	Moscow	
28:15.6	Ron Clarke	AUS	18.12.1963	Melbourne	
27:39.4b	Ron Clarke	AUS	14.7.1965	Oslo	(.89)
27:38.4a	Lasse Viren	FIN	3.9.1972	Munich	(.35)
27:30.8a	David Bedford	GBR	13.7.1973	London	(.80)
27:30.5a	Samson Kimobwa	KEN	30.6.1977	Helsinki	(.47)
27:22.5a	Henry Rono	KEN	11.6.1978	Vienna	(.47)

3000 Metres Steeplechase

(First recognized in 1954)

8:45.4	Horace Ashenfelter	USA	25.7.1952	Helsinki	
8:44.4	Olavi Rinteenpää	FIN	2.7.1953	Helsinki	
The above marks were the best authentic performances prior to recognition.					
8:49.6	Sándor Rozsnyói	HUN	28.8.1954	Berne	
8:47.8	Pentti Karvonen	FIN	1.7.1955	Helsinki	
8:45.4	Pentti Karvonen	FIN	15.7.1955	Oslo	
8:45.4	Vasiliy Vlasenko	USSR	18.8.1955	Moscow	
8:41.2	Jerzy Chromik	POL	31.8.1955	Brno, Czechoslovakia	
8:40.2	Jerzy Chromik	POL	11.9.1955	Budapest	
8:39.8	Semyon Rzhishchin	USSR	14.8.1956	Moscow	
8:35.6	Sándor Rozsnyói	HUN	16.9.1956	Budapest	
8:35.6	Semyon Rzhishchin	USSR	21.7.1958	Tallinn	
8:32.0	Jerzy Chromik	POL	2.8.1958	Warsaw	
8:31.4	Zdzisław Krzyszkowiak	POL	26.6.1960	Tula, USSR	
8:31.2	Grigoriy Taran	USSR	28.5.1961	Kiev	
8:30.4	Zdzisław Krzyszkowiak	POL	10.8.1961	Walcz	
8:29.6	Gaston Roelants	BEL	7.9.1963	Leuven	
8:26.4	Gaston Roelants	BEL	7.8.1965	Brussels	
8:24.2	Jouko Kuha	FIN	17.7.1968	Stockholm	
8:22.2	Vladimir Dudin	USSR	19.8.1969	Kiev	
8:22.0	Kerry O'Brien	AUS	4.7.1970	Berlin, Germany	
8:20.8	Anders Gärderud	SWE	14.9.1972	Helsinki	
8:19.8	Benjamin Jipcho	KEN	19.6.1973	Helsinki	
8:14.0a	Benjamin Jipcho	KEN	27.6.1973	Helsinki	(.91)
8:10.4	Anders Gärderud	SWE	25.6.1975	Oslo	
8:09.8a	Anders Gärderud	SWE	1.7.1975	Stockholm	(.70)
8:08.0a	Anders Gärderud	SWE	28.7.1976	Montreal	(.02)
8:05.4	Henry Rono	KEN	13.5.1978	Seattle	

110 Metres Hurdles

15.0	Forrest Smithson	USA	25.7.1908	London
14.8	Earl Thomson	CAN	18.8.1920	Antwerp
14.8	Sten Pettersson	SWE	18.9.1927	Stockholm
14.6	George Weightman-Smith	RSA	31.7.1928	Amsterdam
14.4	Eric Wennström	SWE	25.8.1929	Stockholm
14.4	Bengt Sjöstedt	FIN	5.9.1931	Helsinki
14.4	Percy Beard	USA	23.6.1932	Cambridge, Mass.
14.4	Jack Keller	USA	16.7.1932	Palo Alto, Calif.
14.4	George Saling	USA	2.8.1932	Los Angeles
14.4	John Morriss	USA	12.8.1933	Budapest
14.4	John Morriss	USA	8.9.1933	Turin
14.3	Percy Beard	USA	26.7.1934	Stockholm
14.2	Percy Beard	USA	6.8.1934	Oslo
14.2	Al Moreau	USA	2.8.1935	Oslo

110 Metres Hurdles (continued)

14.1	Forrest Towns	USA	19.6.1936	Chicago	
14.1	Forrest Towns	USA	6.8.1936	Berlin	
13.7	Forrest Towns	USA	27.8.1936	Oslo	
13.7	Fred Wolcott	USA	29.6.1941	Philadelphia	
13.6	Dick Attlesey	USA	24.6.1950	College Park, Md.	
13.5	Dick Attlesey	USA	10.7.1950	Helsinki	
13.4	Jack Davis	USA	22.6.1956	Bakersfield, Calif.	
13.2b	Martin Lauer	GER	7.7.1959	Zurich	(.56)
13.2	Lee Calhoun	USA	21.8.1960	Berne	
13.2b	Earl McCullouch	USA	16.7.1967	Minneapolis	(.43)
13.2	Willie Davenport	USA	4.7.1969	Zurich	
13.2a	Rodney Milburn	USA	7.9.1972	Munich	(.24)
13.1b	Rodney Milburn	USA	6.7.1973	Zurich	(.41)
13.1	Rodney Milburn	USA	22.7.1973	Siena	
13.1	Guy Drut	FRA	23.7.1975	St Maur	
13.0	Guy Drut	FRA	22.8.1975	Berlin	

13.24	Rodney Milburn	USA	7.9.1972	Munich
13.21	Alejandro Casanas	CUB	21.8.1977	Sofia
13.16	Renaldo Nehemiah	USA	14.4.1979	San José, Calif.
13.00	Renaldo Nehemiah	USA	6.5.1979	Westwood, Calif.

400 Metres Hurdles

55.0	Charles Bacon	USA	22.7.1908	London	
54.2	John Norton	USA	26.6.1920	Pasadena, Calif.	
54.0	Frank Loomis	USA	16.8.1920	Antwerp, Belgium	
53.8	Sten Pettersson	SWE	4.10.1925	Paris	
52.6	John Gibson	USA	2.7.1927	Lincoln, Neb.	
52.0	Morgan Taylor	USA	4.7.1928	Philadelphia	
52.0	Glenn Hardin	USA	1.8.1932	Los Angeles	
51.8	Glenn Hardin	USA	30.6.1934	Milwaukee, Wis.	
50.6	Glenn Hardin	USA	26.7.1934	Stockholm	
50.4	Yuriy Lituyev	USSR	20.9.1953	Budapest	
49.5	Glenn Davis	USA	29.6.1956	Los Angeles	
49.2	Glenn Davis	USA	6.8.1958	Budapest	
49.2	Salvatore Morale	ITA	14.9.1962	Belgrade	
49.1	Rex Cawley	USA	13.9.1964	Los Angeles	
48.8b	Geoff Vanderstock	USA	11.9.1968	S. Lake Tahoe, Calif.	(.94)
48.1a	David Hemery	GBR	15.10.1968	Mexico City	(.12)
47.8a	John Akii-Bua	UGA	2.9.1972	Munich	(.82)

47.82	John Akii-Bua	UGA	2.9.1972	Munich
47.64	Edwin Moses	USA	25.7.1976	Montreal
47.45	Edwin Moses	USA	11.6.1977	Westwood, Calif.

20 Kilometres Walk

1h.39:22.0	Niels Petersen	DEN	30.6.1918	Copenhagen
1h.39:20.4	Armando Valente	ITA	2.12.1926	Bologna
1h.38:53.2	Attilio Callegari	ITA	26.12.1926	Milan
1h.37:42.2	Donato Pavesi	ITA	23.10.1927	Milan
1h.36:34.4	Armando Valente	ITA	25.10.1930	Genoa
1h.34:26.0	Janis Dalinsh	LAT	1.6.1933	Riga
1h.32:28.4	John Michaelsson	SWE	12.7.1942	Växjö
1h.30:26.4	Josef Dolezal	TCH	1.11.1953	Stará Boleslav
1h.30:02.8	Volodymyr Holubnichiy	USSR	2.10.1955	Kiev
1h.28:45.2	Leonid Spirin	USSR	13.6.1956	Kiev

1h.27:58.2	Mikhail Lavrov	USSR	13.8.1956	Moscow
1h.27:38.6	Grigoriy Panichkin	USSR	9.5.1958	Stalinabad
1h.27:05.0	Volodymyr Holubnichiy	USSR	23.9.1958	Simferopol
1h.26:45.8	Gennadiy Agapov	USSR	6.4.1969	Simferopol
1h.25:50.0	Peter Frenkel	GDR	4.7.1970	Erfurt
1h.25:19.4	Peter Frenkel	GDR	24.6.1972	Erfurt
1h.25:19.4	Hans-Georg Reimann	GDR	24.6.1972	Erfurt
1h.24:45.0	Bernd Kannenberg	GER	25.5.1974	Hamburg
1h.23:31.9	Daniel Bautista	MEX	14.5.1977	Fana, Norway
1h.22:59.4	Anatoley Solomin	USSR	26.4.1979	Alushta, USSR
1h.22:19.4	Gerard Leheire	FRA	29.4.1979	Epinay-Sur-Seine
1h.20:58.6	Domingo Colon	MEX	26.5.1979	Fana, Norway

50 Kilometres Walk

4h.34:03.0*	Paul Sievert	GER	5.10.1924	Munich
4h.32:52.0	John Ljunggren	SWE	29.7.1951	Gislaved
4h.31:21.6	Antal Róka	HUN	1.6.1952	Budapest
4h.29:58.0	John Ljunggren	SWE	8.8.1953	Fristad
4h.27:28.4	Ladislav Moc	TCH	13.10.1955	Znojmo
4h.26:05.2	Milan Skřont	TCH	30.4.1956	Krnov
4h.21:07.0	Ladislav Moc	TCH	21.6.1956	Prague
4h.16:08.6	Sergey Lobastov	USSR	23.8.1958	Moscow
4h.14:02.4	Abdon Pamich	ITA	19.11.1961	Rome
4h.10:51.8	Christoph Höhne	GDR	16.5.1965	Potsdam
4h.08:05.0	Christoph Höhne	GDR	18.10.1969	Berlin
4h.04:19.8	Peter Selzer	GDR	3.10.1971	Naumberg
4h.03:42.6	Venjamin Soldatenko	USSR	5.10.1972	Moscow
4h.00:27.2	Gerhard Weidner	GER	8.4.1973	Hamburg
3h.56:51.4	Bernd Kannenberg	GER	16.11.1975	Nerviano, Italy
3h.52:23.5	Raul Gonzalez	MEX	19.5.1978	Føde, Norway
3h.41:39.0	Raul Gonzalez	MEX	25.5.1979	Fana, Norway

*(Performance made on road)

4 x 100 Metres Relay

42.3	GERMAN NATIONAL TEAM (Otto Röhr, Max Hermann, Erwin Kern, Richard Rau)	8.7.1912	Stockholm
42.2	USA NATIONAL TEAM (Jackson V. Scholz, Loren C. Murchison, Morris Kirksey, Charles W. Paddock)	22.8.1920	Antwerp
42.0	BRITISH NATIONAL TEAM (Harold M. Abrahams, Walter Rangeley, Lancelot C. Royle, W. P. Nichol)	12.7.1924	Paris
42.0	DUTCH NATIONAL TEAM (Jan Boot, Henk A. Broos, Jan C. de Vries, Martinus Van den Berghe)	12.7.1924	Paris
41.0	USA NATIONAL TEAM (Frank Hussey, Lous A. Clarke, Loren C. Murchison, J. Alfred Leconey)	13.7.1924	Paris
41.0	NEWARK A.C. USA (Chester Bowman, John Currie, James Pappas, Henry Cumming)	4.7.1927	Lincoln, Nebr.
41.0	SPORT CLUB, EINTRACHT, GERMANY (Ernst Geerling, Friedrich W. Wichmann, Adolf Metzner, Hans Salz)	10.6.1928	Halle
41.0	USA NATIONAL TEAM (Frank C. Wykoff, James Quinn, Charles E. Borah, Henry A. Russell)	5.8.1928	Amsterdam
40.8	GERMAN NATIONAL TEAM (Arthur Jonath, Richard Corts, Hubert Houben, Helmut Körnig)	2.9.1928	Berlin
40.8	SPORT CLUB CHARLOTTENBURG, GERMANY (Helmut Körnig, W. Grosser, H. Alex Natan, Hermann Schlöske)	22.7.1929	Breslau
40.8	UNIVERSITY OF S. CALIFORNIA, USA (R. Delby, Milton Maurer, Maurice Guyer, Frank C. Wykoff)	9.5.1931	Fresno, Calif.
40.6	GERMAN NATIONAL TEAM (Helmut Körnig, Georg Lammers, Erich Borchmeyer, Arthur Jonath)	14.6.1932	Kassel

4 x 100 Metres Relay (continued)

40.0	USA NATIONAL TEAM (Robert A. Keisel, Emmett Toppino, Hector Dyer, Frank C. Wykoff)	7.8.1932	Los Angeles	
39.8	USA NATIONAL TEAM (Jesse Owens, Ralph Metcalfe, Foy Draper, Frank C. Wykoff)	9.8.1936	Berlin	
39.5	USA NATIONAL TEAM (Ira Murchison, Leamon King, W. Thane Baker, Bobby J. Morrow)	1.12.1956	Melbourne	
39.5	GERMAN NATIONAL TEAM (Manfred Steinbach, Martin Lauer, Heinz Fütterer, Manfred Germar)	29.8.1958	Cologne	
39.5	GERMAN NATIONAL TEAM (Bernd Cullmann, Armin Hary, Walter Mahlendorf, Martin Lauer)	7.9.1960	Rome	
39.5	GERMAN NATIONAL TEAM (Bernd Cullmann, Armin Hary, Walter Mahlendorf, Martin Lauer)	8.9.1960	Rome	
39.1	USA NATIONAL TEAM (Hayes Jones, Frank Budd, Charles Frazier, Paul Drayton)	15.7.1961	Moscow	
39.0	USA NATIONAL TEAM (O. Paul Drayton, Gerry Ashworth, Dick Stebbins, Bob Hayes)	21.10.1964	Tokyo	
38.6	UNIVERSITY OF S. CALIFORNIA, USA (Earl McCullouch, Fred Kuller, O. J. Simpson, Lennox Miller)	17.6.1967	Provo, Utah	
38.6a	JAMAICAN NATIONAL TEAM (Errol Stewart, Mike Fray, Clifton Forbes, Lennox Miller)	19.10.1968	Mexico City	(.)
38.3b	JAMAICAN NATIONAL TEAM (Errol Stewart, Mike Fray, Clifton Forbes, Lennox Miller)	19.10.1968	Mexico City	(.39)
38.2a	USA NATIONAL TEAM (Charlie Greene, Mel Pender, Ronnie Ray Smith, Jim Hines)	20.10.1968	Mexico City	(.23)
38.2a	USA NATIONAL TEAM (Larry Black, Robert Taylor, Gerald Tinker, Eddie Hart)	10.9.1972	Munich	(.19)

38.19	USA NATIONAL TEAM (Larry Black, Robert Taylor, Gerald Tinker, Eddie Hart)	10.9.1972	Munich
38.03	USA NATIONAL TEAM (Bill Collins, Steve Riddick, Cliff Wiley, Steve Williams)	3.9.1977	Düsseldorf

4 x 400 Metres Relay

3:18.2	USA NATIONAL TEAM (Harry Schaaf, Melvin W. Sheppard, Harry Gissing, James M. Rosenberger)	4.9.1911	Celtic Park NY	
3:16.6	USA NATIONAL TEAM (Melvin W. Sheppard, Charles D. Reidpath, Ted Meredith, F. J. Lindberg)	15.7.1912	Stockholm	
3:16.0	USA NATIONAL TEAM (Comm. S. Cochrane, Alan B. Helffrich, J. Oliver McDonald, Bill E. Stevenson)	13.7.1924	Paris	
3:14.2	USA NATIONAL TEAM (George Baird, Emerson Spencer, Fred Alderman, Ray Barbuti)	5.8.1928	Amsterdam	
3:13.4	USA NATIONAL TEAM (George Baird, F. Morgan Taylor, Ray Barbuti, Emerson Spencer)	11.8.1928	London	
3:12.6	STANFORD UNIVERSITY, USA (Maynor Shore, Alvin A. Hables, Leslie T. Hables, Ben Eastman)	8.5.1931	Fresno, Calif.	
3:08.2	USA NATIONAL TEAM (Ivan Fuqua, Edgar Ablowich, Karl Warner, Bill Carr)	7.8.1932	Los Angeles	
3:03.9b	JAMAICAN NATIONAL TEAM (Arthur S. Wint, Leslie A. Laing, Herb H. McKenley, V. George Rhoden)	27.7.1952	Helsinki	(.04)
3:02.2b	USA NATIONAL TEAM (Jack Yerman, Earl Young, Glenn Davis, Otis Davis)	8.9.1960	Rome	(.37)
3:00.7	USA NATIONAL TEAM (Ollan Cassell, Mike Larrabee, Ulis Williams, Henry Carr)	21.10.1964	Tokyo	
2:59.6	USA NATIONAL TEAM (Bob Frey, Lee Evans, Tommie Smith, Theron Lewis)	24.7.1966	Los Angeles	
2:56.1b	USA NATIONAL TEAM (Vince Matthews, Ron Freeman II, Larry James, Lee Evans)	20.10.1968	Mexico City	(.16)

High Jump

2.00m/6′7″	George Horine	USA	18.5.1912	Palo Alto, Calif.
2.01m/6′7¼″	Edward Beeson	USA	2.5.1914	Berkeley, Calif.
2.03m/6′8¼″	Harold Osborn	USA	27.5.1924	Urbana, Illinois
2.04m/6′8½″	Walter Marty	USA	13.5.1933	Fresno, Calif.
2.06m/6′9″	Walter Marty	USA	28.4.1934	Palo Alto, Calif.
2.07m/6′9¾″	Cornelius Johnson	USA	12.7.1936	New York
2.07m/6′9¾″	David Albritton	USA	12.7.1936	New York
2.09m/6′10¼″	Mel Walker	USA	12.8.1937	Malmö, Sweden
2.11m/6′11″	Lester Steers	USA	17.6.1941	Los Angeles
2.12m/6′11½″	Walter Davis	USA	27.6.1953	Dayton, Ohio
2.15m/7′0½″	Charles Dumas	USA	29.6.1956	Los Angeles
2.16m/7′1″*	Yuriy Styepanov	USSR	13.7.1957	Leningrad
2.17m/7′1½″	John Thomas	USA	30.4.1960	Philadelphia
2.17m/7′1¾″	John Thomas	USA	21.5.1960	Cambridge, Mass.
2.18m/7′2″	John Thomas	USA	24.6.1960	Bakersfield, Calif.
2.22m/7′3¾″	John Thomas	USA	1.7.1960	Palo Alto, Calif.
2.23m/7′3¾″	Valeriy Brumel	USSR	18.6.1961	Moscow
2.24m/7′4¼″	Valeriy Brumel	USSR	16.7.1961	Moscow
2.25m/7′4½″	Valeriy Brumel	USSR	31.8.1961	Sofia
2.26m/7′5″	Valeriy Brumel	USSR	22.7.1962	Palo Alto, Calif.
2.27m/7′5¼″	Valeriy Brumel	USSR	29.9.1962	Moscow
2.28m/7′5¾″	Valeriy Brumel	USSR	21.7.1963	Moscow
2.29m/7′6¼″	Patrick Matzdorf	USA	3.7.1971	Berkeley, Calif.
2.30m/7′6½″	Dwight Stones	USA	11.7.1973	Munich
2.31m/7′7″	Dwight Stones	USA	5.6.1976	Philadelphia
2.32m/7′7¼″	Dwight Stones	USA	4.8.1976	Philadelphia
2.33m/7′7¾″	Volodymyr Yashchenko	USSR	3.7.1977	Richmond, USA
2.34m/7′8″	Volodymyr Yashchenko	USSR	16.6.1978	Tbilisi

**Made with built-up shoe*

Pole Vault

4.02m/13′2¼″	Marc Wright	USA	8.6.1912	Cambridge, Mass.
4.09m/13′5″	Frank Foss	USA	20.8.1920	Antwerp
4.12m/13′6¼″	Charles Hoff	NOR	3.9.1922	Copenhagen
4.21m/13′9¾″	Charles Hoff	NOR	22.7.1923	Copenhagen
4.23m/13′10½″	Charles Hoff	NOR	13.8.1925	Oslo
4.25m/13′11¼″	Charles Hoff	NOR	27.9.1925	Turku, Finland
4.27m/14′0″	Sabin Carr	USA	27.5.1927	Philadelphia
4.30m/14′1½″	Lee Barnes	USA	28.4.1928	Fresno, Calif.
4.37m/14′4¼″	Bill Graber	USA	16.7.1932	Palo Alto, Calif.
4.39m/14′5″	Keith Brown	USA	1.6.1935	Cambridge, Mass.
4.43m/14′6½″	George Varoff	USA	4.7.1936	Princeton, N. J.
4.54m/14′11″	Bill Sefton	USA	29.5.1937	Los Angeles
4.54m/14′11″	Earle Meadows	USA	29.5.1937	Los Angeles
4.60m/15′1″	Cornelius Warmerdam	USA	29.6.1940	Fresno, Calif.
4.72m/15′5¾″	Cornelius Warmerdam	USA	6.6.1941	Compton, Calif.
4.77m/15′7¾″	Cornelius Warmerdam	USA	23.5.1942	Modesto, Calif.
4.78m/15′8¼″	Bob Gutowski	USA	27.4.1957	Palo Alto, Calif.
4.80m/15′9¼″	Don Bragg	USA	2.7.1960	Palo Alto, Calif.
4.83m/15′10¼″	George Davies	USA	20.5.1961	Boulder, Colorado
4.89m/16′0¾″	John Uelses	USA	31.3.1962	Santa Barbara, Calif.
4.93m/16′2″	Dave Tork	USA	28.4.1962	Walnut, Calif.
4.94m/16′2½″	Pentti Nikula	FIN	22.6.1962	Kauhava
5.00m/16′5″	Brian Sternberg	USA	27.4.1963	Philadelphia
5.08m/16′8″	Brian Sternberg	USA	7.6.1963	Compton, Calif.
5.13m/16′10¼″	John Pennel	USA	5.8.1963	London
5.20m/17′0¾″	John Pennel	USA	24.8.1963	Coral Gables, Fla.
5.23m/17′2″	Fred Hansen	USA	13.6.1964	San Diego, Calif.

Pole Vault (continued)

5.28m/17′4″	Fred Hansen	USA	25.7.1964	Los Angeles
5.32m/17′5½″	Bob Seagren	USA	14.5.1966	Fresno, Calif.
5.34m/17′6¼″	John Pennel	USA	23.7.1966	Los Angeles
5.36m/17′7″	Bob Seagren	USA	10.6.1967	San Diego, Calif.
5.38m/17′7¾″	Paul Wilson	USA	23.6.1967	Bakersfield, Calif.
5.41m/17′9″	Bob Seagren	USA	12.9.1968	S. Lake Tahoe, Calif.
5.44m/17′10¼″	John Pennel	USA	21.6.1969	Sacramento, Calif.
5.45m/17′10½″	Wolfgang Nordwig	GDR	17.6.1970	Berlin
5.46m/17′11″	Wolfgang Nordwig	GDR	3.9.1970	Turin
5.49m/18′0¼″	Christos Papanicolaou	GRE	24.10.1970	Athens
5.51m/18′1″	Kjell Isaksson	SWE	8.4.1972	Austin, Texas
5.54m/18′2″	Kjell Isaksson	SWE	15.4.1972	Los Angeles
5.55m/18′2½″	Kjell Isaksson	SWE	12.6.1972	Helsinki
5.63m/18′5¾″	Bob Seagren	USA	2.7.1972	Eugene, Oregon
5.65m/18′6½″	Dave Roberts	USA	28.3.1975	Gainesville, Fla.
5.67m/18′7¼″	Earl Bell	USA	29.5.1976	Wichita, Kans.
5.70m/18′8¼″	Dave Roberts	USA	22.6.1976	Eugene, Oregon

Long Jump

7.61m/24′11¾″	Peter O'Connor	GBR	5.8.1901	Dublin
7.69m/25′3″	Edwin Gourdin	USA	23.7.1921	Cambridge, Mass.
7.76m/25′5¼″	Robert LeGendre	USA	7.7.1924	Paris
7.89m/25′10¾″	William de Hart Hubbard	USA	13.6.1925	Chicago
7.90m/25′11″	Edward Hamm	USA	7.7.1928	Cambridge, Mass.
7.93m/26′0¼″	Sylvio Cator	HAI	9.9.1928	Paris
7.98m/26′2¼″	Chuhei Nambu	JAP	27.10.1931	Tokyo
8.13m/26′8¼″	Jesse Owens	USA	25.5.1935	Ann Arbor, Mich.
8.21m/26′11¼″	Ralph Boston	USA	12.8.1960	Walnut, Calif.
8.24m/27′0½″	Ralph Boston	USA	27.5.1961	Modesto, Calif.
8.28m/27′2″	Ralph Boston	USA	16.7.1961	Moscow
8.31m/27′3¼″	Igor Ter-Ovanesyan	USSR	10.6.1962	Yerevan
8.31m/27′3¼″	Ralph Boston	USA	15.8.1964	Kingston, Jamaica
8.34m/27′4¼″	Ralph Boston	USA	12.9.1964	Los Angeles
8.35m/27′5″	Ralph Boston	USA	29.5.1965	Modesto, Calif.
8.35m/27′4¾″	Igor Ter-Ovanesyan	USSR	19.10.1967	Mexico City
8.90m/29′2½″	Bob Beamon	USA	18.10.1968	Mexico City

Triple Jump

15.52m/10′11″	Daniel Ahearn	USA	30.5.1911	New York
15.52m/50′11¼″	Anthony Winter	USA	12.7.1924	Paris
15.58m/51′1½″	Mikio Oda	JAP	27.10.1931	Tokyo
15.72m/51′7″	Chuhei Nambu	JAP	4.8.1932	Los Angeles, Calif.
15.78m/51′9¼″	Jack Metcalfe	AUS	14.12.1935	Sydney
16.00m/52′6″	Naoto Tajima	JAP	6.8.1936	Berlin
16.00m/52′6″	Adhemar da Silva	BRA	3.12.1950	São Paulo
16.01m/52′6¼″	Adhemar da Silva	BRA	30.9.1951	Rio de Janeiro
16.12m/52′10¼″	Adhemar da Silva	BRA	23.7.1952	Helsinki
16.22m/53′2½″	Adhemar da Silva	BRA	23.7.1952	Helsinki
16.23m/53′3″	Leonid Shcherbakov	USSR	19.7.1953	Moscow
16.56m/54′4″	Adhemar da Silva	BRA	16.3.1955	Mexico City
16.59m/54′5¼″	Olyeg Ryakhovskiy	USSR	28.7.1958	Moscow
16.70m/54′9½″	Olyeg Fedoseyev	USSR	3.5.1959	Nalchik
17.03m/55′10½″	Józef Schmidt	POL	5.8.1960	Olsztyn

17.10m/56′1¼″	Giuseppe Gentile	ITA	16.10.1968	Mexico City
17.22m/56′6″	Giuseppe Gentile	ITA	17.10.1968	Mexico City
17.23m/56′6¼″	Viktor Saneyev	USSR	17.10.1968	Mexico City
17.27m/56′8″	Nelson Prudencio	BRA	17.10.1968	Mexico City
17.39m/57′0¾″	Viktor Saneyev	USSR	17.10.1968	Mexico City
17.40m/57′1″	Pedro Perez	CUB	5.8.1971	Cali, Colombia
17.44m/57′2¾″	Viktor Saneyev	USSR	17.10.1972	Sukhumi
17.89m/58′8½″	João de Oliveira	BRA	15.10.1975	Mexico City

Shot Put

15.54m/51′0″	Ralph Rose	USA	21.8.1909	San Francisco
15.79m/51′9¾″	Emil Hirschfeld	GER	6.5.1928	Breslau
15.87m/52′0¾″	John Kuck	USA	29.7.1928	Amsterdam
16.04m/52′7½″	Emil Hirschfeld	GER	26.8.1928	Bochum
16.04m/52′7½″	František Douda	TCH	4.10.1931	Brno
16.05m/52′8″	Zygmunt Heljasz	POL	29.6.1932	Poznan
16.16m/53′0½″	Leo Sexton	USA	27.8.1932	Freeport, N. Y.
16.20m/53′1¾″	František Douda	TCH	24.9.1932	Prague
16.48m/54′1″	John Lyman	USA	21.4.1934	Palo Alto, Calif
16.80m/55′1½″	Jack Torrance	USA	27.4.1934	Des Moines, Iowa
16.89m/55′5″	Jack Torrance	USA	30.6.1934	Milwaukee, Wis.
17.40m/57′1″	Jack Torrance	USA	5.8.1934	Oslo
17.68m/58′0¼″	Charles Fonville	USA	17.4.1958	Lawrence, Kans.
17.79m/58′4½″	Jim Fuchs	USA	28.7.1949	Oslo
17.82m/58′5½″	Jim Fuchs	USA	29.4.1950	Los Angeles
17.90m/58′8¾″	Jim Fuchs	USA	20.8.50	Visby, Sweden
17.95m/58′10¾″	Jim Fuchs	USA	22.8.1950	Eskilstuna, Sweden
18.00m/59′0¾″	Parry O'Brien	USA	9.5.1953	Fresno, Calif.
18.04m/59′2¾″	Parry O'Brien	USA	5.6.1953	Compton, Calif.
18.42m/60′5¼″	Parry O'Brien	USA	8.5.1954	Los Angeles
18.43m/60′5¾″	Parry O'Brien	USA	21.5.1954	Los Angeles
18.54m/60′10″	Parry O'Brien	USA	11.6.1954	Los Angeles
18.62m/61′1″	Parry O'Brien	USA	5.5.1956	Salt Lake City
18.69m/61′4″	Parry O'Brien	USA	15.6.1956	Los Angeles
19.06m/62′6¼″	Parry O'Brien	USA	3.9.1956	Eugene, Oregon
19.25m/63′2″	Parry O'Brien	USA	1.11.1956	Los Angeles
19.25m/63′2″	Dallas Long	USA	28.3.1959	Santa Barbara, Calif.
19.30m/63′4″	Parry O'Brien	USA	1.8.1959	Albuquerque, NM
19.38m/63′7″	Dallas Long	USA	5.3.1960	Los Angeles
19.45m/63′10″	Bill Nieder	USA	19.3.1960	Palo Alto, Calif.
19.67m/64′6½″	Dallas Long	USA	26.3.1960	Los Angeles
19.99m/65′7″	Bill Nieder	USA	2.4.1960	Austin, Texas
20.06m/65′10″	Bill Nieder	USA	12.8.1960	Walnut, Calif.
20.08m/65′10½″	Dallas Long	USA	18.5.1962	Los Angeles
20.10m/65′11½″	Dallas Long	USA	4.4.1964	Los Angeles
20.20m/66′3¼″	Dallas Long	USA	29.5.1964	Los Angeles
20.68m/67′10″	Dallas Long	USA	25.7.1964	Los Angeles
21.52m/70′7¼″	Randy Matson	USA	8.5.1965	College Stn. Tex.
21.78m/71′5½″	Randy Matson	USA	22.4.1967	College Stn. Tex
21.82m/71′7″	Allan Feuerbach	USA	5.5.1973	San José, Calif.
21.85m/71′8½″	Terry Albritton	USA	21.2.1976	Honolulu
22.00m/72′2¼″	Aleksandr Baryshnikov	USSR	10.7.1976	Paris
22.15m/72′8″	Udo Beyer	GDR	6.7.1978	Gothenburg

Discus

47.58m/156′1″	James Duncan	USA	27.5.1912	New York
47.61m/156′2″	Thomas Lieb	USA	14.9.1924	Chicago
47.89m/157′2″	Glenn Hartranft	USA	2.5.1925	San Francisco
48.20m/158′2″	Clarence Houser	USA	3.4.1926	Palo Alto, Calif.
49.90m/163′8″	Eric Krenz	USA	9.3.1929	Palo Alto, Calif.
51.03m/167′5″	Eric Krenz	USA	17.5.1930	Palo Alto, Calif.
51.73m/169′9″	Paul Jessup	USA	23.8.1930	Pittsburgh
52.42m/172′0″	Harald Andersson	SWE	25.8.1934	Oslo
53.10m/174′2″	Willi Schröder	GER	28.4.1935	Magdeburg
53.26m/174′9″	Archie Harris	USA	20.6.1941	Palo Alto, Calif.
53.34m/175′0″	Adolfo Consolini	ITA	26.10.1941	Milan
54.23m/177′11″	Adolfo Consolini	ITA	14.4.1946	Milan
54.93m/180′3″	Robert Fitch	USA	8.6.1946	Minneapolis
55.33m/181′6″	Adolfo Consolini	ITA	10.10.1948	Milan
56.46m/185′3″	Fortune Gordien	USA	9.7.1949	Lisbon
56.97m/186′11″	Fortune Gordien	USA	14.8.1949	Hömeenlinna, Finland.
57.93m/190′0″	Sim Iness	USA	20.6.1953	Lincoln, Nebr.
58.10m/190′7″	Fortune Gordien	USA	11.7.1953	Pasadena, Calif.
59.28m/194′6″	Fortune Gordien	USA	22.8.1953	Pasadena, Calif.
59.91m/196′6″	Edmund Piatkowski	POL	14.6.1959	Warsaw
59.91m/196′6″	Rink Babka	USA	12.8.1960	Walnut, Calif.
60.56m/198′8″	Jay Silvester	USA	11.8.1961	Frankfurt/Main
60.72m/199′2″	Jay Silvester	USA	20.8.1961	Brussels
61.10m/200′5″	Al Oerter	USA	18.5.1962	Los Angeles
61.64m/202′3″	Vladimir Trusenyov	USSR	4.6.1962	Leningrad
62.45m/204′10″	Al Oerter	USA	1.7.1962	Chicago
62.62m/205′5″	Al Oerter	USA	27.4.1963	Walnut, Calif.
62.94m/206′6″	Al Oerter	USA	25.4.1964	Walnut, Calif.
64.55m/211′9″	Ludvík Daněk	TCH	2.8.1964	Turnov
65.22m/213′11″	Ludvík Daněk	TCH	12.10.1965	Sokolov
66.54m/218′4″	Jay Silvester	USA	25.5.1968	Modesto, Calif.
68.40m/224′5″	Jay Silvester	USA	18.9.1968	Reno, Nev.
68.40m/224′5″	Rickard Bruch	SWE	5.7.1972	Stockholm
68.48m/224′8″	John van Reenan	RSA	14.3.1975	Stellenbosch
69.08m/226′8″	John Powell	USA	4.5.1975	Long Beach, Calif.
69.18m/226′11″	Mac Wilkins	USA	24.4.1976	Walnut, Calif.
69.80m/229′0″	Mac Wilkins	USA	1.5.1976	San José, Calif.
70.24m/230′5″	Mac Wilkins	USA	1.5.1976	San José, Calif.
70.86m/232′6″	Mac Wilkins	USA	1.5.1976	San José, Calif.
71.16m/233′5″	Wolfgang Schmidt	GDR	9.8.1978	East Berlin

Hammer

57.77m/189′6″	Patrick Ryan	USA	17.8.1913	New York
59.00m/193′7″	Erwin Blask	GER	27.8.1938	Stockholm
59.02m/193′7″	Imre Németh	HUN	14.7.1948	Tata
59.57m/195′5″	Imre Németh	HUN	4.9.1949	Katowice, Poland
59.88m/196′5″	Imre Németh	HUN	19.5.1950	Budapest
60.34/197′11″	József Csermák	HUN	24.7.1952	Helsinki
61.25m/100′11″	Sverre Strandli	NOR	14.9.1952	Oslo
62.36m/204′7″	Sverre Strandli	NOR	5.9.1953	Oslo
63.34m/207′9″	Mikhail Krivonosov	USSR	29.8.1954	Berne
64.05m/210′1″	Stanislav Nyenashev	USSR	12.12.1954	Baku
64.33m/211′0″	Mikhail Krivonosov	USSR	4.8.1955	Warsaw
64.52m/211′8″	Mikhail Krivonosov	USSR	19.9.1955	Belgrade
65.85m/216′0″	Mikhail Krivonosov	USSR	25.4.1956	Nalchik
66.38m/217′9″	Mikhail Krivonosov	USSR	8.7.1956	Minsk
67.32m/220′10″	Mikhail Krivonosov	USSR	22.10.1956	Tashkent

68.54m/224′10″	Harold Connolly	USA	2.11.1956	Los Angeles
68.68m/225′4″	Harold Connolly	USA	20.6.1958	Bakersfield, Calif.
70.33m/230′9″	Harold Connolly	USA	12.8.1960	Walnut, Calif.
70.67m/231′10″	Harold Connolly	USA	21.7.1962	Palo Alto, Calif.
71.06m/233′2″	Harold Connolly	USA	29.5.1965	Ceres, Calif.
71.26m/233′9″	Harold Connolly	USA	20.6.1965	Walnut, Calif.
73.74m/241′11″	Gyula Zsivótzky	HUN	4.9.1965	Debrecen
73.76m/242′0″	Gyula Zsivótzky	HUN	14.9.1968	Budapest
74.52m/244′6″	Romuald Klim	USSR	15.6.1969	Budapest
74.68m/245′0″	Anatoliy Bondarchuk	USSR	20.9.1969	Athens
75.48m/247′8″	Anatoliy Bondarchuk	USSR	12.10.1969	Rovno
76.40m/250′8″	Walter Schmidt	GER	4.9.1971	Lahr
76.60m/251′4″	Reinhard Theimer	GDR	4.7.1974	Leipzig
76.66m/251′6″	Aleksey Spiridonov	USSR	11.9.1974	Munich
76.70m/251′8″	Karl-Hans Riehm	GER	19.5.1975	Rehlingen
77.56m/254′4″	Karl-Hans Riehm	GER	19.5.1975	Rehlingen
78.50m/257′6″	Karl-Hans Riehm	GER	19.5.1975	Rehlingen
79.30m/260′2″	Walter Schmidt	GER	14.8.1975	Frankfurt/Main
80.14m/262′11″	Boris Zaichuk	USSR	9.7.1978	Moscow
80.32m/263′6″	Karl-Hans Riehm	GER	6.8.1978	Heidenheim

Javelin

62.32m/204′5″	Erik Lemming	SWE	29.9.1912	Stockholm
66.10m/216′10″	Jonni Myyrä	FIN	25.8.1919	Stockholm
66.62m/218′7″	Gunnar Lindström	SWE	12.10.1924	Eksjö
69.88m/229′3″	Eino Penttilä	FIN	8.10.1927	Viipuri
71.01m/232′11″	Erik Lundqvist	SWE	15.8.1928	Stockholm
71.57m/234′9″	Matti Järvinen	FIN	8.8.1930	Viipuri
71.70m/235′3″	Matti Järvinen	FIN	17.8.1930	Tampere
71.88m/235′10″	Matti Järvinen	FIN	31.8.1930	Vaasa
72.93m/239′3″	Matti Järvinen	FIN	14.9.1930	Viipuri
74.02m/242′10″	Matti Järvinen	FIN	27.6.1932	Turku
74.28m/243′8″	Matti Järvinen	FIN	25.5.1933	Mikkeli
74.61m/244′9″	Matti Järvinen	FIN	7.6.1933	Vaasa
76.10m/249′8″	Matti Järvinen	FIN	15.6.1933	Helsinki
76.66m/251′6″	Matti Järvinen	FIN	7.9.1934	Turin
77.23m/253′4″	Matti Järvinen	FIN	18.6.1936	Helsinki
77.87m/255′5″	Yrjö Nikkanen	FIN	25.8.1938	Karhula
78.70m/258′2″	Yrjö Nikkanen	FIN	16.10.1938	Kotka
80.41m/263′10″	Bud Held	USA	8.8.1953	Pasadena, Calif.
81.75m/268′2″	Bud Held	USA	21.5.1955	Modesto, Calif.
83.56m/274′1″	Soini Nikkinen	FIN	24.6.1956	Kuhmoinen
83.66m/274′5″	Janusz Sidło	POL	30.6.1956	Milan
85.71m/281′2″	Egil Danielsen	NOR	26.11.1956	Melbourne
86.04m/282′3″	Al Cantello	USA	5.6.1959	Compton, Calif.
86.74m/284′7″	Carlo Lievore	ITA	1.6.1961	Milan
87.12m/285′10″	Terje Pedersen	NOR	1.7.1964	Oslo
91.72m/300′11″	Terje Pedersen	NOR	2.9.1964	Oslo
91.98m/301′9″	Jānis Lūsis	USSR	23.6.1968	Saarijärvi, Finland
92.70m/304′1″	Jorma Kinnunen	FIN	18.6.1969	Tampere
93.80m/307′9″	Jānis Lūsis	USSR	6.7.1972	Stockholm
94.08m/308′8″	Klaus Wolfermann	GER	5.5.1973	Leverkusen
94.58m/310′4″	Miklós Németh	HUN	26.7.1976	Montreal

Decathlon

POINTS TABLES 1920	1962					100m	long jump	shot put	high jump	400m	110m hurdles	discus throw	pole vault	javelin throw	1500m
7481.69	6270	Aleksander Klumberg	EST	16/17.9.1922	Helsinki	12.3	659	1292	175	55.0	17.0	3964	340	6220	5:11.3
7710.775	6668	Harold Osborn	USA	11/12.7.1924	Paris	11.2	692	1143	197	53.2	16.0	3451	350	4669	4:50.0
7821.93	6651	Paavo Yrjölä	FIN	17/18.7.1926	Viipuri	11.8	654	1397	185	52.4	16.9	3731	330	5670	4:41.1
7995.19	6768	Paavo Yrjölä	FIN	16/17.7.1927	Helsinki	11.7	673	1427	185	52.8	16.8	4076	320	5740	4:41.8
8053.29	6774	Paavo Yrjölä	FIN	3/4.8.1928	Amsterdam	11.8	672	1411	187	53.2	16.6	4209	330	5570	4:44.0
8255.475	7036	Akilles Järvinen	FIN	19/20.7.1930	Viipuri	11.1	689	1314	180	50.0	15.4	3647	360	5815	4:54.2
8462.235	6896	James Bausch	USA	5/6.8.1932	Los Angeles	11.7	695	1532	170	54.2	16.2	4458	400	6191	5:17.0
8467.62	6999	Hans-Heinrich Sievert	GER	22/23.7.1933	Hamburg	11.4	709	1455	182	54.0	16.2	4666	340	5958	4:59.8
1934	1962														
7824	7292	Hans-Heinrich Sievert	GER	7/8.7.1934	Hamburg	11.1	748	1531	180	52.2	15.8	4723	343	5832	4:58.8
7900	7421	Glenn Morris	USA	7/8.8.1936	Berlin	11.1	697	1410	185	49.4	14.9	4302	350	5452	4:33.2
8042	7453	Bob Mathias	USA	29/30.6.1950	Tulare, Calif.	10.9	709	1448	185	51.0	14.7	4462	398	5559	5:05.1
1950	1962/1977														
7887	7731	Bob Mathias	USA	25/26.7.1952	Helsinki	10.9	698	1530	190	50.2	14.7	4689	400	5921	4:50.8
7985	7758	Rafer Johnson	USA	10/11.6.1955	Kingsburg, Calif.	10.5	749	1380	185	49.7	14.5	4720	387	5909	5:01.5
8014	7760	Vasiliy Kuznyetsov	USSR	17/18.5.1958	Krasnodar	11.0	730	1449	175	49.1	14.5	4750	400	6616	4:50.0
8302	7896	Rafer Johnson	USA	27/28.7.1958	Moscow	10.6	717	1469	180	48.2	14.9	4906	395	7259	5:05.0
8357	7957	Vasiliy Kuznyetsov	USSR	16/17.5.1959	Moscow	10.7	735	1468	189	49.2	14.7	4994	420	6506	5:04.6
8683	8063	Rafer Johnson	USA	8/9.7.1960	Eugene, Oregon	10.6	755	1585	178	48.6	14.5	5198	397	7109	5:09.9
	8089	Yang Chuan-Kwang	ROC	27/28.4.1963	Walnut, Calif.	10.7	717	1322	192	47.7	14.0	4099	484	7175	5:02.4
	8230	Russ Hodge	USA	23/24.7.1966	Los Angeles	10.5	751	1725	185	48.9	15.2	5044	410	6449	4:40.4
	8319	Kurt Bendlin	GER	13/14.5.1967	Heidelberg	10.6	755	1450	184	47.9	14.8	4631	410	7485	4:19.4
	8417	Bill Toomey	USA	10/11.12.1969	Los Angeles	10.3	776	1438	193	47.1	14.3	4649	427	6574	4:39.4
	8454/8456	Mykola Avilov	USSR	7/8.9.1972	Munich	11.00	768	1436	212	48.45	14.31	4698	455	6166	4/22.8
	8524	Bruce Jenner	USA	9/10.8.1975	Eugene, Oregon	10.7	717	1525	201	48.7	14.6	5000	470	6552	4:16.6
	8538	Bruce Jenner	USA	25/26.6.1976	Eugene, Oregon	10.7	719	1404	200	48.6	14.3	5168	460	6928	4:16.4
	8618/8617	Bruce Jenner	USA	29/30.7.1976	Montreal	10.94	722	1535	203	47.51	14.84	5004	480	6852	4:12.6

Women

100 Metres

11.7	Stanisława Walasiewicz	POL	26.8.1934	Warsaw	
11.6	Stanisława Walasiewicz	POL	1.8.1937	Berlin	
11.5	Fanny Blankers-Koen	HOL	13.6.1948	Amsterdam	
11.5b	Marjorie Jackson	AUS	22.7.1952	Helsinki	(.65)
11.4	Marjorie Jackson	AUS	4.10.1952	Gifu, Japan	
11.3	Shirley de la Hunty	AUS	4.8.1955	Warsaw	
11.3	Vera Krepkina	USSR	13.9.1958	Kiev	
11.3	Wilma Rudolph	USA	2.9.1960	Rome	
11.2	Wilma Rudolph	USA	19.7.1961	Stuttgart	
11.2	Wyomia Tyus	USA	15.10.1964	Tokyo	
11.1	Irena Kirszenstein	POL	9.7.1965	Prague	
11.1	Wyomia Tyus	USA	31.7.1965	Kiev	
11.1	Barbara Ferrell	USA	2.7.1967	Santa Barbara, Calif.	
11.1	Ludmila Samotyosova	USSR	15.8.1968	Leninakan	
11.1b	Irena Szewińska	POL	14.10.1968	Mexico City	(.19)
11.0b	Wyomia Tyus	USA	15.10.1968	Mexico City	(.08)
11.0	Chi Cheng	ROC	18.7.1970	Südstadt, Austria	
11.0	Renate Meissner	GDR	2.8.1970	Berlin	
11.0	Renate Stecher	GDR	31.7.1971	Berlin	
11.0	Renate Stecher	GDR	3.6.1972	Potsdam	
11.0	Ellen Stropahl	GDR	15.6.1972	Potsdam	
11.0	Eva Glesková	TCH	1.7.1972	Budapest	
10.9	Renate Stecher	GDR	7.6.1973	Ostrava	
10.8	Renate Stecher	GDR	20.7.1973	Dresden	(.07)
11.08	Wyomia Tyus	USA	15.10.1968	Mexico City	
11.07	Renate Stecher	GDR	2.9.1972	Munich	
11.04	Inge Helten	GER	13.6.1976	Fürth	
11.01	Annegret Richter	GER	25.7.1976	Montreal	
10.88	Marlies Oelsner	GDR	1.7.1977	Dresden	

200 Metres

23.6	Stanisława Walasiewicz	POL	15.8.1935	Warsaw	
23.6b	Marjorie Jackson	AUS	25.7.1952	Helsinki	(.74
23.4b	Marjorie Jackson	AUS	25.7.1952	Helsinki	(.59)
23.2	Betty Cuthbert	AUS	16.9.1956	Sydney	
23.2	Betty Cuthbert	AUS	7.3.1960	Hobart, Tasmania	
22.9	Wilma Rudolph	USA	9.7.1960	Corpus Christi, Texas	
22.9	Margaret Burvill	AUS	22.2.1964	Perth	
22.7	Irena Kirszenstein	POL	8.8.1965	Warsaw	
22.5a	Irena Szewińska	POL	18.10.1968	Mexico City	(.58
22.4	Chi Cheng	ROC	12.7.1970	Munich	
22.4a	Renate Stecher	GDR	7.9.1972	Munich	(.40)
22.1a	Renate Stecher	GDR	21.7.1973	Dresden	(.38)
22.21	Irena Szewińska	POL	13.6.1974	Potsdam	
22.06	Marita Koch	GDR	28.5.1978		
22.03	Marita Koch	GDR	3.6.1978	Leipzig	
21.71	Marita Koch	GDR	10.6.1979	Karl-Marx-Stadt	

400 Metres

57.0	Marlene Mathews	AUS	6.1.1957	Sydney	
57.0	Marise Chamberlain	NZL	16.2.1957	Christchurch	
56.3	Nancy Boyle	AUS	24.3.1957	Sydney	
55.2	Polina Lazareva	USSR	10.5.1957	Moscow	
54.0	Maria Itkina	USSR	8.6.1957	Minsk	
53.6	Maria Itkina	USSR	6.7.1957	Moscow	
53.4	Maria Itkina	USSR	12.9.1959	Krasnodar	
53.4	Maria Itkina	USSR	14.9.1962	Belgrade	
51.9	Shin Geum Dan	PRK	23.10.1962	Pyongyang	
51.7a	Nicole Duclos	FRA	18.9.1969	Athens	(.73)
51.7b	Colette Besson	FRA	18.9.1969	Athens	(.75)
51.0a	Marilyn Neufville	JAM	23.7.1970	Edinburgh	(.02)
51.0b	Monika Zehrt	GDR	4.7.1972	Paris	(.08)
49.9	Irena Szewińska	POL	22.6.1974	Warsaw	

50.14	Riita Salin	FIN	4.9.1974	Rome
49.77	Christine Brehmer	GDR	9.6.1974	Dresden
49.75	Irena Szewińska	POL	22.6.1976	Bydgoszcz
49.29	Irena Szewińska	POL	29.7.1976	Montreal
49.19	Marita Koch	GDR	2.7.1978	Leipzig
49.02	Marita Koch	GDR	19.8.1978	Potsdam
48.94	Marita Koch	GDR	31.8.1978	Prague
48.89	Marita Koch	GDR	29.7.1979	Potsdam
48.60	Marita Koch	GDR	4.8.1979	Turin

800 Metres

2:16.8	Lina Batschauer-Radke	GER	2.8.1928	Amsterdam	
2:15.9	Anna Larsson	SWE	28.8.1944	Stockholm	
2:14.8	Anna Larsson	SWE	19.8.1945	Hälsingborg	
2:13.8	Anna Larsson	SWE	30.8.1945	Stockholm	
2:13.0	Yevdokiya Vasilyeva	USSR	17.7.1950	Moscow	
2:12.2	Valentina Pomogayeva	USSR	26.7.1951	Moscow	
2:12.0	Nina Pletnyova	USSR	26.8.1951	Minsk	
2:08.5	Nina Pletnyova	USSR	15.6.1952	Kiev	
2:07.3	Nina Otkalenko	USSR	27.8.1953	Moscow	
2:06.6	Nina Otkalenko	USSR	16.9.1954	Kiev	
2:05.0	Nina Otkalenko	USSR	24.9.1955	Zagreb, Yugoslavia	
2:04.3	Lyudmila Shevtsova	USSR	3.7.1960	Moscow	
2:04.3b	Lyudmila Shevtsova	USSR	7.9.1960	Rome	(.50)
2:01.2	Dixie Willis	AUS	3.3.1962	Perth	
2:01.1	Ann Packer	GBR	20.10.1964	Tokyo	
2:01.0	Judy Pollock	AUS	28.6.1967	Helsinki	
2:00.5	Vera Nikolić	YUG	20.7.1968	London	
1:58.5a	Hildegard Falck	GER	11.7.1971	Stuttgart	(.45)
1:57.5	Svetla Zlateva	BUL	24.8.1973	Athens	
1:56.0	Valentina Gerasimava	USSR	12.6.1976	Kiev	
1:54.9a	Tatyana Kazankina	USSR	26.7.1976	Montreal	(.94)

1500 Metres

4:17.3	Anne Smith	GBR	3.6.1967	London	
4:15.6	Maria Gommers	HOL	24.10.1968	Sittard	
4:12.4	Paola Pigni	ITA	2.7.1969	Milan	
4:10.7	Jaroslava Jehlicková	TCH	20.9.1969	Athens	
4:09.6	Karin Burneleit	GDR	15.8.1971	Helsinki	
4:06.9	Lyudmila Bragina	USSR	18.7.1972	Moscow	
4:06.5a	Lyudmila Bragina	USSR	4.9.1972	Munich	(.47)
4:05.1a	Lyudmila Bragina	USSR	7.9.1972	Munich	(.07)
4:01.4a	Lyudmila Bragina	USSR	9.9.1972	Munich	(.38)
3:56.0	Tatyana Kazankina	USSR	28.6.1976	Podolsk	

1 Mile

4:37.0	Anne Smith	GBR	3.6.1967	London
4:36.8	Maria Gommers	HOL	14.6.1969	Leicester, England
4:35.3	Ellen Tittel	GER	20.8.1971	Sittard, Neths.
4:29.5	Paola Cacchi	ITA	8.8.1973	Viareggio
4:23.8	Natalia Marasescu	ROM	21.5.1977	Bucharest
4:22.1	Natalia Marasescu	ROM	27.1.1979	Auckland, NZ.

3000 Metres

8:52.8a	Lyudmila Bragina	USSR	6.7.1974	Durham, N. C.	(.74)
8:46.6	Greta Waitz	NOR	24.6.1975	Oslo	
8:45.4	Greta Waitz	NOR	21.6.1976	Oslo	
8:27.2b	Lyudmila Bragina	USSR	7.8.1976	College Park, Md.	(.12)

100 Metres Hurdles

13.3	Karin Balzer	GDR	20.6.1969	Warsaw	
13.3	Teresa Sukneiwicz	POL	20.6.1969	Warsaw	
13.0	Karin Balzer	GDR	27.7.1969	Leipzig	
12.9	Karin Balzer	GDR	5.9.1969	Berlin	
12.8	Teresa Sukniewicz	POL	20.6.1970	Warsaw	
12.8	Chi Cheng	ROC	12.7.1970	Munich	
12.7	Karin Balzer	GDR	26.7.1970	Berlin	
12.7	Teresa Sukniewicz	POL	20.9.1970	Warsaw	
12.7	Karin Balzer	GDR	25.7.1971	Berlin	
12.6	Karin Balzer	GDR	31.7.1971	Berlin	
12.5	Annelie Ehrhardt	GDR	15.6.1972	Potsdam	
12.5	Pamela Ryan	AUS	28.6.1972	Warsaw	
12.3b	Annelie Ehrhardt	GDR	22.7.1973	Dresden	(.68)

12.59	Annelie Ehrhardt	GDR	8.9.1972	Munich
12.48	Grazyna Rabsztyn	POL	10.6.1978	Furth
12.48	Grazyna Rabsztyn	POL	18.6.1979	Warsaw

400 Metres Hurdles

56.51	Krystyna Kacperczyk	POL	13.7.1974	Augsburg, Germany
55.74	Tatyana Storozheva	USSR	26.6.1977	Karl-Marx-Stadt, GDR
55.63	Karin Rossley	GDR	14.8.1977	Helsinki
55.44	Krystyna Kacperczyk	POL	18.8.1978	Berlin
55.31	Tatyana Zelentsova	USSR	19.8.1978	Podolsk
54.89	Tatyana Zelentsova	USSR	2.9.1978	Prague
54.78	Marina Makeyera	USSR	27.7.1979	Moscow

4 x 100 Metres Relay

46.4	GERMAN NATIONAL TEAM (Emmy Albus, Kathe Krauss, Marie Dollinger, Ilse Dörffeldt)	8.8.1936	Berlin	
46.1b	AUSTRALIAN NATIONAL TEAM (Verna Johnson, Shirley B de la Hunty, Winsome Cripps, Marjorie Jackson)	27.7.1952	Helsinki	(.23)
45.9b	USA NATIONAL TEAM (Mae Faggs, Babara Jones, Janet Moreau, Catherine Hardy)	27.7.1952	Helsinki	(.14)
45.9b	GERMAN NATIONAL TEAM (Ursula Knab, Maria Sander, Helga Klien, Marga Petersen)	27.7.1952	Helsinki	(.18)
45.6	USSR NATIONAL TEAM (Vyera Kalashnikova, Zinaida Safronova, Irina Turova, Nadyezhda Dvalishvili)	20.9.1953	Bupapest	
45.6	USSR NATIONAL TEAM (Lidia Polinichenko, Galina Vinogradova, Zinaida Safronova, Maria Itkina)	11.9.1955	Moscow	
45.2	USSR NATIONAL TEAM (Vyera Krepkina, Olga Kosheleva, Maria Itkina, Irina Bochkaryova)	27.7.1956	Kiev	
45.1	GERMAN NATIONAL TEAM (Erika Fisch, Gisela Köhler, Christa Stubnick, Bärbel Mayer)	30.9.1956	Dresden	
44.9	AUSTRALIAN NATIONAL TEAM (Shirley B de la Hunty, Norma Croker, Fleur Mellor, Betty Cuthbert)	1.12.1956	Melbourne	
44.9	GERMAN NATIONAL TEAM (Maria Sander, Christa Stubnick, Gisela Köhler, Bärbel Mayer)	1.12.1956	Melbourne	
44.5b	AUSTRALIAN NATIONAL TEAM (Shirley B de la Hunty, Norma Croker, Fleur Mellor, Betty Cuthbert)	1.12.1956	Melbourne	(.65)
44.4	USA NATIONAL TEAM (Martha Hudson, Lucinda Williams, Barbara Jones, Wilma Rudolph)	7.9.1960	Rome	
44.3	USA NATIONAL TEAM (Willye White, Ernestine Pollards, Vivianne Brown, Wilma Rudolph)	15.7.1961	Moscow	
43.9	USA NATIONAL TEAM (Willye White, Wyomia Tyus, Marilyn White, Edith McGuire)	21.10.1964	Tokyo	
43.9b	USSR NATIONAL TEAM (Lilia Tkachenko, Galina Bukharina, Vyera Poplova, Lyudmila Samotyosova)	16.8.1968	Leninakan	
43.6	USSR NATIONAL TEAM (Lyudmila Zharkova, Galina Bukharina, Vyera Poplova, Lyudmila Samotyosova)	27.9.1968	Mexico City	
43.4b	USA NATIONAL TEAM (Barbara Ferrell, Margaret Bailes, Mildrette Netter, Wyomia Tyus)	19.10.1968	Mexico City	(.50)
43.4b	DUTCH NATIONAL TEAM (Wilma van den Berg, Mieke Sterk, Truus Hennipman, Corrie Bakker)	19.10.1968	Mexico City	(.49)
42.8b	USA NATIONAL TEAM (Barbara Ferrell, Margaret Bailes, Mildrette Netter, Wyomia Tyus)	20.10.1968	Mexico City	(.87)
42.8a	GERMAN NATIONAL TEAM (Christiane Krause, Ingrid Mickler, Annegret Richter, Heide Rosendahl)	10.9.1972	Munich	(.81)
42.6	GDR NATIONAL TEAM (Petra Kandarr, Renate Stecher, Christine Heinich, Doris Selmigkeit)	1.9.1973	Potsdam	
42.6	GDR NATIONAL TEAM (Doris Maletzki, Renate Stecher, Christine Heinich, Bärbel Eckert)	24.8.1974	Berlin	
42.5a	GDR NATIONAL TEAM (Doris Maletzki, Renate Stecher, Christine Heinich, Bärbel Eckert)	8.9.1974	Rome	(.51)

42.51	GDR NATIONAL TEAM (Doris Maletzki, Remate Stecher, Christine Heinich, Bärbel Eckert)	8.9.1974	Rome	
42.50	GDR NATIONAL TEAM (Marlies Oelsmer, Renate Stecher, Carla Bodendorf, Martina Blos)	29.5.1976	Karl-Marx-Stadt	
42.27	GDR NATIONAL TEAM (Johanna Xlier, Monika Hanann, Carla Bodendorf, Marlies Gohr)	19.8.1978	Potsdam	
42.09	GDR NATIONAL TEAM (Marita Koch, Romy Schneider, Ingrid Auerswald, Marlies Gohr)	10.6.1979	Karl-Marx-Stadt	
42.09	GDR NATIONAL TEAM (Christine Brehmer, Romy Schneider, Ingrid Auerswald, Marlies Gohr)	4.8.1979	Turin	

4 x 400 Metres Relay

3:47.4	MOSCOW TEAM (Lyubov Finogenova, Tatyana Medvedeva, Olga Klein, Tamara Voytenko)	30.5.1969	Moscow	
3:43.2	LATVIA TEAM (Lilita Zagere, Ingrida Verbele, Sarmite Shtula, Anna Dundare)	1.6.1969	Minsk	
3:37.6	GB & NI TEAM (Jenny Pawsey, Pauline Attwood, Janet Simpson, Lillian Board)	22.6.1969	London	
3:34.2	FRENCH NATIONAL TEAM (Michèle Mombet, Eliane Jacq, Nicole Duclos, Colette Besson)	6.7.1969	Paris	
3:33.9	GERMAN NATIONAL TEAM (Christa Czekay, Antje Gleichfeld, Inge Eckhoff, Christel Frese)	19.9.1979	Athens	
3:30.8	GB & NI NATIONAL TEAM (Rosemary Stirling, Pat Lowe, Janet Simpson, Lillian Board)	20.9.1969	Athens	
3:30.8	FRENCH NATIONAL TEAM (Bernadette Martin, Nicole Duclos, Eliane Jacq, Colette Besson)	20.9.1969	Athens	
3:29.3a	GDR NATIONAL TEAM (Rita Kühne, Ingelore Lohse, Helga Seidler, Monika Zehrt)	15.8.1971	Helsinki	(.28)
3:28.8	GDR NATIONAL TEAM (Dagmar Käsling, Helga Seidler, Monika Zehrt, Brigitte Rohde)	5.7.1972	Paris	
3:28.5	GDR NATIONAL TEAM (Dagmar Käsling, Rita Kühne, Helga Seidler, Monika Zehrt)	9.9.1972	Munich	(.48)
3:23.0a	GDR NATIONAL TEAM (Dagmar Käsling, Rita Kühne, Helga Seidler, Monika Zehrt)	10.9.1972	Munich	(.95)
3:19.2a	GDR NATIONAL TEAM (Doris Maletzki, Brigitte Rohde, Ellen Streidt, Christa Brehmer)	31.7.1976	Montreal	(.23)

High Jump

1.65m/5′5″	Jean Shiley	USA	7.8.1932	Los Angeles
1.65m/5′5″	Mildred Didrikson	USA	7.8.1932	Los Angeles
1.66m/5′5¼″	Dorothy Odam	GBR	29.5.1939	Brentwood
1.66m/5′5¼″	Esther Van Heerden	RSA	29.3.1941	Stellenbosch
1.66m/5′5¼″	Ilsebill Pfenning	SUI	29.7.1941	Lugano
1.71m/5′7¼″	Fanny Blankers-Koen	HOL	30.5.1943	Amsterdam
1.72m/5′7½″	Sheila Lerwill	GBR	7.7.1951	London
1.73m/5′8″	Aleksandra Chudina	USSR	22.5.1954	Kiev
1.74m/5′8½″	Thelma Hopkins	GBR	5.5.1956	Belfast
1.75m/5′8½″	Iolanda Balas	ROM	14.7.1956	Bucharest
1.76m/5′9¼″	Mildred McDaniel	USA	1.12.1956	Melbourne
1.76m/5′9¼″	Iolanda Balas	ROM	13.10.1957	Bucharest
1.77m/5′9¾″	Cheng Feng-jung	CPR	17.11.1957	Peking
1.78m/5′10″	Iolanda Balaş	ROM	7.6.1958	Bucharest
1.80m/5′10¾″	Iolanda Balaş	ROM	22.6.1958	Cluj
1.81m/5′11¼″	Iolanda Balaş	ROM	31.7.1958	Poiana Stalin
1.82m/5′11¾″	Iolanda Balaş	ROM	4.10.1958	Bucharest
1.83m/6′0″	Iolanda Balaş	ROM	18.10.1958	Bucharest
1.84m/6′0½″	Iolanda Balaş	ROM	21.9.1959	Bucharest
1.85m/6′0¾″	Iolanda Balaş	ROM	6.6.1960	Bucharest
1.86m/6′1¼″	Iolanda Balaş	ROM	10.7.1960	Bucharest
1.87m/6′1½″	Iolanda Balaş	ROM	15.4.1961	Bucharest
1.88m/6′2″	Iolanda Balaş	ROM	18.6.1961	Warsaw
1.90m/6′2¾″	Iolanda Balaş	ROM	8.7.1961	Budapest
1.91m/6′3¼″	Iolanda Balaş	ROM	16.7.1961	Sofia
1.92m/6′3½″	Ilona Gusenbauer	AUT	4.9.1971	Vienna
1.92m/6′3½″	Ulrike Meyfarth	GER	4.9.1972	Munich
1.94m/6′4½″	Yordanka Blagoyeva	BUL	24.9.1972	Zagreb
1.94m/6′4½″	Rosemarie Witschas	GDR	24.8.1974	Berlin
1.95m/6′5″	Rosemarie Witschas	GDR	8.9.1974	Rome
1.96m/6′5¼″	Rosemarie Ackermann	GDR	8.5.1976	Dresden
1.96m/6′5¼″	Rosemarie Ackermann	GDR	3.7.1977	Dresden
1.97m/6′5½″	Rosemarie Ackermann	GDR	14.8.1977	Helsinki
1.97m/6′5½″	Rosemarie Ackermann	GDR	26.8.1977	Berlin, Germany
2.00m/6′6¾″	Rosemarie Ackermann	GDR	26.8.1977	Berlin, Germany
2.01m/6′7″	Sara Simeoni	ITA	4.8.1978	Brescia
2.01m/6′7″	Sara Simeoni	ITA	31.8.1978	Prague

Long Jump

5.98m/19′7½″	Kinue Hitomi	JAP	20.5.1928	Osaka
6.12m/20′1″	Christel Schulz	GER	30.7.1939	Berlin
6.25m/20′6″	Fanny Blankers-Koen	HOL	19.9.1943	Leiden
6.28m/20′7½″	Yvette Williams	NZL	20.2.1954	Gisborne
6.28m/10′7½″	Galina Vinogradova	USSR	11.9.1955	Moscow
6.31m/20′8½″	Galina Vinogradova	USSR	18.11.1955	Tbilisi
6.35m/20′10″	Elżbieta Krzesińska	POL	20.8.1956	Budapest
6.35m/20′10″	Elżbieta Krzesińska	POL	27.11.1956	Melbourne
6.40m/21′0″	Hildrun Claus	GDR	7.8.1960	Erfurt
6.42m/21′0¾″	Hildrun Claus	GDR	23.6.1961	Berlin
6.48m/21′3¼″	Tatyana Shchelkanova	USSR	16.7.1961	Moscow
6.53m/21′5¼″	Tatyana Shchelkanova	USSR	10.6.1962	Leipzig
6.70m/21′1¾″	Tatyana Shchelkanova	USSR	4.7.1964	Moscow
6.76m/22′2¼′	Mary Rand	GBR	14.10.1964	Tokyo
6.82m/22′4½″	Viorica Viscopoleanu	ROM	14.10.1968	Mexico City
6.84m/22′5¼″	Heide Rosendahl	GER	3.9.1970	Turin

6.92m/22′8½″	Angela Voigt	GDR	9.5.1976	Dresden
6.99m/22′11¼″	Sigrun Siegl	GDR	19.5.1976	Dresden
7.07m/23′2¼″	Vilma Bardauskiene	USSR	19.8.1978	Moscow
7.07m/23′2¼″	Vilma Bardauskiene	USSR	19.8.1978	Moscow
7.09m/23′3¼″	Vilma Bardauskiene	USSR	29.8.1978	Prague

Shot

14.38m/47′2¼″	Gisela Mauermayer	GER	15.7.1934	Warsaw
14.59m/47′10½″	Tatyana Sevryukova	USSR	4.8.1948	Moscow
14.86m/48′9″	Klavdiya Tochonova	USSR	30.10.1949	Tbilisi
15.02m/49′3½″	Anna Andreyeva	USSR	9.11.1950	Ploesti, Rumania
15.28m/50′1¾″	Galina Zybina	USSR	26.7.1952	Helsinki
15.37m/50′5¼″	Galina Zybina	USSR	20.9.1952	Frunze
15.42m/50′7¼″	Galina Zybina	USSR	1.10.1952	Frunze
16.20m/53′1¾″	Galina Zybina	USSR	9.10.1953	Malmö, Sweden
16.28m/53′5″	Galina Zybina	USSR	14.9.1954	Kiev
16.29m/53′5½″	Galina Zybina	USSR	5.9.1955	Leningrad
16.67m/54′8¼″	Galina Zybina	USSR	15.11.1955	Tbilisi
16.76m/55′0″	Galina Zybina	USSR	13.10.1956	Tashkent
17.25m/56′7¼″	Tamara Press	USSR	26.4.1959	Nalchik
17.42m/57′2″	Tamara Press	USSR	16.7.1960	Moscow
17.78m/58′4″	Tamara Press	USSR	13.8.1960	Moscow
18.55m/60′10½″	Tamara Press	USSR	10.6.1962	Leipzig
18.55m/60′10½″	Tamara Press	USSR	12.9.1962	Belgrade
18.59m/61′0″	Tamara Press	USSR	19.9.1965	Kassel
18.67m/61′3″	Nadyezhda Chizhova	USSR	28.4.1968	Sochi
18.87m/61′11″	Margitta Gummel	GDR	22.9.1968	Frankfurt/Oder
19.07m/62′6¾″	Margitta Gummel	GDR	20.10.1968	Mexico City
19.61m/64′4″	Margitta Gummel	GDR	20.10.1968	Mexico City
19.72m/64′8½″	Nadyezhda Chizhova	USSR	30.5.1969	Moscow
20.09m/65′11″	Nadyezhda Chizhova	USSR	13.7.1969	Chorzow, Poland
20.10m/65′11¼″	Margitta Gummel	GDR	11.9.1969	Berlin
20.10m/65′11½″	Nadyezhda Chizhova	USSR	16.9.1969	Athens
20.43m/67′0½″	Nadyezhda Chizhova	USSR	16.9.1969	Athens
20.43m/67′0½″	Nadyezhda Chizhova	USSR	29.8.1971	Moscow
20.63m/67′8¼″	Nadyezhda Chizhova	USSR	19.5.1972	Sochi
21.03m/69′0″	Nadyezhda Chizhova	USSR	7.9.1972	Munich
21.20/69′6¾″	Nadyezhda Chizhova	USSR	28.8.1973	Lvov
21.60m/70′10½″	Marianne Adam	GDR	6.8.1975	Berlin
21.67m/71′1¼″	Marianne Adam	GDR	30.5.1976	Karl-Marx-Stadt
21.87m/71′9″	Ivanka Khristova	BUL	3.7.1976	Belmeken
21.89m/71′9¾″	Ivanka Khristova	BUL	4.7.1976	Belmeken
31.99m/72′2″	Helena Fibingerová	TCH	26.9.1976	Opava
22.32m/73′3″	Helena Fibingerová	TCH	20.8.1977	Nitra

Discus

48.31m/158'6"	Gisela Mauermayer	GER	11.7.1936	Dresden
53.25m/174'8"	Nina Dumbadze	USSR	8.8.1948	Moscow
53.37m/175'1"	Nina Dumbadze	USSR	27.5.1951	Gori
53.61m/175'11"	Nina Romashkova	USSR	9.8.1952	Odessa
57.04m/187'2"	Nina Dumbadze	USSR	18.10.1952	Tbilisi
57.15m/187'6"	Tamara Press	USSR	12.9.1960	Rome
57.43m/188'5"	Tamara Press	USSR	15.7.1961	Moscow
58.06m/190'6"	Tamara Press	USSR	1.9.1961	Sofia
58.98m/193'6"	Tamara Press	USSR	20.9.1961	London
59.29m/194'6"	Tamara Press	USSR	18.5.1963	Moscow
59.70m/195'10"	Tamara Press	USSR	11.8.1965	Moscow
61.26m/201'1"	Liesel Westermann	GER	5.11.1967	Sao Paulo
61.64m/202'3"	Christine Spielberg	GDR	26.5.1968	Regis Breitingen
62.54m/205'2"	Liesel Westerman	GER	24.7.1968	Werdohl
62.70m/205'8"	Liesel Westermann	GER	18.6.1969	Berlin
63.96m/209'10"	Liesel Westermann	GER	27.9.1969	Hamburg
64.22m/210'8"	Faina Melnyk	USSR	12.8.1971	Helsinki
64.88m/212'10"	Faina Melnyk	USSR	4.9.1971	Munich
65.42m/214'7"	Faina Melnyk	USSR	31.5.1972	Moscow
65.48m/214'10"	Faina Melnyk	USSR	24.6.1972	Augsburg, Germany
66.76m/219'0"	Faina Melnyk	USSR	4.8.1972	Luzhniki
67.32m/220'10"	Argentina Menis	ROM	23.9.1972	Constanza
67.44m/221'3"	Faina Melnyk	USSR	25.5.1973	Riga
67.58m/221'9"	Faina Melnyk	USSR	10.7.1973	Moscow
69.48m/227'11"	Faina Melnyk	USSR	7.9.1973	Edinburgh
69.90m/229'4"	Faina Melnyk	USSR	27.5.1974	Prague
70.20m/230'4"	Faina Melnyk	USSR	20.8.1975	Zurich
70.50m/231'3"	Faina Melnyk	USSR	24.4.1976	Sochi
70.72m/232'0"	Evelyn Jahl	GDR	12.8.1978	Dresden

Javelin

46.74m/153'4"	Nan Gindele	USA	18.6.1932	Chicago
47.24m/155'0"	Anneliese Steinheuer	GER	21.6.1942	Frankfurt/Main
48.21m/158'2"	Herma Bauma	AUT	29.6.1947	Vienna
48.63m/159'6"	Herma Bauma	AUT	12.9.1948	Vienna
49.59m/162'8"	Natalya Smirnitskaya	USSR	25.7.1949	Moscow
53.41m/175'2"	Natalya Smirnitskaya	USSR	5.8.1949	Moscow
53.56m/175'8"	Nadyezhda Konyayeva	USSR	5.2.1954	Leningrad
55.11m/180'9"	Nadyezhda Konyayeva	USSR	22.5.1954	Kiev
55.48m/182'0"	Nadyezhda Konyayeva	USSR	6.8.1954	Kiev
55.73m/182'10"	Dana Zátopková	TCH	1.6.1958	Prague
57.40m/188'4"	Anna Pazera	AUS	24.7.1958	Cardiff, GBR
57.49m/188'7"	Birute Zalogaitite	USSR	30.10.1958	Tbilisi
57.92m/190'0"	Elvira Ozolina	USSR	3.5.1960	Leselidze
59.55m/195'4"	Elvira Ozolina	USSR	4.6.1960	Bucharest
59.78m/196'1"	Elvira Ozolina	USSR	3.7.1963	Moscow
62.40m/204'8"	Yelena Gorchakova	USSR	16.10.1964	Tokyo, Japan
62.70m/205'8"	Ewa Gryziecka	POL	11.6.1972	Bucharest
65.06m/213'5"	Ruth Fuchs	GDR	11.6.1972	Potsdam
66.10m/216'10"	Ruth Fuchs	GDR	7.9.1973	Edinburgh, GBR
67.22m/220'6"	Ruth Fuchs	GDR	3.9.1974	Rome
69.12m/226'9"	Ruth Fuchs	GDR	10.7.1976	Berlin
69.32m/227'5"	Kate Schmidt	USA	11.9.1977	Fürth, Germany
69.52m/228'1"	Ruth Fuchs	GDR	13.6.1979	Dresden

Pentathlon

POINTS TABLES

1954		shot put	long jump	100m	high jump	javelin throw
4155		Gisela Mauermayer	GER	9/11.8.1933	London	
		1344	551	13.0	152	3290
4391		Gisela Mauermayer	GER	16/17.7.1938	Stuttgart	
		1307	562	12.4	156	3690
1954		**shot put**	**high jump**	**200m**	**80 hurdles**	**long jump**
4692		Fanny Blankers-Koen	HOL	15/16.9.1951	Amsterdam	
		1150	160	24.4	11.4	588
4704		Aleksandra Chudina	USSR	8/9.8.1953	Bucharest	
		1342	163	25.5	11.6	581
4747		Nina Martynenko	USSR	6/7.7.1955	Leningrad	
		1354	162	25.8	11.3	592
4750		Aleksandra Chudina	USSR	6/7.7.1955	Moscow	
		1399	164	26.3	11.5	604
4767		Nina Vinogradova	USSR	11/12.8.1956	Moscow	
		1323	157	25.4	10.9	588
4846		Galina Bystrova	USSR	15/16.10.1957	Odessa	
		1273	158	25.2	10.8	617
4872		Galina Bystrova	USSR	1/2.11.1958	Tblisi	
		1381	160	25.5	10.8	600
4880		Irina Press	USSR	13/14.9.1959	Krasnodar	
		1420	158	24.8	10.9	582
4902		Irina Press	USSR	21/22.5.1960	Tula	
		1500	157	24.3	11.2	576
4959		Irina Press	USSR	25/26.6.1960	Tula	
		1518	150	24.5	10.9	617
4972		Irena Press	USSR	17/18.10.1960	Kiev	
		1534	163	24.7	10.8	558
5137	1971	Irina Press	USSR	8/9.10.1961	Tbilisi	
		1526	162	24.2	10.9	624
5246		Irena Press	USSR	16/17.10.1964	Tokyo	
		1716	163	24.7	10.7	624
5352	4727	Liese Prokop	AUT	4/5.10.1969	Vienna	
		1495	175	24.6	13.5	662w
5406	4775	Burglinde Pollak	GDR	5/6.9.1970	Erfurt	
		1557	175	23.8	13.3	620
	4801a	Mary Peters	GBR	2/3.9.1972	Munich	
		1602	182	24.08	13.29	598
	4831a	Burglinde Pollak	GDR	12.8.1973	Sofia	
		1540	174	23.70	13.21	645
	4932a	Burglinde Pollak	GDR	22.9.1973	Bonn	
		1585	178	23.35	13.21	647
	1971	**100m hurdles**	**shot put**	**high jump**	**long jump**	**800m**
	4765a	Eva Wilms	GER	24.5.1977	Göttingen	
		13.70	2062	174	603	2:19.9
	4823a	Eva Wilms	GER	18.6.1977	Bernhausen	
		13.83	2095	174	629	2:19.7
	4839a	Nadyezhda Tkachenko	USSR	18.9.1977	Lille, France	
		13.49	1593	180	649	2:10.6

Note Tkachenko's 800m time was 2:10.62, i.e. 2:10.7 under current (1979) rules, reducing her score by 1 point to 4838.

Index

Page numbers in italic refer to illustrations